Baseball in Crisis

ALSO BY FRANK P. JOZSA, JR.

Baseball, Inc.: The National Pastime as Big Business (McFarland, 2006)

Baseball in Crisis

Spiraling Costs, Bad Behavior,
Uncertain Future

FRANK P. JOZSA, JR.

McFarland & Company, Inc., Publishers
Jefferson, North Carolina, and London

LIBRARY OF CONGRESS CATALOGUING-IN-PUBLICATION DATA

Jozsa, Jr., Frank P., 1941–
    Baseball in crisis : spiraling costs, bad behavior, uncertain
future / Frank P. Jozsa, Jr.
        p.   cm.
    Includes bibliographical references and index.

    ISBN-13: 978-0-7864-3331-5
    softcover : 50# alkaline paper ∞

    1. Baseball — United States.   2. Professional sports —
United States.   I. Title.
    GV863.A1J69   2008
    796.3570973 — dc22   2008027616

British Library cataloguing data are available

Cover image ©2008 Shutterstock

Manufactured in the United States of America

*McFarland & Company, Inc., Publishers
    Box 611, Jefferson, North Carolina 28640
    www.mcfarlandpub.com*

To current and future
baseball fans

ACKNOWLEDGMENTS

I owe acknowledgments to a number of people and organizations that assisted in my efforts.

To provide me with comments and about any issues relevant to the popularity of baseball, during 2006 these sports fans stated what troubled them the most with respect to the sport or big leagues. The insights of Loras College professor of economics Laddie Sula, Winthrop University professor of economics Gary Stone, Pfeiffer University's assistant dean for student services at the Charlotte campus, Michael Utsman, orthodontist John Roshel, Jr., of Terre Haute, Indiana, were meaningful and, in part, have been included in various chapters of *Baseball in Crisis*.

Since early 2000, some administrators at Pfeiffer University have generously granted me time to concentrate on the study of professional team sports. These persons include former vice president for academic affairs and dean of the undergraduate college Bettie Starr, and professor of accounting and director of the master of business administration program Bob Spear. For seven years Bettie and Bob have not required me to participate on many university committees and projects, or to become involved in the school's extracurricular activities. Their cooperation, trust and support are very much appreciated.

To be accurate, informative and interesting, this title contains many examples about events that had occurred with respect to the regular seasons and postseasons of the American League and National League, and to various teams, coaches and players. To that end, Brand Keys Inc.'s president Dr. Robert Passikof provided me with some special assistance. He explained his Sports Loyalty Index and Customer Loyalty Index measures and how these indexes are applied to the operations of professional sports franchises.

Becky Wallace, who works for a Chicago-based company named Team Marketing Report, promptly answered questions about the organization's generation and publication of ticket prices and fan cost indexes for MLB clubs and other professional sports league teams. Howard Bloom and other sports writers published articles practically each day about the operation and business of professional sports on the web site sportsbusinessnews.com. This information is cited throughout *Baseball in Crisis*. Thus, my thanks and best wishes to Dr. Passikof, Becky and Team Marketing Report, and Howard Bloom.

As he did with my previous sports books, Pfeiffer University's director of information services at the Charlotte, North Carolina, campus, Frank Chance, was the primary source for me any of the literature I needed on general and specific topics in baseball. He never hesitated to scan databases and obtain books on interlibrary loan, to download articles for me from journals, magazines and newspapers, and to locate and confirm hard-to-find numbers about MLB's regular seasons and postseasons, teams and players. By successfully completing these tasks, Frank saved me from spending many hours on a computer to research the literature. Moreover, his knowledge of library holdings and sports meant that the information he had acquired was both current and complete. Without Frank, this look could not have been written using the most relevant and up-to-date references and periodicals. So Frank, my special thanks to you for your input into the production of the manuscript.

For ten years, I've used a room at Maureen Fogle's residence, in a certain city of northeast South Carolina, as an office housing my computer and printer, as well as baseball books and assorted documents and files. To be near a desk, these materials were scattered on the floor of the office, in a chair and within a closet, while some folders neatly rested on a bed in another room. Although Maureen occasionally complained about the messy appearance of these two rooms, she never forced me to move the stuff to another room in an inconvenient place. Also we shared the cost of purchasing and maintaining the printer. Because of Maureen, there was a quiet and out-of-the-way space for me to complete any of the tasks related to my classes at Pfeiffer University, and to write sports books.

Besides such academic benefits, in 2005 Maureen and I agreed to co-own a friendly and sweet basset/beagle mix named Lucy. Lucy has been a constant companion, and we relish her love and affection for us. In short, Maureen — who favors the Boston Red Sox — and Lucy — who enjoys dog agility tournaments on television's Animal Planet — are respectively my soul mate and our pet, and the real reasons for my being an economics professor who has the discipline and ambition to author this book about some past, current and potential issues in baseball, and the short and long run business, financial and social problems that involve MLB and the American and National League teams.

TABLE OF CONTENTS

PREFACE

After playing a total of 17 years as an amateur athlete while a student in elementary and high school, and at Indiana State University in Terre Haute, I have an interest in studying the business aspects of the professional sports industry based in the United States. This interest developed during three distinct periods. The first period was in the mid-to-late 1970s, when Georgia State University professors Larry Schroeder and David Sjoquist had guided me to write a dissertation on sports as a final requirement for a doctorate in economics. Because of their assistance, my dissertation, titled "An Economic Analysis of Franchise Relocation and League Expansion in Professional Team Sports, 1950–1975," was completed in 1977. Besides being the leading members of my dissertation committee, Larry and David also played basketball for fun, and so we competed against each other in pick-up games after classes on Friday afternoons at the school's gymnasium. In retrospect, the microeconomics team beat macroeconomics in most of the games.

During the second period, which was the late 1970s to mid–1990s, I wrote a few articles about professional sports for various journals and newspapers, and also attended some academic conferences to present research. Then, in the mid-to-late 1990s, period three, my first book was published. It was titled *Relocating Teams and Expanding Leagues in Professional Sports: How the Major Leagues Respond to Market Conditions* (Quorum, 1999). Professor John J. Guthrie, Jr., who taught history and basic economics for several years at Daytona Beach Community College in Florida, edited the manuscript and co-authored the book. Sadly, in 2000, John died at the age of 44 from the complications of an illness. Even so, in ten years he accomplished a significant amount of scholarly work as an author and co-author, and as an instruc-

1

tor and researcher. In his honor, DBCC officials planted a tree on the campus in memory of John's contributions in education and for being an outstanding professor, inspiration, and role model to his students.

I wrote four books between 2000 and 2006, and each focused on the business, economics and finance of professional team sports. These four titles were *American Sports Empire: How the Leagues Breed Success* (Praeger, 2003), *Sports Capitalism: The Foreign Business of American Professional Leagues* (Ashgate, 2004), *Baseball, Inc.: The National Pastime as Big Business* (McFarland, 2006); and *Big Sports, Big Business: A Century of League Expansions, Mergers, and Reorganizations* (Praeger, 2006).

In researching the history of major league baseball (MLB) and learning all about the league and after reading about the current status of baseball in urban areas and rural communities across America, and the conduct of major league players, it became evident that MLB is influenced by significant business, demographic and economic trends, which present a variety of challenges for the league to confront. The purpose of this book is to analyze these matters.

Baseball in Crisis contains plenty of dollar amounts, numbers and statistics, and other information that were reported in the readings. Any typographical errors that were missed during the editing of the manuscript, and any mistakes in the historical facts and records, are my responsibility.

INTRODUCTION

Since they were established and became distinguished as national organizations between the late 1800s early 2000s, each of America's prominent professional sports leagues and their respective franchises have anticipated and responded to the public's demands by implementing policies and rules to reform their operations as businesses, and thus effectively compete against each other for fans and market share, and to earn more revenues and profits. From a historical perspective, foremost among these organizations is Major League Baseball (MLB) and its American League (AL) and National League (NL). Surviving economic recessions, world wars and other destabilizing events such as baseball team scandals, player union strikes and MLB work stoppages, the AL and NL have been independent entities, but linked together because they joined to form big league baseball in 1901. After that year, some of the other existing sports leagues were eventually organized and officially named. These groups include, for example, the National Hockey League (NHL) in 1917, National Football League (NFL) in 1922, National Basketball Association (NBA) in 1949 and Major League Soccer (MLS) in 1995.

As an organization within the sports and entertainment industries and throughout the twentieth century, MLB experienced and resolved a number of threatening challenges that, to some extent, affected each of the leagues and baseball's current and future image, growth and structure. To illustrate, before 1950, there was much illegal gambling on baseball games by several big league players; the enactment and enforcement of antitrust laws involving baseball, and the entry of rival professional leagues and their exit from the sport. Then, after 1950, some new clubs were admitted into the AL and NL, a few baseball franchises decided to move their teams to other cities, and free

3

agency was adopted by MLB to benefit players. Besides these matters, the majority of team owners received increasing amounts of revenues from local, regional and national television and radio broadcast rights, the market value of various franchises skyrocketed, players' salaries soared, and new ballparks that cost $100 million and more were constructed primarily taxpayer funds. Despite these events, MLB not only survived as a sport and entertainment business but also generally prospered during the century-plus it has existed in the present, two-league structure.

For various reasons, however, since the early-to-mid–1990s the public's demand for baseball has significantly declined. This trend has been documented in several studies by reputable media companies. For example, in "Americans to Rest of World: Soccer Not Really Our Thing," the Pew Research Center surveyed 2,250 adults during February-March 2006 and determined that only 13 percent of them selected baseball as their favorite sport, while 34 percent chose football, 14 percent preferred basketball, and 4 percent enjoyed soccer. Interestingly, when broken down by race, baseball was the favorite of 14 percent of whites, 4 percent of blacks, and 15 percent of Hispanics. Furthermore, the Pew Research Center article contained statistics from a Gallup poll that noted the following changes in responses to the question, "What is your favorite sport to watch?" From August 1994 to December 2004 baseball had declined from 21 to 10 percent among adult respondents, while football increased from 35 to 38 percent and basketball from 11 to 13 percent, and soccer remained at 2 percent. Therefore, as the favorite sport viewed by adults in 2004, baseball was inferior to football, about equal to basketball, and superior to soccer and other team sports such as ice hockey, as well as to individual sports including boxing, golf, ice skating, tennis and wrestling.[1]

Based, in part, on data from surveys, and on other sources listed in the literature, and given the information contained in my five prior sports books, *Baseball in Crisis* identifies and examines the most, persistent and substantial issues that have most likely restricted MLB's popularity as a professional sport. Likewise, these and other issues may limit the league's current and future stability, its growth and prosperity as a business entity, and the AL and NL as member units within the group. Moreover, although average attendances at regular season and postseason baseball games — and most teams' total revenues and their market values — have steadily increased in recent years, MLB's 30 franchises lag relatively behind NFL and NBA teams in popularity, television viewers and income growth, but ahead of the NHL and MLS clubs with respect to these sports-specific and financial matters.

As further evidence of market erosion in big league baseball, Chapters

1–5 of this book reveal that a smaller proportion of sports fans are participating in fantasy baseball games; the auctioning of several naming rights to investors for big league ballparks have netted, on average, smaller increases in these revenues for MLB franchises; some well-known sports periodicals are publishing more articles about professional football and basketball news than about baseball; and recent television ratings for MLB's annual All-Star game, postseason divisional playoffs, league championships and World Series are a major disappointment to baseball officials and team owners, to the broadcast network executives, to baseball's partners, licensees, sponsors and vendors, and to the print media. To analyze these problems and other matters, this book includes a combination of demographic, economic and financial information, plus baseball-specific data, statistics and values.[2]

Before outlining the challenges to baseball that will be discussed in each of the five chapters, and recommending specific reforms in Chapter 6, the next section contains a representative sample of the literature that was consulted to researched *Baseball in Crisis*. As listed in the bibliography, my sources include a number of enlightening articles, books, Internet sources, dissertations, media guides and reports.

Baseball Literature

I researched a wide variety of baseball books, as well as other printed and online publications, which were then incorporated into one or more chapters. Interestingly, this literature provided numerous facts and different perspectives about when and why the game of baseball, and MLB, had gradually decreased in market share among United States sports fans. Furthermore, the literature discloses why thousands of these fans have reordered their preferences for entertainment, especially since the early-to-mid–1990s, and switched from watching MLB games to becoming followers of the other American-based professional sports leagues including minor league, baseball, and to attending events of other sports organizations, such as the National Association for Stock Car Automobile Racing (NASCAR). Anyway, the majority of these readings in the literature reported useful insights that revealed the current status of MLB, and its AL and NL teams. The following are a few of these sources with respect to professional baseball and the sport and entertainment business.

Team Marketing Report (TMR) is a commercial media company that is based in Chicago, Illinois. This firm publishes each year at least two detailed publications about professional sports leagues and teams. One document, in part, lists the average ticket prices of the 30 MLB teams for a regular season, while the other document consists of a Fan Cost Index (FCI) for each of the clubs. After making adjustments for ticket price and volume discounts, TMR weighs and indexes the seating capacities of all big league ballparks to determine the average value of a ticket so that each of the FCIs measure what it costs, in total, for a family of four to attend the MLB teams' regular season games. Even though these TMR publications are timely and comprehensive, more information about ballpark ticket prices and other game costs are available on the web sites of the big league teams and also reported on the AL and NL primary online site mlb.com.

Besides the publications of TMR, there are numerous sources for researchers of the sports industry to obtain specific facts and statistics, and to read general information about the business, economic and financial operations of franchises and the history of professional baseball teams, players and seasons. These sources include, for example, such Internet sites as ball parks.com, baseballalmanac.com, baseballlibrary.com, cnnsi.com, sabr.org, sportsbusinessnews.com, sports.espn.com, wikipedia.org and yahoo.com. Other literature concerning the performances of various coaches, general managers, players and teams, and about the AL and NL, are the *Official Major League Baseball Fact Book 2005 Edition* (2005), *The New Bill James Historical Baseball Abstract* (2003), *Baseball Between the Numbers* (2006), and *The Numbers Game: Baseball's Lifelong Fascination with Statistics* (2004). Of these publications, the two most valuable sources for this book were sportsbusinessnews.com and the *Official Major League Baseball Fact Book 2005 Edition*.

In fact, to read more about the causes and realities of MLB's deteriorating market share and fan base, it was productive for me to thoroughly research any books, media guides, newspapers and periodicals that provided the regular seasons' and postseasons' attendances of baseball teams and these franchises' total revenues and players' payrolls; that reported the estimated and actual costs to build and operate new ballparks and renovate existing stadiums; that published the television ratings of regular season and postseason MLB games and such special events as an All-Star Game; that listed the numbers and dates of division titles, league championships and World Series won by various clubs; and that contained reports regarding the AL and NL, and perhaps particular teams' policies, regulations and rules.[3]

Since the late 1980s, several prominent books have been published that discuss big league baseball's history and its structure and performance from various business, cultural, economic, financial, legal and/or social perspectives. In total, these titles delve into major and minor issues and the operation of the sport, and also how MLB has evolved and matured by establishing relationships with local businesses and communities, and baseball fans, players and teams, and franchise owners and investors. As such, each book contains information that relates to concerns in professional baseball.

For example, in 1989 economist and university professor Gerald W. Scully authored *The Business of Major League Baseball*. Generally, Scully modeled and critiqued the sport's economic issues, and then he specifically examined the rules of baseball and their impact on the sport and society, the business aspects of baseball, and the supply and demand conditions of the market for professional baseball players. After an analysis of these issues Professor Scully concluded, in part, that there existed a compelling case for self-regulation in organized baseball; that the effects of television broadcasts on baseball have been mixed although the benefits were greater in 1988–1989 than during earlier years; that as an economic cartel, baseball has not been very efficient; and that to the mid-to-late 1980s, the cartel had mismanaged its wars with the Major League Baseball Players Association (MLBPA), the demands for expansion of the minor leagues, and its relationships with communities and players. As Scully viewed baseball's future, his forecast was stated as follows: "The period 1989–90 and after promises to be turbulent. Yet baseball is in its second century. History suggests that the leagues will, at the very least, blunder through and that the game which is our national pastime will endure."[4]

During 1992, Basic Books published educator and consultant Andrew Zimbalist's *Baseball and Billions*. The book's primary topics included such matters as the evolution of legal and labor relations, baseball's barons, franchises' finances, player performances and salaries, and the minor leagues, metropolises, and the media. Because of the sport's antitrust exemption and its behavior as a monopoly, Zimbalist declared that big league baseball had some serious problems to confront and solve. These were, in part, the competitive imbalances that existed between teams in the AL and NL, MLB's tenuous relationships with cities and governments, and the arrogance of team owners with their wealth, huge egos, and overwhelming authority to dominate all aspects of the sport.

According to Zimbalist, it is commercialism, greed and mismanagement that will threaten the future of the game. As a result, he advocated for an internal reorganization of the league, and also the implementation of policy initiatives by government to restore competition and establish a more equitable distribution of economic benefits between the owners of franchises and these teams' players. To achieve socially efficient results, Zimbalist proposed the removal of MLB's antitrust exemption and an increase in revenue sharing, reform of the league's television contract with the networks to allow for off-air broadcasts of games in all markets, and an aggressive expansion of the big leagues to 40 or more clubs before 2002. In the concluding section of his book, Zimbalist remarks: "With a modicum of management intelligence, cohesion, and vision there is every reason to believe that MLB can continue to be a growth industry."

Besides the publication of Zimbalist's *Baseball and Billions* in 1992, that year Paul M. Sommers edited *Diamonds Are Forever: The Business of Baseball.* Organized into four parts with each part containing a series of readings, this title discussed some of baseball's most intense and troublesome issues. These problems involved such topics as franchise relocations, collective bargaining processes, commercialization of the game, owners' collective response to free agency, concerns about racial discrimination, and linkages between player performances and pay. Basically the authors of the book's ten articles applied economic models to analyze the operating and financial risks of these issues, and how they had affected the business of baseball despite several years of prosperity that benefited the sport's fans, players and franchise owners. In the end, *Diamonds Are Forever* recommended similar but not identical organizational reforms and public policies as those proposed in *The Business of Major League Baseball* and *Baseball and Billions.*

In 1997 editor Daniel R. Marburger's *Stee-Rike Four! What's Wrong with the Business of Baseball?* was published by Praeger. As a group, this book's 13 readings explored how labor economics had affected the game of professional baseball. Readers of *Stee-Rike Four!* are provided with analyses of such familiar matters as collective bargaining strategies, free agency, salary arbitration, lockouts and strikes, luxury taxes, salary caps, revenue sharing, the plight of baseball teams in small markets, and the sport's antitrust exemption. Despite its historical problems as an economic cartel, baseball in the late 1990s, according to Marburger, had a bright future. In his view of labor relations and sports, it is free-market capitalism, efficient allocation of resources, and the profit motive that will most benefit baseball fans. That is because team owners and union representatives are essentially motivated to base their decisions on whether to, respectively, initiate lockouts or player strikes only after rationally evaluating the economic short- and long-run rewards, costs and risks of approving of work stoppages. Thus after the 1995 regular season, the AL and NL officials, franchise owners and players, and the players' union, had learned that the best policy for them in the future was to make use of the collective bargaining process rather than losing baseball's fan base by canceling regular season games, the playoffs, and a World Series. In the concluding remarks section of his book, Marburger said: "Baseball proved the power of the free market. If you spend too much time arguing over how to share the wealth, the wealth may vanish."

Published by Broadway Books in 2001, Bob Costas's book *Fair Ball: A Fan's Case for Baseball* condemns the behavior of players who, after productive seasons with a team, become free agents and then quit their teams to sign lucrative contracts with other clubs. Besides criticizing these players' greediness and disloyalty, Costas also contends that MLB's problems are caused by such things as the designated hitter rule, interleague games, the wild card system, and the increasing payroll disparities between teams in small versus large markets. To resolve these issues, Costas—an Emmy Award–winning television sports broadcaster—would abolish the designated hitter rule, eliminate interleague competition except for World Series games, permit only the six division winners in the AL and NL to qualify for the playoffs, and establish payroll limits—that is, floors and caps—to partially control the relative salary differentials between clubs that play home and away games in the various markets. It is likely, however, that MLB Commissioner Bud Selig, franchise owners and the MLBPA would each unanimously reject Costas's reforms because they are too radical and would not equally benefit the leagues, the 30 teams and their players. Indeed, as one reviewer of his book stated: "*Fair Ball* offers a good overview of both baseball's problems and solutions. It's meant as a rallying cry for baseball fans, not a negotiation plan for owners and players."

In his 2006 book *In the Best Interests of Baseball?*, sports economist and columnist Andrew Zimbalist declares that as MLB's full-time commissioner since the mid-to-late 1990s, Bud Selig has been a success. According to Zimbalist, former Milwaukee Brewers owner Selig has been a consensus-building leader and a shrewd diplomat in mediating with the teams' executives. Furthermore, he is very impartial at meting out justice, open-minded about accepting new concepts that appeal to the interests of baseball fans, and most importantly, he sincerely believes in treating the union and baseball players with respect.

In Zimbalist's book, some economic issues are addressed that do not receive enough attention in the sports pages of local newspapers and national baseball magazines. These matters include the deficiencies in baseball's revenue sharing plan, the devious and selfish strategies of those owners who sell or offer to sell their MLB franchises, the implicit tax ramifications of the sport's business practices, and the innovative remedies to close the revenue gaps between clubs in metropolitan areas with small and large populations. Besides exploring these topics, Zimbalist also discusses the roles of previous MLB commissioners such as Judge Kenesaw Mountain Landis, Ford Frick and

Peter Ueberroth. Written for anyone who is concerned about how the sport operates as a business cartel and the effectiveness of Bud Selig's leadership, *In the Best Interests of Baseball?* is a recent and thoughtful addition to the literature. In retrospect, it is authors Scully, Zimbalist, Sommers, Marburger and Costas who primarily identified the current and future problems in baseball.

The final book to be highlighted in this literature review is *Baseball, Inc.: The National Pastime as Big Business*, which was published by McFarland in early 2006. The book, also by this author, is organized into five parts, each of which is composed of essays that examine various topics of Major and Minor League Baseball, such as of the sport's history, competitiveness, progress, and business operation. Consequently there are detailed discussions about such matters as the redistribution of revenues among teams; he history of player unionization; the global marketing of baseball by AL and NL officials, strategies of how franchise owners create, develop and promote their brands; teams' average ticket prices and fan cost indexes for various regular seasons; success or failure of former league expansions and team relocations, the growth and impact of professional international baseball players; an evaluation of teams' coaches and general managers; baseball's drug culture and its television and radio broadcasting contracts, and clubs' social investments in their local communities, charities and events. After reading my essays, the readers of *Baseball, Inc.* learn when, why and how professional baseball became a popular leisure activity and a top-notch sport in the U.S. and somewhat in Canada, and about MLB's efforts to expand the game into Asia, Western Europe and Latin America.

Book Organization

To discuss the most persistent challenges facing American baseball and especially MLB, there are six chapters in *Baseball in Crisis*. Although the first five chapters focus on specific issues, the contents of the book are so interrelated that certain matters may be mentioned in sections of more than one chapter. For example, the dedication displayed by baseball fans for their local teams — as highlighted in Chapter 2 — are influenced, in part, by several factors contained in other chapters, such as the inflated price of seats at ballparks, the opening of a new stadium, a team's total wins for regular seasons in its division, the salaries, personalities and performances of rookies and veteran players, the success of clubs located in the same metropolitan area, and coverage of the games in local newspapers.

Chapter 1 deals with the effects and implications of inflationary player, team and game costs. In professional baseball, the financial topic of major concern for franchise owners is the nominal and annual increases in the dollar amounts — and in percentage growths — of player salaries and team payrolls, while for typical fans — individuals as well as families and other groups — it is the higher average ticket prices and other ballpark expenses to attend teams' home and away regular season games, the playoffs, and the World Series. Simply put, this chapter reveals how historical changes in these types of costs have tended to destabilize some players' and teams' performances, and thus have directly affected the clubs' attendances, revenues and market values.[5]

In contrast, Chapter 2 reveals how MLB's fan base has evolved in recent decades and why it has shifted among various age, gender and ethnic groups, and among households in different income classes. Indeed, a number of these changes have resulted in cultural, economic and social challenges for big league teams. Also, these changes have created business risks for one or more clubs in the AL and NL, and for other organizations affiliated with MLB, such as fans in local communities, baseball's licensees, partners, sponsors and vendors, and radio stations and television broadcast networks. Finally, the chapter includes elements of cost and price inflation, and contrasts some of the changes in performances and market values that have occurred between teams located in small, midsized and large metropolitan areas.[5]

Chapter 3 analyzes a variety of historical and business-related information pertaining to the cities where professional baseball clubs are or have previously been located in the U.S. and Canada. Identifying and describing the location and size of these places, the chapter reveals how congested baseball markets are with respect to the numbers of current and perhaps future sports franchises. Then some international cities are portrayed as being either potentially attractive or undesirable sites to host new and/or relocated major league, and perhaps minor league, professional baseball clubs.[6]

Chapter 4 discusses some of the irresponsible behaviors and decisions, and illegal practices and scandals that involved at one time or another have MLB players and the players' union, and also team owners and league officials. The chapter relates how these events undermine the sport's interests and have damaged relationships with baseball's fans, local communities and governments, and perhaps with the media. Such activities include reports of players abusing drugs, committing crimes and initiating domestic violence; franchise owners' selfishness and disinvestment in the short-run competitiveness and long-run development of their clubs; owners' threats to move their team to another city if local taxpayers do not fund the construction of a new home ballpark; and collective bargaining disputes and contractual conflicts that have led to several lockouts and player strikes, and to canceling portions of regular seasons, and the entire playoffs and the World Series in 1994. Although these and similar problems have occurred in other U.S. professional team sports, they seem to have been more frequent in the behavior of big league baseball.[7]

Alternatively, Chapter 5 exposes the misallocation of power among the 30 big league franchises. Key differences and trends are examined about AL and NL teams' metropolitan areas and performances, and their payrolls, revenues and estimated market values. Despite a redistribution of income because of revenue sharing and a luxury tax on the clubs with the highest annual payrolls, small market teams, such as those who play at home in Cleveland, Kansas City, Miami, Milwaukee, Pittsburgh and Tampa Bay, generally struggle each season for wins. Even teams located in various midsized markets like Arlington, Baltimore, Denver, Seattle, Toronto and Washington, D.C., each finished the 2006 season more than eight games behind their division leaders.[8]

In retrospect, below-average performance by these mediocre clubs tends to diminish their image among local, regional and national sports fans, discourages baseball fans from attending these teams' regular season home games, constrains the growth of their revenues from the sales of tickets, merchandise and concessions at their home ballparks, causes their owners to cut payroll in future regular seasons and perhaps to not invest in player development and minor league programs, prevents these clubs from competing for division titles and league championships, and motivates their general managers to trade the teams' most valuable players and even raise ticket prices. In short, this chapter focuses on the distribution of power among the 14 clubs in the AL and 16 in the NL.

Chapter 6 recommends the, implementation and enforcement of selected reforms in the big leagues that will strategically increase the efficiency and popularity of baseball and MLB, and will improve the decisions made by the commissioner, league and union officials, and franchise owners, general managers, coaches and players. Such reforms may include one or more of the following items.

First, the adoption of a more equitable redistribution of revenues and/or luxury taxes between small, midsized and large market franchises in each league; second, the consistent application of regulations and standards as established by the league and team owners, and the MLBPA; third, more severe but prompt and equitable penalizing of players who violate teams' and the union's rules when they consume performance-enhancing drugs and other illegal substances, commit crimes, and engage in violent actions; fourth, the implementation of a system by the league to periodically evaluate foreign cities as potential sites for expansion and relocating teams; fifth, imposition by the team owners of some type of limits on clubs who unjustifiably increase their ticket prices to home games and thereby gouge local baseball fans; and sixth, creation by the commissioner's office of incentives for the AL and NL to aggressively market the sport to various age, gender and ethnic groups in nations across the globe, and especially to baseball fans in Asian and Latin American countries.

Certainly the literature contains a number of reforms as proposed by academic experts, baseball officials and blue-ribbon committees. Furthermore, successful policies in other professional sports may be feasible to adopt by teams in MLB and even by their affiliated minor league clubs.[9]

1

TEAM PRICES, COSTS, AND VALUES

Since they co-exist and interact within the sports industry, the American League (AL) and National League (NL) franchises and their teams in Major League Baseball (MLB) are compelled to perform as competitive businesses. Consequently, each of these baseball organizations must establish goals. To that end, the primary economic goal is to maximize profits or alternatively, to minimize losses. So in order to accomplish a team's objective, it is the responsibility of a franchise owner and his or her general manager and administrative staff to implement short- and long-run organizational strategies and jointly make important financial decisions, and to hire a competent field manager and coaching staff who will inspire, develop and lead ballplayers to win enough regular season games against rivals in a division to qualify for the AL or NL playoffs.[1]

From a purely business perspective, the operation and success of MLB franchises are greatly affected by local, regional and national market forces. That is, by changes in such variables as income per capita and population growth, and by fluctuations in inflation and in interest and unemployment rates. In turn, these and other variables tend to influence the cash flows, revenue streams, and expenses of teams, and likewise their earnings after taxes. Furthermore, a professional baseball club's success or failure each season depends on its ability to establish a proportionately large and enthusiastic fan base within its local community and metropolitan area, to win exciting baseball games against opponents in its home ballpark, and to generate support from the hometown media. In short, there are several internal and external demographic, economic, financial and sport-specific variables that determine the current and future expectations for the performances of MLB franchises.

Beginning in the early-to-mid–1990s, and especially after the AL and NL had canceled some regular season games and the playoffs and the World Series in 1994 and then failed to open the 1995 season as scheduled, the public's demand for professional baseball gradually deteriorated. This decline occurred even though the United States national economy and securities markets, and thousands of private businesses and a majority of households, generally prospered during the period. Thus, to explain why MLB was economically troubled several reasons have been proposed by academic researchers and sports analysts, and by journalists, practitioners and pundits. Undoubtedly the league's lockout of players during late 1994 and early 1995 disillusioned the public and educated the media about the unique and complex economics of baseball. It also alerted sports fans to how much money was being earned each season by professional baseball players and by teams, and provided information to communities about how these amounts had incrementally raised the market values of franchises and financially benefited those in the sport, including very wealthy franchise owners.

In other words, professional baseball seemingly became an overvalued sport to millions of fans. It seemed that players, the Major League Baseball Players Association (MLBPA) and team owners were unnecessarily arrogant and greedy, and basically out of touch with their affiliates and allies. As a result of this exposure, MLB has subsequently declined in popularity for many years, becoming a disappointment as a competitive sport for large numbers of people who may watch baseball games on television and read about them in newspapers, and who may purchase expensive season tickets to attend games and buy the merchandise and other products of the teams.

This chapter examines why inflationary prices, costs and valuations have limited the prosperity of MLB relative to the other professional sports in America, and how this issue has marginally constrained the expansion of pubic goodwill and social benefits to teams' players and the MLBPA, and to franchise owners. Specifically, the focus of this chapter is on four effects: the steady growth of big league baseball's ticket prices at ballparks; the rising costs for families with children to attend regular season and postseason games; the ever-higher payrolls spent by owners to acquire their teams' players; finally, the dilemmas that occur when the valuations of some franchises temporarily peak to amounts in the several hundreds of millions of dollars.

Consequences of Inflating Ticket Prices

According to Table 1.1, between 1993 and 2006 the ticket prices at regular season games of MLB teams averaged approximately $15. Meanwhile, on average the price per ticket to attend an NBA game was about $39, NHL game $40, and NFL game $44. Indeed, during this range of 14 consecutive seasons—excluding, however, 1993 and 2004 in the NHL—the average ticket price of each of these four professional sports had increased, respectively, by 114 percent in baseball, versus 66 percent in basketball, 24 percent in ice hockey, and 121 percent in football.[2]

Specifically in MLB, the four largest percentage increases year-to-year occurred when tickets rose by 15 percent for the 1999 regular season, 11 percent for the 1994 season, and 10 percent for the 1996 and 2005 seasons. Interestingly, because of attacks by terrorists in America during September of 2001, which resulted in immediate cutbacks of consumer and business spending and a slowdown of the United States economy, there was a significant drop that year in average ticket prices to watch NBA, NFL and NHL games, but surprisingly, not of the prices to attend MLB games. Perhaps baseball's franchise owners had decided that their fans, markets and revenue streams would not be adversely affected by these attacks. So the group of owners marginally increased the average price of tickets at their ballparks, that is, by more than six percent in 2001, and then between five and six percent in 2002 and again in 2003.

Based in part on these changes and other seasons when ticket prices were inflated, big league baseball has struggled to recover its entire fan base since 1993 and a year later, when the league had to cancel some regular season games, its playoffs and the World Series, and also a number of games in the early portion of the 1995 season. As a result, baseball teams' average attendance declined, in thousands, from 31.2 per game in 1994 to 28.8 in 2005 although the league's total attendance increased from 50.4 million to 74.9 million (see Table 2.1). But in 1993, which was one year before the players struck, MLB's average attendance per game and total attendance were, respectively, 30.9 thousand and 70.2 million. In other words, while attendance per game was greater in 1993 than in 2005, the totals have increased because of such actions as the Brewers' shift from the AL to NL after the 1997 season; the placement of new expansion teams in Phoenix and Tampa Bay in 1998; the batting competition between Mark McGwire and Sammy Sosa to break Babe Ruth's single season home run record of 60, and the movement of the Expos from Montreal to Washington, D.C., in early 2005, after which the team was renamed the Washington Nationals.

Table 1.1 Leagues Average Ticket Prices
By Sport League and Leagues Per Season, 1993–2006

League	1993	1994	1995	1996	1997	1998	1999	2000	2001	2002	2003	2004	2005	2006
MLB	9	10	10	11	12	13	15	16	17	18	19	19	21	22
NBA	27	30	31	34	36	42	48	51	41	43	44	45	45	47
NFL	28	30	33	35	39	42	45	49	47	50	52	54	58	62
NHL	NA	33	34	38	42	42	46	47	41	41	43	—	41	43
Average	21	25	27	29	32	34	38	40	36	38	39	39	41	43

Note: The sports leagues are abbreviated as MLB for Major League Baseball, NBA for the National Basketball Association, NFL for the National Football League, and NHL for the National Hockey League. The average ticket prices of teams are reported in dollars and represent the 1993–2006 regular seasons in each sport. NA means the data was not available in 1993 and the dash (—) indicates that the NHL's 2004 regular season was canceled.

Source: "Major League Baseball," at http://www.teammarketing.com cited 10 September 2006; "National Basketball Association," at http://www.teammarketing.com cited 10 September 2006; "National Football League," at http://www.teammarketing.com cited 10 September 2006; "National Hockey League," at http://www.teammarketing.com cited 10 September 2006.

During 16 seasons, former Oakland Athletics and St. Louis Cardinals slugger Mark McGwire hit 583 homers and batted in 1,414 runs, and was selected to 11 All-Star teams. Although he did not admit to abusing drugs as a player, on the first ballot McGwire received only 25 percent of the votes necessary to be elected into the Baseball Hall of Fame. [National Baseball Hall of Fame Library, Cooperstown, N.Y.]

Despite relatively higher ticket prices per game, the NBA, NFL and NHL have experienced proportionately larger increases in attendance than in MLB. For example, between 1993 and 2005 the changes in the average and total attendances of these three sports were as follows: 16.2 to 17.5 thousand per game and 17.9 to 21.5 million in the NBA; 62.3 to 67.5 thousand per game and 13.9 to 17.3 million in the NFL; and 14.7 to 16.9 thousand per game and 16.1 to 20.8 million in the NHL. It is apparent, therefore, that baseball's steady increases in average ticket prices since the early 1990s have contributed to impeding the growth in attendance per game despite the league's two highest totals of 74.9 million in the 2005 season, and one year later, more than 76 million. This outcome implies, in part, that average ticket prices to attend regular season games in MLB are moderately too expensive relative to in the other three professional sports, even though in 2006 an average price of $22 per ticket in baseball was approximately 50 percent or less than tickets to games in the NBA, NFL and NHL.

To determine how much more in dollars and percentages that tickets cost in the other three sports leagues relative to those in MLB during selected regular seasons, ratios of prices were calculated and compared for 1993, 1994, 2000 and 2006. To illustrate, based on the average prices that are listed in column two of Table 1.1, in 1993 a fan paid $18, or 200 percent, more for a ticket to attend a game between, for example, the Philadelphia 76ers and Boston Celtics than a game priced at $9 between the St. Louis Cardinals and Chicago Cubs. Also in that year the average price of a ticket to any professional sports game was $21, which was $12, or 133 percent, more than a single game in MLB. Given this illustration, the ratios of ticket prices among the four leagues for three years reveal some interesting consequences.

First, during 1994 the average price for a spectator to attend a big league game between clubs such teams as the Los Angeles Dodgers and Arizona Diamondbacks was $10. In turn, it cost on average $20, or 200 percent, more to watch the regular season games played between NBA teams and among NFL teams, and $23, or 230 percent, more to see the NHL clubs compete against each other. Thus, prior to the players' strike in the summer of 1994, baseball's franchise owners had made it relatively inexpensive for consumers to buy tickets and attend MLB games than did the owners of teams in the other professional sports. As a result, before the players struck, there was above average attendances at ballparks during the majority of games in MLB. In fact, baseball's prices remained almost the same in 1995 after the players had returned to complete the regular season and then the playoffs and the World Series.

Second, six years after 1994, ticket prices between the four sports leagues had changed in dollars and percentages. Relative to MLB's average ticket price of $16, in 2000 it cost $35, or 218 percent, more for spectators to watch a typical game in the NBA; $33, or 206 percent, more in the NFL; and $31, or 193 percent, more in the NHL. Therefore, despite the prosperity of MLB clubs during the latter 1990s, the sport's 30 franchise owners had not gouged baseball fans by overpricing the tickets to their home games. Alternatively, it became more expensive in dollars and percentages for fans to see games in the NBA and NFL, but not as much so on a percentage basis in the NHL, since the demand for ice hockey games by American sports fans was not as robust as in the other sports.

Third, in 2006 a ticket to a big league game averaged $22. Meanwhile to attend an NBA game it cost fans $25, or 113 percent, more than in MLB; $40, or 181 percent, more for them at NFL games; and $21, or 95 percent, more for NHL games. Clearly, between 2000 and 2006, the percentage differences per game between the leagues had decreased. In other words, during the early 2000s MLB teams had increased their average ticket prices at a greater rate than did the franchise owners of clubs in the other sports. This pricing strategy, in part, was implemented in baseball because of such factors as the growth in attendance at big league games, recovery of the U.S. economy after 2001–2002, relatively low national inflation, interest and unemployment rates, more competition between teams in divisions within the AL and NL and during the playoffs, MLB's new four-year collective bargaining agreement in 2002, and the improvements of clubs like the AL Angels, Red Sox and White Sox, and NL Cardinals, Diamondbacks and Marlins, who each won a World Series and thus prevented the New York Yankees from repeating as champions (see Table A.1.1).

Table 1.2 denotes how average ticket prices (rounded to whole dollars) had varied among the 30 MLB teams each year between 1993 and 2006. From my perspective, the increases in ticket prices implemented by teams to open the majority of their 14 or fewer seasons, the different prices between clubs in the AL and NL and among all of them, and the ranges in prices of teams located in small, midsized and large markets, have each affected these franchises' attendances, revenues and estimated values, and likely their seasons' and players' annual performances.

Historically, for example, the average ticket prices listed in the table have been highest for such large market clubs as the AL Boston Red Sox and New York Yankees, and the NL Chicago Cubs and New York Mets. In turn, these four teams have each earned a large amount of revenues from their ticket sales. Except for the Yankees, however, they are not perennial winners of their divisions and league titles, of multiple World Series. Alternatively,

Table 1.2 MLB Teams Average Ticket Prices By Leagues and Teams Per Season, 1993–2006

Team	1993	1994	1995	1996	1997	1998	1999	2000	2001	2002	2003	2004	2005	2006
AL														
Angels	8	8	8	9	11	13	13	11	11	15	16	16	17	18
Athletics	10	10	10	11	10	10	10	11	14	14	15	16	17	22
Blue Jays	13	13	13	13	15	16	16	16	15	15	18	17	19	23
Brewers	9	9	9	9	9	—	—	—	—	—	—	—	—	—
Devil Rays	—	—	—	—	—	15	15	12	16	15	14	16	13	17
Indians	8	12	12	14	15	17	18	20	22	22	22	20	21	21
Mariners	7	9	9	11	13	14	19	23	22	24	24	24	24	24
Orioles	11	11	13	13	17	19	19	19	18	18	20	22	22	22
Rangers	8	12	12	11	13	16	19	19	18	18	18	16	16	15
Red Sox	11	13	13	15	17	20	24	28	34	39	38	40	44	46
Royals	9	10	10	9	9	10	11	11	12	12	12	13	13	13
Tigers	9	11	10	10	10	10	12	24	20	20	19	17	18	18
Twins	9	9	9	10	8	8	8	9	10	11	13	14	16	17
White Sox	11	12	12	14	13	14	15	14	18	18	22	21	25	26
Yankees	13	14	15	14	18	20	23	25	24	24	24	24	27	28
AL Average	9	10	11	11	12	14	15	17	18	18	19	19	21	22
NL														
Astros	8	8	8	10	11	11	13	20	17	18	20	22	24	26
Braves	9	12	12	13	17	17	19	19	20	20	17	17	17	17
Brewers	—	—	—	—	—	10	11	11	16	17	16	16	16	18
Cardinals	9	9	9	9	12	15	16	17	21	21	23	23	25	29
Cubs	11	13	13	13	14	14	17	17	21	24	24	28	32	34

Diamondbacks	—	—	—	—	14	16	16	13	13	15	17	19	19
Dodgers	9	9	9	11	12	13	15	15	16	16	16	18	20
Expos	8	8	9	8	9	9	10	9	9	10	10	—	—
Giants	9	10	10	11	11	12	21	19	20	21	21	23	24
Marlins	9	9	10	10	12	12	12	12	12	12	12	15	16
Mets	10	10	11	13	16	19	24	22	22	23	23	23	25
Nationals	—	—	—	—	—	—	—	—	—	—	—	21	20
Padres	8	9	9	10	11	11	13	13	15	16	21	20	20
Phillies	8	9	11	11	11	13	13	14	15	17	26	26	26
Pirates	9	9	10	9	9	10	11	19	20	19	17	17	17
Reds	7	7	7	8	8	9	10	15	16	18	18	17	17
Rockies	7	10	10	12	15	15	16	15	15	15	15	14	14
NL Average	8	9	10	11	12	14	15	16	17	18	18	21	21
MLB Average	9	10	11	12	13	15	16	17	18	19	19	21	22

Note: The average ticket price of a team is a weighted average of season ticket prices for seating categories within a ballpark. It is determined by factoring the tickets in each price range as a percentage of the total number of seats available in each ballpark. The table excludes luxury seats but includes season ticket prices. Team Marketing Report first reported the average ticket prices for children in 1999. The Brewers moved from the AL to NL in 1998 and that year, the Devil Rays joined the AL and Diamondbacks the NL. In 1997, the Angels' first name changed from California to Anaheim, and then in 2005 the Anaheim Angels became the Los Angeles Angels of Anaheim. Canadian prices are converted to U.S. dollars for the AL Blue Jays and NL Expos. A dash (—) indicates that no MLB team existed at the site in that season.

Source: The teams' average ticket prices were contained in "Major League Baseball," at http://www.teammarketing.com cited 10 September 2006.

such small market clubs as the AL Kansas City Royals, Minnesota Twins and Tampa Bay Devil Rays, and the NL Florida Marlins, Cincinnati Reds and Pittsburgh Pirates each charge spectators at their ballparks among the lowest average ticket prices per season. These clubs have generally struggled to be competitive in their divisions and to qualify for the postseason playoffs. Surprisingly, the Colorado Rockies, Texas Rangers, and Atlanta Braves have tended to have average or below-average ticket prices because of the support of local sports fans for popular NFL teams that play at home in Denver (Broncos), Arlington (Cowboys) and Atlanta (Falcons). Thus, competition from these and other professional sports teams in their hometown markets have constrained some AL and NL teams from raising prices more than necessary to maximize profits. While this type of pricing behavior could result in more or fewer fans who attend these baseball teams' home games, the MLB clubs may also receive lower cash flows from ticket sales than if their prices were established at or above the league averages (see Table A.1.2).

Based on the information in Table 1.2, it is obvious that some franchise owners significantly hiked their ticket prices when their clubs started playing of regular season home games in a new ballpark. These increased prices occurred, for example, in 1994 for the AL Cleveland Indians at Jacobs Field and in 2000 for the Seattle Mariners at Safeco Field, and in the NL, for the San Francisco Giants at Pacific Bell Park in 2000 and the Milwaukee Brewers at Miller Park in 2001. However, after those four specific seasons were completed, the Indians, Mariners and Giants, but not the Brewers, had each implemented annual ticket price changes that remained above average with respect to the other clubs in their specific leagues. In short, the pricing of tickets to single games and weekend series, and for the 81 home-game regular season, are issues that require each MLB team owner to be less short-sighted and ambitious, and more conscientious and rational in making this type of business decision.

Impact of Rising Costs

Besides the cost of single and season tickets, the families who attend baseball games might also incur other costs associated with this event. These non-ticket costs, of course, are variable based on a family's purchases of clothing, food and merchandise, and other items and products before, during and after a game. As one of its more useful sports statistics for fans and researchers, the Chicago-based Team Marketing Report (TMR) provides an estimate each year of these costs for all MLB, NBA, NFL and NHL franchises. This statis-

Table 1.3 Fan Cost Indexes
By Sport League and Per Season Averages, 1993–2006

League	1993	1994	1995	1996	1997	1998	1999	2000	2001	2002	2003	2004	2005	2006
MLB	91	96	97	103	107	115	121	132	140	145	151	155	164	171
NBA	168	182	192	204	216	241	268	281	244	254	261	263	267	274
NFL	172	180	199	208	227	241	256	279	278	290	301	321	329	346
NHL	NA	195	203	219	234	238	258	264	239	240	253	—	247	258
Average	143	163	172	183	196	208	225	239	225	232	241	246	251	262

Note: The leagues' Fan Cost Indexes are reported in American dollars. An index includes the estimated costs per game of four each average-priced tickets, soft drinks and hot dogs, and two each beers, game programs and adult-sized caps, and an amount for parking fees. NA means Not Available since the NHL's FCI was not estimated by TMR in 1993. The years are each sports league's 1993–2006 regular seasons and the dash (—) indicates that the NHL's 2004 season was cancelled.

Source: See Table 1.1.

tic is titled a Fan Cost Index (FCI) and TMR has published it for MLB, NBA and NFL teams since 1993, and for NHL clubs since 1994. Expressed in American dollars, a 14-year history of FCIs for the three earlier sports leagues—and a 12-year history for the NHL—have been entered as rounded dollar amounts into Table 1.3 and are defined in the note that appears below the table.

As measured by TMR for each of the four leagues' indexes, from the most to least expensive items to purchase by families—after paying for two adult and two child tickets—are respectively caps, parking fees, hot dogs, beers and sodas, and game programs. Typically the costs of tickets are approximately 55 to 65 percent of a professional sports team's FCI. Table 1.3 indicates how a number of FCIs have varied among the four professional leagues based on the games played at home by teams in their regular seasons (see Table A.1.3).

Similar to the listings of ticker prices as depicted in Table 1.1, the highest index of costs in 2006 was $346, which was spent on average by a family who attended an NFL game, while the lowest index of costs that year was $171, which was paid by a family who observed an MLB game or doubleheader. During the several seasons that included costs for each league, MLB's average FCI was $127 and the NBA's $233, NHL's $235 and NFL's $259. Thus, a four-person family could attend one MLB game between the Baltimore Orioles and Toronto Blue Jays for about one-half to two-thirds of what it would cost the same group to watch, for example, a game played between the NBA Miami Heat and Phoenix Suns, or NHL Detroit Red Wings and New York Islanders, or NFL Green Bay Packers and Chicago Bears.

In fact, the distribution of FCIs by sport appears to show an excellent bargain for hometown fans of MLB teams. Nevertheless, since 81 regular season games are played at each of the home-site ballparks in baseball versus eight in football, and 41 each in basketball and ice hockey, families who are not season ticket holders are likely to attend more than one or two home and/or away MLB games per year, and thus spend proportionately more of their discretionary income to see MLB games than to attend games in the other three sports for which the FCIs are significantly higher. Moreover, MLB teams—and their affiliated clubs in the minor leagues—tend to promote their home games as a fun event for households with children.

As such, this marketing strategy means that a portion of the audiences at games will be families with children. Consequently, when an FCI rises in MLB, families with children are especially affected by the costs, so they may remain at home and watch regular season games on cable or a television network. Therefore, a decision by families to not drive to a local ballpark for a game will cumulatively diminish baseball teams' home attendance, and thus franchises' ticket sales, general revenues, and operating profits.

Based on the dollar amounts contained in Table 1.3, the MLB FCIs increased in percentages above the nation's inflation rates in each season except for 1995. That year, baseball's FCI rose by exactly 1.0 percent while the increase in the Consumer Price Index (CPI) was reported as 2.8 percent and in the Gross Domestic Product Deflator (GDPD) as 1.8 percent. Because of the players' strike that cancel a major portion of the 1994 season, the AL and NL playoffs, and a World Series, on average MLB owners decided to keep their ticket prices nearly constant in 1995 while some of the teams' vendors had marginally raised the retail costs of baseball caps, food, memorabilia, and other items that were available for sale at big league ballparks. Furthermore, the table reveals that MLB's FCI increased by six percent in 2001, while the NFL's fell by .5 percent, the NHL's decreased by 10 percent, and the NBA's declined by 13 percent. These differences in percentage changes indicate why the total cost of attending MLB games became relatively more expensive in 2001 and as a result, the 30 teams' home attendances averaged approximately 29.5 thousand per game in the 2000 and 2001 regular seasons.[3]

Similar to the growth in amounts and percentage differences that were discussed in this chapter about teams' average ticket prices in various years, it is interesting to reveal how the leagues' cost indexes—in dollars and percentages—varied relative to each other during particular seasons. So for 1993, 1994, 2000 and 2006, the ratios of leagues' FCIs relative to MLB's were calculated and ranked. To illustrate, based on the second column in Table 1.3, it cost a family of four $91 to attend an MLB game in 1993. In contrast to MLB's FCI, that year an NBA game was $77, or 85 percent, more for a family while an NFL game was $81, or 89 percent, more in total costs. Furthermore, in 1993 the average FCI of $143 for the three leagues exceeded baseball's by $52 or 57 percent. For sure, during the early 1990s families who attended MLB games paid less on average for tickets, beverages and food, clothing and other products at ballparks than did the families who watched games in NBA arenas and NFL stadiums.

During the year that baseball players had struck for higher salaries and benefits, there were only marginal differences in dollars and percentages across the leagues in their FCIs as opposed to the previous year. To be exact, based on an FCI of $96 in MLB, in 1994 it cost families $86, or 90, percent more to attend NBA games than big league baseball games. Moreover, the NFL and NHL games were increasingly expensive for families. Relative to MLB's FCI in 1994 these costs were higher by, respectively, $84 or 87 percent, and $99 or 103 percent. Besides these percentages and values, in 1994 the average FCI of all sports leagues was $163, a $20 increase from 1993, and also 70 percent higher than big league baseball's $96. Thus, because of relatively

Table 1.4 MLB Teams Fan Cost Indexes
By Leagues and Teams Per Season, 1993–2006

Team	1993	1994	1995	1996	1997	1998	1999	2000	2001	2002	2003	2004	2005	2006
AL														
Angels	84	90	90	92	101	113	121	117	110	113	130	133	125	134
Athletics	99	100	101	104	94	98	92	94	120	124	139	145	152	170
Blue Jays	116	113	101	95	106	107	112	112	114	121	155	145	164	182
Brewers	91	87	86	85	94	–	–	–	–	–	–	–	–	–
Devil Rays	–	–	–	–	–	131	120	120	132	138	149	156	143	129
Indians	87	103	99	115	116	126	133	142	150	161	161	152	156	157
Mariners	85	95	95	106	118	125	136	179	180	173	175	173	172	186
Orioles	102	105	113	113	124	135	139	138	131	141	148	158	158	158
Rangers	92	99	100	101	113	127	139	156	150	150	139	130	136	134
Red Sox	100	102	112	117	129	144	160	168	209	228	238	263	276	287
Royals	86	98	98	96	85	96	110	100	119	113	112	120	120	120
Tigers	92	103	96	109	108	102	108	165	160	160	157	149	157	162
Twins	82	90	97	100	97	97	97	102	130	121	127	131	146	149
White Sox	97	106	110	118	115	120	123	122	138	159	159	160	188	191
Yankees	113	115	118	117	134	148	166	174	178	178	182	183	193	208
AL Average	94	100	101	104	109	119	125	134	144	148	155	157	163	169
NL														
Astros	80	86	87	94	105	108	120	161	143	157	165	177	182	191
Braves	97	113	113	121	135	134	144	160	156	155	154	144	145	145
Brewers	–	–	–	–	–	97	95	100	124	130	128	124	130	131
Cardinals	78	91	91	91	105	129	127	133	151	151	168	170	177	207

Cubs	103	108	112	116	121	120	134	135	166	181	172	194	210	219
Diamondbacks	—	—	—	—	—	119	124	120	112	115	119	132	145	147
Dodgers	88	90	90	96	104	111	123	140	142	145	147	153	158	175
Expos	86	82	86	90	86	93	87	88	76	84	100	108	—	—
Giants	87	100	102	121	110	108	110	161	163	169	178	184	191	201
Marlins	98	92	86	92	93	102	100	104	110	110	112	114	147	154
Mets	86	91	91	104	114	132	154	175	175	177	182	186	186	207
Nationals	—	—	—	—	—	—	—	—	—	—	—	—	169	169
Padres	85	83	82	86	101	102	114	124	127	133	146	154	176	180
Phillies	82	91	91	111	100	94	121	126	131	137	149	188	188	193
Pirates	91	93	93	96	86	94	99	107	150	151	147	143	143	138
Reds	77	79	81	81	82	89	96	104	129	127	140	140	145	156
Rockies	81	82	99	103	116	132	135	130	138	141	141	140	141	140
NL Average	87	91	93	100	104	110	117	129	137	141	146	153	164	172
MLB Average	90	95	97	102	106	115	121	132	140	145	150	155	163	171

Note: Each team's Fan Cost Index, which is rounded into whole dollars, includes the prices of two adult and two children tickets, and a combination of beers, sodas, hot dogs, parking fees, game programs, and baseball caps. For more specific details about these prices and costs, see the note below Table 1.3. The dash (—) means that a team did not exist at the site during that season.

Source: "Major League Baseball," at http://www.teammarketing.com cited 10 September 2006.

lower costs, families with children had a greater incentive to attend MLB games than to be spectators at NBA, NFL and NHL games.

Six years later, in the 2000 regular season families spent an average of $132 to attend each MLB game. Nevertheless, despite this amount, in 2000 MLB games were reasonable in price for families relative to the games being played in three other sports leagues. Indeed, families who attended games in the NBA, NFL and NHL paid much more in dollars and on a percentage basis than in MLB. To be specific, for NBA games it was $149, or 112 percent, more; $147, or 111 percent greater, for NFL games; and $132, or 100 percent, higher per game in the NHL. Consequently, when compared to MLB, the FCIs of the NBA and NFL had increased in dollars and percentages relative to 1994, but the differences remained about the same in 1994 and 2000 for the percentage differences in FCIs of MLB and NHL games. In short, families with children must have realized that big league baseball games were an even better bargain in 2000 than in 1994.

By 2006, however, the gap in FCIs had narrowed among the four sports leagues. Given an average cost of $171 for a family to attend a game in MLB, it was only $103, or 60 percent, more for this group of four at NBA games; $175, or 102 percent, more at NFL games, and $87, or 51 percent, more at NHL games. Besides inflated ticket prices to root for the Boston Red Sox and the other 29 big league teams, during the early 2000s families had to spend increasing amounts of money at MLB games for their beverages, food, souvenirs, baseball uniforms and parking fees. These costs had risen for several reasons, such as an increase in demand for professional baseball, an expanding U.S. economy, more expenditures for services at teams' renovated or new ballparks, and to the higher salaries of players, coaches and general managers, and to franchises' profits. If this trend in FCIs continues, before 2012 families will spend about the same amounts to attend MLB games as they would have at games in the other sports leagues.

Table 1.4 evaluates the FCIs of each MLB club and how much these costs have varied per season. The table reveals some interesting and important facts about the operations and businesses of these professional baseball teams. First, in 2006, six or 20 percent of the teams had indexes that exceeded $200 per game for a typical family. In other words, a weekend series of three games between the Red Sox and Yankees at Fenway Park in Boston cost a family of four people an estimated $861. Even so, because Red Sox-Yankees games have always been extremely popular, all of the games' tickets were sold and the two teams shared the revenues generated from the event.

In contrast, an FCI of $120 per game in 2006 for the Royals in Kansas City may be an unreasonable and exorbitant expense for baseball fans and households in that city. That is, when the Royals compete at home against other small market AL teams such as the Cleveland Indians, Minnesota Twins and Tampa Bay Devil Rays, the Royals' crowds in Kauffman Stadium are usually well below capacity due, in part, to the club's FCI of $120. In turn, this means that the Royals and perhaps other small market teams in each of the leagues are at a financial disadvantage to the big city teams. These revenue disparities have existed for many seasons in MLB, and as a result, the competitive gap has continued to expand among many of the AL and NL teams and especially between those that are located in small and large metropolitan areas. In short, there are endemic inequalities among MLB teams despite the two leagues' implementation and enforcement of a revenue sharing system, and the imposition of a luxury tax on high-payroll clubs (see Table A.1.4).

Second, the extreme percentage changes in FCIs among some of the large and small market clubs in each league are a challenge to maintain the growth of the sport. In the NL, for example, between 1993 and 2006 the percentage increases in the FCIs were 140 percent for the big city Mets and 112 percent for the Cubs, but also 111 and 102 percent, respectively, for the Padres and Reds, who each play in relatively small metropolitan areas. Since the Mets at Shea Stadium in New York and the Cubs at Wrigley Field in Chicago each play their home games before fans who earn above-average incomes, these two teams are better able to withstand—with respect to their home-site attendances—any steady but sizable increases in their FCIs than such clubs as the San Diego Padres at Petco Park in southern California and the Cincinnati Reds at the Great American Ballpark in southwestern Ohio.

Third, the FCIs between large and small market clubs have also generally increased in seasons from 1993 to 2006. To illustrate, the cost indexes of the NL Los Angeles Dodgers and Pittsburgh Pirates were nearly equal in 1993. But 13 years later, their FCIs per game differed by $37. Since ticket prices are a major portion of each team's FCI, families now pay proportionately more to attend a Dodgers home game in southern California than a Pirates game in western Pennsylvania. Therefore, the impact of an increasingly higher FCI and greater attendances for the Dodgers has resulted in relatively more revenues from ticket sales for this club at Dodger Stadium than collected by the Pirates at Heinz Field. Simply put, this means that the payrolls and thus competitiveness between the two teams were different in 2006 than in 1993, and most certainly to the Dodgers' advantage.

An aside: during the regular seasons that are listed in Table 1.4, the AL's FCI increased by approximately 80 percent while the NL's expanded by 98 percent. Perhaps the unequal percentage growths between the two leagues

Table 1.5 Team Payrolls
By League and Team Per Season, 1998–2006

Team	1998	1999	2000	2001	2002	2003	2004	2005	2006
AL									
Anaheim/LA Angels	48.3	51.8	54.3	49.4	62.4	79.9	115.6	96.9	103.6
Baltimore Orioles	71.8	78.9	69.3	77.1	62.9	72.1	56.8	81.0	72.5
Boston Red Sox	59.4	59.5	75.5	114.3	116.6	108.4	130.3	116.6	120.1
Chicago White Sox	35.1	24.5	35.6	62.8	57.2	63.2	64.6	73.1	102.8
Cleveland Indians	59.5	68.0	78.3	95.3	77.8	53.4	42.6	40.6	56.7
Detroit Tigers	19.2	34.1	54.8	51.1	56.5	55.3	58.8	68.7	82.3
Kansas City Royals	35.6	23.7	25.9	36.1	52.2	45.4	44.7	34.9	47.2
Minnesota Twins	24.5	19.2	16.7	27.4	41.8	56.9	54.7	6.3	63.8
New York Yankees	65.6	84.2	95.2	114.4	138.4	169.5	187.9	207.1	198.6
Oakland Athletics	22.4	23.2	30.3	39.7	40.9	51.3	60.2	8.4	62.3
Seattle Mariners	43.6	49.9	59.8	79.9	88.3	95.7	81.8	70.5	88.3
Tampa Bay Devil Rays	27.3	33.9	61.2	50.9	35.8	27.4	24.4	26.6	35.4
Texas Rangers	60.5	74.8	57.8	86.8	108.8	103.3	79.2	49.8	65.4
Toronto Blue Jays	34.1	44.5	54.5	74.2	69.2	58.8	50.6	45.6	71.9
AL Average	43.3	47.8	54.9	68.5	72.1	74.3	75.1	73.2	83.6
NL									
Atlanta Braves	61.7	73.3	87.5	94.8	94.7	97.9	79.4	85.8	92.4
Arizona Diamondbacks	31.6	66.0	77.2	85.1	109.5	83.7	68.4	60.8	59.2
Chicago Cubs	49.8	60.1	59.4	72.8	74.9	84.1	100.6	76.5	94.8
Cincinnati Reds	20.7	33.1	42.3	43.9	44.5	50.6	46.2	49.5	59.4
Colorado Rockies	47.7	55.8	63.9	68.6	52.0	66.8	69.4	32.5	41.1

Team									
Florida Marlins	15.1	18.8	22.1	38.0	43.6	55.8	50.3	56.2	14.9
Houston Astros	48.3	51.6	50.1	66.4	66.6	72.8	81.9	76.1	92.5
Los Angeles Dodgers	62.8	79.2	88.8	115.4	103.1	113.2	101.6	87.7	99.1
Milwaukee Brewers	31.8	41.3	36.9	46.6	49.8	43.3	29.5	42.7	56.7
Montreal Expos	8.3	16.1	27.2	34.6	36.6	47.2	39.3	–	–
New York Mets	58.6	62.4	82.2	93.1	102.8	112.8	103.1	103.9	102.9
Philadelphia Phillies	28.6	30.2	45.7	46.9	61.4	71.5	97.3	94.8	88.2
Pittsburgh Pirates	13.6	22.1	33.6	46.6	47.1	53.2	32.5	30.1	46.8
San Diego Padres	53.0	47.8	54.2	38.6	40.5	50.8	65.9	66.3	69.7
San Francisco Giants	48.5	44.9	50.4	67.5	82.5	89.1	82.4	83.3	90.8
St. Louis Cardinals	44.0	45.6	69.1	76.1	73.8	93.1	92.8	87.3	88.4
Washington Nationals	–	–	–	–	–	–	–	62.8	63.2
NL Average	39.0	46.7	55.6	64.6	67.7	68.0	71.2	68.5	72.5
MLB Average	41.0	47.1	55.1	66.1	69.6	71.0	72.8	70.6	77.0

Note: The payroll amounts are expressed in tens of millions of dollars. The dash (–) indicates that a team did not exist at the site during that season. For the Anaheim/LA Angels, in 2005 the nickname of the Anaheim Angels was changed to Los Angeles Angels of Anaheim.

Source: "Payroll Comparison," at http://si.printthis.clickability.com cited 2 January 2005; "1998 Team Payrolls," at http://www.usa today.com cited 19 May 1999; "Payrolls For Every MLB Team," at http://www.augustasports.com cited 6 September 2001; "2005 Baseball Final Payrolls, List," at http://sportsillustrated.netscape.cnn.com cited 7 January 2006; "Baseball Payrolls List by Team," at http://sportsillustrated.netscape.cnn.com cited 6 April 2006.

occurred, for one reason, because NL teams had more pricing power and produced more entertainment value for the fans in their respective markets than
did hometown clubs in the AL. Indeed, according to some baseball experts
the NL teams have become a superior group of business enterprises. Furthermore, an imbalance in FCIs may have prevailed throughout some of the regular seasons because of such weak AL franchises as the Kansas City Royals,
Minneapolis Twins, and Tampa Bay Devil Rays, and despite inferior NL
teams such as the Cincinnati Reds, Milwaukee Brewers, and Pittsburgh
Pirates. So if the differences in power and FCIs between the AL and NL franchises continue to enlarge, MLB will aggravate its resource and finance allocation problems and be forced to realign divisions or initiate other reforms
that provide incentives to better balance the income opportunities for the 14
AL franchises with those of the 16 in the NL.[4]

Implications of Higher Team Payrolls

Annual price and cost inflation numbers, when expressed in percents,
are financially important statistics to all sports leagues because these percentages are reflected in the payroll amounts of the teams. In MLB the relationship trends between inflation rates, ticket prices and other game costs, and
team payrolls have ramifications that involve competition and parity between
clubs in the AL and NL, which in turn affects the growth of their attendances, revenues and profits. Table 1.5 lists the amounts of payrolls per team
in millions of dollars during nine or fewer consecutive MLB seasons, and
represents how much these values changed from one season to the next. For
our purposes, the main implications of the table are first, whether these values are in the best interests of the two big league groups the individual 30
teams, and their franchise owners and players, and second, whether they are
of benefit to fans and communities, and to professional baseball.

Between 1998 and 2006, the 14 AL teams' payrolls increased by 93 percent and the 16 NLs by 86 percent. Although these two percentages are reasonably close, there were vast differences among the clubs, and especially
between the teams small and large metropolitan areas. In the AL, for example, the Yankees' payroll expanded from 1998 to 2006 by $133 million, or
202 percent, while the Devil Rays' amount increased by $8 million, or eight
percent. In the NL, however, the Pirates' payroll rose by $33 million, or 244
percent, during the nine seasons, while the Mets' payout increased by slightly
more than $44 million, or 75 percent. Despite the growth in payrolls of these
four clubs, the majority of teams such as the Blue Jays, Indians, Pirates, Rock-

ies and Marlins each cut their payrolls at least once after competing in the four seasons 1998. Indeed, the Washington Nationals were the only team in MLB that continued to increase its payroll, during the club's well-publicized two-year history in the NL East Division after relocating as the Expos from Montreal Canada in 2005.

Based on the data in Table 1.5, baseball fans should be curious but alarmed about the excessive amounts of money—and differences in these amounts—per season, and since 1998, about the growth in payrolls of the 30 MLB franchises. Although consumer price inflation in the U.S. has averaged about 2.5-3 percent per year since the late 1990s, the salaries of players have soared in terms of both dollars and percentages. Accordingly it seems that some of the team owners and general managers, and of course the players and MLBPA, are not overly concerned or knowledgeable about the personal incomes of their fans, and/or are indifferent about how much it costs for an individual or family to attend more than a few games during a regular season, and to buy tickets for the leagues' playoffs and a World Series (see Table A.1.5).

Even with the increasing price and cost inflation in big league baseball, and despite Americans' preferences for football and basketball games and their interests, in other team sports such as outdoor soccer, a number of MLB clubs have established attendance records at their ballparks in recent years. However, if the growth in salaries of big league players continues to accelerate after the 2006 season, in AL the payroll of the Yankees in 2015 will be more than $600 million, the White Sox in excess of $300 million, and the Red Sox at least $240 million. For these three large market franchises, their estimated payrolls will likely be controversial but affordable.

But, for small market clubs, it will be exceedingly difficult for their franchise owners to pay greatly increased salaries and also satisfy other debts. To illustrate, in 2015 the annual payrolls of the NL Reds, Pirates and Brewers are estimated to be, respectively, $170 million, $161 million and $101 million. Consequently, unless baseball's commissioner, the 30 team owners, and the MLBPA agree in collective bargaining to further increase revenue sharing and/or raise the luxury tax on the wealthiest teams, in the 2010s some of the small market clubs will be forced to fold their operations or request approval from their respective league organizations to move their franchises into larger metropolitan areas of the U.S. or elsewhere.[5]

Effects of Inflated Valuations

Since the early-to-mid–1990s, the estimated market values of most MLB franchises have risen above expectations, given that they are competitive sports

Table 1.6 Estimated Values of MLB Teams
By League and League Averages, Selected Seasons

Team	1992	1995	1998	2001	2004	2005	2006
AL							
Anaheim/LA Angels	105	90	157	198	241	294	368
Baltimore Orioles	130	168	323	335	296	341	359
Boston Red Sox	136	143	230	339	533	563	617
Chicago White Sox	123	144	214	215	248	262	315
Cleveland Indians	81	125	322	372	292	319	352
Detroit Tigers	97	106	137	290	235	239	292
Kansas City Royals	111	80	108	138	171	187	239
Milwaukee Brewers	86	71	127	—	—	—	—
Minnesota Twins	95	74	94	99	168	178	216
New York Yankees	160	209	362	635	832	950	1026
Oakland Athletics	124	97	118	149	186	185	234
Seattle Mariners	86	92	251	332	396	415	428
Tampa Bay Devil Rays	—	—	—	150	152	176	209
Texas Rangers	106	138	254	342	306	326	353
Toronto Blue Jays	155	152	141	161	169	214	286
AL Average	106	120	202	268	301	332	378
NL							
Atlanta Braves	88	163	299	407	374	382	405
Arizona Diamondbacks	—	—	—	245	276	286	305
Chicago Cubs	101	140	204	247	358	398	448
Cincinnati Reds	103	99	136	187	245	255	274

Team							
Colorado Rockies	—	133	303	334	285	290	298
Florida Marlins	—	98	159	128	172	206	226
Houston Astros	87	97	190	318	320	357	416
Los Angeles Dodgers	135	147	236	381	399	424	482
Montreal Expos	86	68	87	92	145	—	—
Milwaukee Brewers	—	—	—	209	174	208	235
New York Mets	145	131	193	454	442	505	604
Philadelphia Phillies	96	103	131	158	281	392	424
Pittsburgh Pirates	95	62	133	211	217	218	250
San Diego Padres	103	67	161	176	265	329	354
San Francisco Giants	103	122	188	333	368	381	410
St. Louis Cardinals	98	112	174	243	314	370	429
Washington Nationals	—	—	—	—	—	310	440
NL Average	103	110	185	257	289	330	375
MLB Average	105	115	193	262	294	331	377

Note: The estimated values of teams are reported in either tens or hundreds of millions of dollars. The dash (—) means that a team did not exist at the location during that year or its value was not estimated.

Source: "MLB Cash Flows," at http://www.baseballguru.com cited 9 November 2004; Michael K. Ozanian, "Selective Accounting," *Forbes* (14 December 1998), 124(134; "The Boys of Summer," at http://www.forbes.com cited 9 November 2004; "Forbes Financial 2004 Valuation For MLB Franchise," at http://www.sportsbusinessnews.com cited 5 October 2004; "MLB Teams: 2005 Valuations," at http://www.forbes.com cited 12 September 2006; Michael K. Ozanian and Lesley Kump, "Steinbrenner's Tax Shelter," *Forbes* (8 May 2006), 60, 64.

businesses that play baseball games for entertainment. Likewise, the valuations of these franchises have achieved high annual growth rates because of their being invested in highly specialized human resources and fixed assets. Expressed as values, the dollar amounts per franchise are reported for a sample of seven years in Table 1.6. Altogether it is estimated that the 30 MLB teams' average value increased from $105 million in 1992 to $377 million in 2006, which is a change of about 260 percent. More specifically, from 1992 to 2006, AL teams averaged a percentage growth in value of 256 percent while NL values increased by 264 percent.[6]

Because of the construction of new AL ballparks in Arlington, Baltimore, Chicago and Cleveland, and new NL stadiums in Atlanta and Denver, during the 1990s, and due to the extraordinary performances of many elite baseball players and some of the teams, the MLB franchises' largest three-year percentage growth in their estimated values was 68 percent, which occurred from 1995 to 1998. Alternatively, the two three-year periods with below-average growth in values of the AL and NL franchises were 1992 to 1995 and then 2001 to 2004.

Financially, the dramatic dollar and percentage increases in the absolute and relative valuations of MLB teams have created problems between clubs in small and large markets, and also has created some controversial issues for current and prospective owners of baseball franchises. Indeed, any current owner who decides to sell his team for profit as a short run strategy needs to be pragmatic and persuasive, and to hype in the marketplace the economic benefits of operating a professional baseball franchise. Then this individual or group must seek out and evaluate potential buyers who are willing and able to purchase an MLB club above the offer price. Since the average value of a big league team in 2006 was approximately $377 million, the available supply of interested and qualified buyers—that is, individuals or groups—are few in number and probably inexperienced as entrepreneurs in the baseball business.

Thus selling a franchise at a profit is a complex, risky, time-consuming, and costly transaction for a team's current and potential owners. In 2006 it would require more than $600 million for a buyer to acquire the Red Sox or Mets, and at least $1 billon to operate the Yankees. Consequently, in the future it will become increasingly difficult for MLB franchises to be sold and purchased because of the financial commitments and other requirements that must be met by prospective buyers, and because of the business demands and peculiar economics of the professional sports business.

Due to their locations, most of the lower-valued small market MLB clubs are at a competitive and financial disadvantage to those teams that exist in such metropolitan areas as Atlanta, Philadelphia and Washington, D.C., and especially in Chicago, Los Angeles and New York. As a result, baseball fans who live in relatively small cities such as Cincinnati, Kansas City, Milwaukee and Tampa Bay, and who are dissatisfied with the performances of their local MLB team, may not agree with the administrative policies and decisions of the current franchise owner and therefore refuse to attend, or watch on television, any regular-season home games. Since the Reds, Royals, Brewers and Devil Rays, and the other AL and NL small market baseball teams, are not likely to be sold to new owners after completing one or more losing seasons, it is sports fans in these communities will experience low morale about the performance and ownership of their home team, and in the long run may have little or no passion for MLB and the sport of baseball. In short, these are some of the direct and indirect effects of the inflated valuations of big league franchises.

Finally, some recent transactions have occurred in MLB that indicate the enormous discrepancies between the estimated values of franchises as reported in the media and the actual sales prices of these teams. During the 1990s, for example, eight big league clubs were sold to various individuals, families, or business groups. In total, four of these franchises were sold at prices that exceeded their estimated market values. Those clubs were the Houston Astros and Seattle Mariners in 1992, St. Louis Cardinals in 1995, and Los Angeles Dodgers in 1998. Meanwhile, the other four franchises were sold to new owners at prices below their estimated market values. These included the Detroit Tigers and San Francisco Giants in 1992, Oakland Athletics in 1995, and Texas Rangers in 1998.

Since the average difference between actual price and estimated value per transaction was $30 million—which was a small to moderate percentage of each final sales amount—the predicted and actual demand for MLB franchises by current and potential owners is ambiguous and imprecise. This suggests that the financial market for baseball teams is inefficient and in disequilibrium. Furthermore, because of too low or high estimated values, the current proprietors of baseball teams are reluctant to sell their assets and rights as owners. In short, the market for existing MLB teams implies a misallocation of resources in the sports business.

To conclude, increasing prices, costs and values involving MLB franchise owners, their teams and players, and their communities, are a type of inflation that directly affects current and future baseball fans and sports markets. As investors in franchises, owners are primarily concerned about their teams' attendances during each regular season and perhaps postseason, and financially about their organization's payrolls and revenues. The teams' baseball players, who on average earned about $3 million in 2006, seek more income based on their contribution to their teams' performances on the field. Baseball markets, meanwhile, consist of fans who demand to be entertained and are sensitive to higher ticket prices and other costs at the local MLB ballpark, but nonetheless root for their home team to win division titles, league championships, and a World Series.

In contrast to some of the other American-based professional sports leagues, MLB has struggled in recent years and gradually its teams have lost market share to those in football and basketball because of the inflation of its prices, costs and values. However, another reason for baseball's dilemma is a shift in the sport's geographical fan base and among various age, ethnic and racial groups in America. This topic is addressed in Chapter 2.[7]

2

SPORTS FANS
ABANDON BASEBALL

According to data reported in the *2004 Entertainment, Media & Advertising Market Research Handbook*, 17 percent of American children selected Major League Baseball as their favorite sport. Furthermore, baseball fans in the United States were 53 percent male and 73 percent white, and 60 percent had a household income of at least $49,999. In contrast, these same statistics for fans of three other professional sports leagues were reported, respectively, in the *2004 Handbook* as follows: 31, 54, 61, and 62 percent for the NBA; 24, 56, 71, and 61 percent for the NFL; and 5, 59, 76, and 56 percent for the NHL. Thus in percentages, MLB ranked third of the leagues as the favorite sport of children, fourth among male and second among white fans, and third in terms of household incomes. In short, these rankings revealed that in 2004 big league baseball had placed only ahead of the NHL in percentages among children and in household incomes, last of the leagues in percentages among males, and second in percentages to the NHL among whites.[1]

Besides a Pew Research Center survey that was briefly discussed in the introduction of this book, other results extracted from polls denote that the U.S. public has serious and specific business, personal and social issues with MLB. For example, a recent USA Today/CNN/Gallup poll found that 33 percent of sports fans follow baseball much less closely than they did three years ago, while nearly 40 percent of the poll's respondents believe the game of baseball has major problems or is in a state of crisis. In fact, thousands of sports fans contend that MLB has become less popular—and is the professional sports organization with the most difficulties—because of such issues as its history of management-labor disputes, Commissioner Bud Selig's decision during the early 2000s to eliminate some inferior teams in the American League (AL) and National League (NL), concerns about the operations and competitiveness of small market clubs, players' consumption of amphetamines, steroids, and other performance-enhancing drugs such as human growth hormones, and the flagrant cheating conducted by elite players like the Chicago Cubs' Sammy Sosa, who was caught by an umpire hitting with cork in his bat. In other words, MLB's controversies and ethical problems, and a few wrong-headed decisions by Commissioner Selig and some team owners and players, and by the Major League Baseball Players Association (MLBPA), have collectively damaged the sport's reputation among fans and other groups in American society.[2]

As a result, a large number of children, teenagers, and young and middle-age adults have temporarily or permanently lost their interest in baseball games and/or loyalty to MLB teams, and perhaps become fans of clubs in the National Football League (NFL), National Basketball Association (NBA) and National Hockey League (NHL), or in other professional sports leagues. Before this topic is addressed, however, it is necessary to establish a few terms, guidelines and parameters that relate to this chapter's contents (see Table A.2.1).

First, although the very early history and pre-modern era of baseball are interesting and relevant to investigate, the specific baseball seasons analyzed here are essentially from the early 1990s to 2000s. Second, as clarified in other studies but modified for our purposes, MLB fans are individuals and families—male and female kids, teenagers and adults—who during one or more previous MLB regular seasons have either attended a big league baseball game or viewed a game on cable or network television, or have listened to a game on the radio, or have expressed a stong or moderate interest in baseball as the nation's pastime.

Third, to determine the behavior of sports fans, the research that I performed included a variety of topics and diverse aspects about the sport. These topics involved such matters as MLB's policies, regulations and rules, AL and NL teams' home attendances and on-the-field performances during various seasons, published studies of baseball fans' experiences, loyalties and values; the former and current geographical locations and ballpark sites of professional baseball franchises; the populations of baseball teams' home cities; the numbers of division and playoff titles won by clubs and their World Series championships, if any; and a combination of selected age, ethnic, gender, racial, business, economic, financial, and socioeconomic data (see Table A.2.2).

Cuban native Rafael Palmeiro clouted 569 home runs and 3,020 hits, and had a .288 batting average during his 20-year career in the big leagues. Despite his great achievements as a player, Palmeiro used steroids and may never be admitted into the Baseball Hall of Fame. [National Baseball Hall of Fame Library, Cooperstown, N.Y.]

After 17 seasons in the big leagues, the Dominican Republic's Sammy Sosa had hit 588 home runs and batted in 1,575 runs, and in 1988 won the National League Most Valuable Player Award. In 2003, Sosa was ejected by an umpire from a game and suspended for seven games by the commissioner for hitting with a corked bat. [National Baseball Hall of Fame Library, Cooperstown, N.Y.]

In part, it is likely that some fans became disillusioned with big league baseball and stopped attending or listening to MLB games because of their dissatisfaction with the actions or inactions of the league commissioner and AL and NL presidents, with franchise owners and the MLBPA, and/or with specific teams, general managers, coaches and players. As discussed earlier, some reputable consumer polls of fans clearly indicate that the sport has very serious issues which have existed for several seasons. These matters are complex and difficult to solve, and involve a combination of circumstances, factors and events. Therefore I assumed that fans are aware MLB is experiencing its share of troubles relative to the other professional sports leagues, even though many aspects about MLB are still perceived as favorable.

Baseball Fan Demographics

In contrast to the pre–1980s, the typical fans of a recent MLB team—that is, from the early-to-mid–1990s to early 2000s—have been white males who were at least 21 years old, had graduated from high school and tended to live in the metropolitan area or suburb of a medium-to-large city, and earned an income that averaged $40–$50 thousand per year. As a group, baseball fans are not as likely to be minorities, or women, children or teenagers, or to live in a small city or rural area, or to be very poor or extremely affluent.[3]

Some studies have therefore determined that the consumer market for big league teams has gradually shifted away from African Americans, kids and young adults, and from families with two or more children. So at home and away games of the New York Yankees, for example, and at games of the other 29 MLB teams, the majority of the people at the ballpark will generally be casual and avid fans who have demographic and economic profiles as previously described. In contrast, for their choices of entertainment, some individuals and groups of local fans, who fit different demographic profiles, have increasingly become more attracted to other sports leagues rather than MLB, and root for teams primarily in professional football and basketball, and secondarily in ice hockey and perhaps outdoor soccer. There are some fundamental reasons why these trends among sports fans have occurred, and why it is that baseball and MLB have been negatively affected. Some reasons for this phenomenon are discussed as follows.

Since the mid-to-late 1970s to early 2000s, the proportions of African American players on MLB teams' rosters have declined from approximately 25 to 9 percent. Meanwhile, the percentages of native Hispanics and foreign athletes—including Latinos—on big league teams have increased from about 10 to 35 percent. As a result, there are fewer African American players as role models on MLB teams for inner city black kids, teenagers, and young adults to emulate and idolize. At the sametime, thousands of minority athletes have tended to specialize by position and compete on basketball and football teams while enrolled in elementary and secondary schools and in colleges. This shift has significantly decreased demand among African Americans to purchase tickets and attend MLB games, or watch them on television and listen to them on the radio. Furthermore, black fans have largely stopped studying the box scores of baseball games that are reported in newspapers, or making an effort to read articles about local amateur and professional baseball teams and their coaches, managers and players.[4]

Besides their children's and teenager's decisions to become involved in other sports, a majority of black heads of households in both rural and urban areas are not willing or able to spend their discretionary income on baseball clothing and equipment. This means that African American children are not prepared for, nor interested in, becoming active in the sport by playing on a Little League team or in other organized baseball groups.

In the literature, other reasons have been cited that explain the low participation rates and interest of the African American population in baseball. First, the numbers of baseball diamonds in America's inner cities have gradually declined because of urban redevelopment projects and the conversion of vacant land into residential housing and commercial properties; second, problems with affording ever-higher ticket prices and other costs at ballparks; third, an absence of any black investors and business entrepreneurs who are majority or primary owners of MLB franchises; and fourth, the inadequate promotion of big league baseball to the black segment of the U.S. population, which totals almost 13 percent. Consequently young African American males have displayed little interest and enjoyed few opportunities to associate with their friends, fellow athletes and classmates to play on organized baseball teams. Also, blacks have hardly any unoccupied spaces and sandlots in their neighborhoods to create a baseball field and play games.

As young and talented male black athletes participate in other sports activities for fun and recreation, and for competition while attending elementary and secondary schools, they are less inclined to become casual or diehard fans of amateur or MLB teams. Meanwhile, the opposite trend has been happening for Hispanic kids who live in American cities and in such countries as the Dominican Republic, Mexico, Panama, Puerto Rico and Venezuela. These youngsters, who are very likely to be living in poverty or at least in substandard housing, have strong economic and social incentives to become successful athletes. Thus, they are eager to play organized baseball beginning at an early age. As a result, MLB teams have invested resources in baseball academies and have conducted clinics in Latin American countries and other foreign nations to get the kids to become committed baseball players, to convince the best foreign athletes to sign professional contracts with big league clubs, to develop the skills of these professional players, and then to move them to the U.S. so that they have an opportunity to play on a AAA, AA, or A minor league team or on a club in a rookie league.

Although some Hispanics from Latin American countries have eventually become superb MLB players, their immediate families and close relatives and friends usually remain at home rather than relocate to the athlete's host city in the U.S. The reluctance to live in America, in turn, prevents some foreign individuals and households from becoming enthusiastic fans who might have attended MLB or minor league games in the U.S. and cheered for their sons, cousins, nephews, and/or acquaintances or the field. In other words, the influx of athletes from Central and South America since the mid-to-late 1970s has not offset the decline of African American baseball players in schools and the major and minor leagues, and the monetary and social contributions that were made by black families, athletes, and fans to the sport.

Women, meanwhile, have tended to be short run or temporary fans of amateur baseball organizations and MLB teams. As such, they become involved as long as their kids play on teams in the Pony League and Little League and their teenage sons participate on a local high school and/or Babe Ruth League and American Legion clubs. Then, when these young athletes graduate from high school and forego baseball to focus on their academics and other sports in college, or decide to join the military or work for a local business, their mothers will likely lose interest in baseball and thus do not become avid or long run fans of the sport. So female youth, teenagers and adults are segments of sports markets that the AL and NL have not yet successfully attracted.

Nevertheless, despite these developments about women, one study reported that the proportion of loyal female MLB fans had increased from 12 percent in 1998 to 28 percent in 2002. Even, so there were also marginal percentage increases in the numbers of women fans of all professional sports, which occurred during the latter 1990s and early 2000s. This trend in sports took place with respect to the fractions of women who became rabid fans of teams in the NFL, NBA and NHL, and of drivers and races in the National Association for Stock Car Racing (NASCAR), and especially of clubs in the Women's National Basketball Association (WNBA) and of female golfers in the Women's Professional Golf Association (WPGA). Because of the strong competition from—and the marketing expenditures and hype about—these and other non-baseball leagues, it is questionable whether MLB will ever be able to sustain any growth in its market share of very young and teenage females and of women in America.[5]

Because of the average ticket prices and Fan Cost Indexes that are listed for each of the AL and NL teams in, respectively, Tables 1.2 and 1.4 of Chapter 1, it is a significant burden for families to attend more than one or two MLB games per season at ballparks in large metropolitan areas, and somewhat expensive for families to view the single games of big league clubs that play at their home sites in small and midsized cities. Rather, in the majority of cases, dads are more likely to bring a son to see at least one or two regular season games featuring their home team at a local MLB ballpark while the other family members, such as mothers and daughters, will engage in other activities at home. Alternatively, a family that enjoys outdoor sports as a group may decide to attend a local minor league baseball game, or they may visit a neighborhood park and play a game of baseball, or arrange other outdoor events that involve sports. In short, because of increasingly higher ticket prices per season, plus the supplemental costs of purchasing food and buying gasoline when driving to and from a ballpark, it is likely that a weekday baseball game or weekend series at MLB ballpark is not the first option of outdoor entertainment for families with children during the months of late spring, summer, and early fall.

Despite the implementation of various innovative marketing programs designed to increase the numbers of baseball fans among African Americans, young and adult women, and families with children, MLB has tough challenges in appealing to these three segments of the U.S. population. For African Americans, it is partly because young blacks as male and female athletes realize that careers in professional basketball and football (for males) are more attainable and financially attractive than becoming a big leaguer in baseball; that at least one NBA and NFL team has a minority franchise owner or some African American investors and proportionately more executives, general managers, coaches and players who are role models for pre-adult and adult blacks; and that basketball and football games are more fun and easier to organize in such locations as neighborhood parks and schoolyards than are baseball games.

For women, the WNBA and WPGA are more popular professional sports groups because females dominate these gender-specific leagues; also, women have social activities and jobs, and household responsibilities that are priorities within their families; and finally, when their children leave home to enter college and eventually join companies and perhaps marry and then become homemakers, most women lose interest in amateur and professional baseball as desirable types of sports entertainment.

For families with children and other kinds of households, MLB games are increasingly expensive and time-consuming to attend while local minor league baseball games are more economical, convenient and entertaining as sports events; furthermore, some families prefer to attend popular and less costly sports games such as those in amateur basketball, football, ice hockey and outdoor soccer. Simply put, MLB's efforts to allocate additional resources to lure African Americans, women, and families with children into being life-long baseball fans have produced only small incremental attendances at games and may or may not have generated even average financial returns.

Other aspects of fan demographics may have positively or negatively influenced the demand for baseball. For example, as the rosters of MLB teams have expanded with more and more players who are citizens of other nations, some traditional baseball fans fail—either intentionally or unintentionally—to identify with these foreign athletes, or to respect their talents and contributions to the sport. Although they are highly skilled, competitive and successful ballplayers, the Boston Red Sox' David Ortiz, the St. Louis Cardinals' Albert Pujois, and the New York Yankees' Hideki Matsui were not born in nor did they America, primarily develop as young players on teams within the U.S. As a result, their achievements and abilities as hitters, infielders or outfielders are less important to—and not recognized by—some local baseball fans than would be the case if they were natives of an American state like California, Indiana, or Texas. This type of player discrimination likely emanates from retired and elderly baseball fans who may have rooted for such great Hall of Famers and former sluggers as Ted Williams of the Red Sox, Stan Musial of the Cardinals and Mickey Mantle of the Yankees.

Consequently, some MLB teams realize they have fewer passionate, dedicated and senior-aged male fans because these and other clubs use a number of foreign athletes as players, who may start at key on-the-field positions and be instrumental in winning or losing games, titles and championships. Given my experience and knowledge about this topic, there are likely a number of American-born fans who have concluded that MLB and minor league baseball are now an international sport, and not our national pastime. If so, this discriminatory belief and attitude has damaged the game of baseball and, if widespread, has probably affected the attendances, revenues and profits of big league clubs that recruit a high proportion of foreign players, including the Florida Marlins, Houston Astros, Kansas City Royals and Los Angeles Dodgers.

Besides the economic, financial and social issues, and the conditions and problems that have been discussed thus far in this and the previous chapter, there are some relevant statistics about MLB and the league's AL and NL teams that reflect the short- and long-run growth of baseball's fan base across America and in several metropolitan areas. It is important, therefore, to focus on some numerical facts about the relationships between big league baseball, a selection of its teams, and these teams' fans.

To that end, the locations and preferences of fans as groups are highlighted in the next sections of this chapter. These topics are explored in the following ways: first, by the totals of—and changes in—each of the MLB team's regular season home attendances since 1993 and by other characteristics of these teams; second by an analysis of a well-publicized measurement of baseball fans' loyalty to their respective club(s) for eight years; and third, by the ranking of each team's ballpark with respect to what attributes sports fans demand in a baseball facility.

After an 18-year career with the New York Yankees, outfielder Mickey Mantle was inducted into the Baseball Hall of Fame in 1974. Although a very popular and outstanding player, Mantle had engaged in extramarital affairs and also suffered from alcoholism. [National Baseball Hall of Fame Library, Cooperstown, N.Y.]

Teams Attendances and Characteristics

Various non-sports statistics and some baseball-specific data measure, in part, the numbers, loyalties and locations of MLB fans with respect to each of the AL and NL teams. Even though these 30 clubs play their 81 home games during regular seasons in ballparks in small, midsized large metropolitan areas, there are no perfect empirical models, or all-inclusive formulas or sets of equations that precisely identify how many people are casual and avid baseball fans during one or more seasons of teams in the big leagues. Nevertheless such big cities as Chicago, Los Angeles and New York have, a larger potential market and more accommodative infrastructure for baseball fans than in smaller towns like Milwaukee, Pittsburgh and Tampa Bay. In other words, the NL Cubs, Dodgers and Mets each have a larger estimated population of sports fans to attract in their respective market areas than do the NL Brewers, Pirates and Devil Rays. Based on the limited types and amounts of non-sports and sports information available, I decided in the following sections of this chapter to use any historical facts and documents that could be applied to measure trends and reveal insights about the numbers and whereabouts of professional baseball fans and whether they have a weak, moderate, or strong passion for specific MLB teams.

To distinguish between the groups of fans of the current 14 AL and 16 NL clubs, these teams' per game attendances—for up to 14 consecutive regular seasons—are listed in columns 2–15 of Table 2.1. To briefly highlight and compare the two leagues and also the home attendance patterns of some teams in each league during particular years, I derived the following findings.

First, except for 1995 the NL average attendances per game were greater than those numbers in the AL. This particular statistic denotes that, in 13 of the 14 regular seasons listed in the table, baseball fans on average had purchased more tickets to home games of the group of small, midsized and large market clubs in the NL because of the entertainment value of seeing games played between such intense rivalries as the East Division's Mets and Phillies, the Central Division's Cardinals and Cubs, and the West Division's Dodgers and Giants.

Second, the NL average attendances peaked at 32.5 thousand spectators in 1993 and the AL at 30.3 thousand in 1994 and 2006. Consequently, it was in 2006 that baseball's fans again attended NL and AL games that averaged, respectively, almost 33 thousand and 31 thousand at ballparks. This occurred primarily because of such factors as the nation's low inflation and interest and unemployment rates, booming real estate and stock markets, and the strong growth of the American economy. It is unlikely, however, that these macroeconomic conditions will continue for many years beyond 2006–2007 due to such risks as the business cycle, the threat of domestic and international terrorism, the decline of the U.S. dollar, and higher energy prices, inflation and interest rates.

Third, MLB's average attendance finally set an all-time record in the 2006 season after it had peaked in 1994. Nevertheless, if more elite players

Table 2.1 Teams Home Attendances
Per Game, by League and Regular Seasons, 1993–2006

Team	1993	1994	1995	1996	1997	1998	1999	2000	2001	2002	2003	2004	2005	2006
AL														
Angels	25.4	26.3	24.1	22.6	21.8	31.1	27.8	25.5	24.7	28.2	37.7	41.6	42.0	42.1
Athletics	25.1	21.8	16.3	14.1	15.6	15.2	17.7	19.7	26.3	26.7	27.3	27.1	26.0	24.4
Blue Jays	50.1	50.5	39.2	31.8	31.7	30.3	26.7	21.0	23.6	20.0	22.2	23.4	24.7	28.4
Brewers	20.8	22.0	15.1	16.2	17.9	–	–	–	–	–	–	–	–	–
Devil Rays	–	–	–	–	–	30.9	21.6	17.8	16.0	13.1	13.0	16.1	14.0	16.9
Indians	26.8	35.3	39.4	41.2	42.2	42.8	42.8	42.6	39.6	32.3	21.3	22.4	24.6	24.6
Mariners	25.3	19.7	22.6	33.8	39.4	32.9	35.9	35.9	43.3	43.7	40.3	36.3	33.6	30.6
Orioles	45.0	45.2	43.0	44.4	45.8	45.4	42.3	40.7	38.6	32.9	30.3	34.3	32.4	26.5
Rangers	27.7	43.9	27.5	35.4	36.3	36.1	34.2	31.9	34.9	29.3	25.8	31.8	31.4	29.4
Red Sox	29.9	0.8	30.0	28.5	27.4	28.5	30.2	31.9	32.4	32.7	33.6	35.0	35.1	36.1
Royals	23.8	24.3	17.1	17.8	18.8	18.5	18.7	19.3	18.9	17.1	22.8	21.0	17.5	17.1
Tigers	24.3	20.6	16.4	14.4	16.8	17.4	25.1	30.1	24.0	18.7	17.1	23.9	25.3	32.0
Twins	25.2	24.7	14.6	17.7	17.4	14.3	14.9	12.3	22.2	23.6	24.0	23.4	25.1	28.2
White Sox	31.8	30.0	22.2	20.5	23.1	17.1	16.6	24.0	22.0	20.7	23.9	24.4	28.9	36.5
Yankees	29.8	29.6	23.5	27.7	31.8	36.4	40.6	37.7	40.8	43.3	42.7	47.7	50.4	51.8
AL Average	29.3	30.3	25.1	26.1	27.6	28.3	28.2	27.9	28.9	27.3	27.3	29.1	25.6	30.3
NL														
Astros	25.7	27.1	18.9	24.3	25.2	30.3	33.4	37.7	35.8	31.0	30.2	38.1	34.5	37.3
Braves	47.9	44.5	35.5	35.8	42.7	41.4	40.5	39.9	34.8	32.1	30.3	29.3	31.5	31.8
Brewers	–	–	–	–	–	22.3	21.4	19.4	34.7	24.3	20.9	25.4	27.2	28.8
Cardinals	35.1	32.4	24.5	32.7	32.5	39.4	40.1	41.1	38.3	37.1	35.9	37.6	43.6	42.5

Team	1993	1994	1995	1996	1997	1998	1999	2000	2001	2002	2003	2004	2005	2006
Cubs	32.5	32.6	26.6	27.2	27.0	32.1	34.7	34.4	35.1	34.4	37.0	39.1	38.7	39.0
Diamond-backs	—	—	—	—	—	44.5	37.2	36.3	33.7	39.4	34.6	31.1	25.4	25.8
Dodgers	39.1	39.6	38.4	39.3	40.9	38.1	38.2	35.5	37.2	38.5	38.7	43.0	44.4	46.4
Expos	20.1	22.3	18.1	19.9	18.4	11.2	9.5	11.4	7.9	9.8	12.6	9.3	—	—
Giants	32.1	29.6	17.2	17.4	20.8	23.6	25.6	40.9	40.8	40.1	40.3	40.2	39.2	38.6
Marlins	37.8	33.6	23.7	21.5	29.1	21.3	16.9	15.0	15.7	9.8	16.2	22.0	22.7	14.3
Mets	23.1	20.3	17.6	19.6	21.8	28.2	33.4	34.8	32.8	35.9	28.1	28.9	35.2	43.3
Nationals	—	—	—	—	—	—	—	—	—	—	—	—	33.6	26.5
Padres	16.9	20.3	14.4	27.0	25.7	31.5	31.1	29.0	29.7	27.4	25.0	37.5	35.0	32.8
Phillies	38.7	39.8	28.3	22.2	18.4	21.1	22.5	19.9	22.8	20.4	28.9	40.5	33.3	34.2
Pirates	20.3	21.4	12.5	16.4	20.4	19.2	20.3	21.5	30.8	22.5	20.9	21.1	23.0	23.2
Reds	30.2	33.0	25.5	22.9	22.0	22.1	25.2	31.8	23.7	23.1	29.0	28.2	23.9	26.3
Rockies	55.3	56.0	47.0	47.7	48.0	46.8	39.9	40.6	39.0	33.8	28.8	29.5	23.9	25.9
NL Average	32.5	32.1	24.9	26.7	28.1	29.6	29.3	30.6	30.6	28.7	28.5	31.3	32.1	32.3
MLB Average	30.9	31.2	25.0	26.5	27.8	29.0	28.8	29.3	29.8	28.0	28.0	30.2	28.8	31.3

Note: Reported in tens of thousands, home attendances are the average number of tickets sold per game and not the actual turnstile count. A dash (—) means that a MLB team did not exist at the site in that season.

Source: The data for the 1993–2003 seasons was reported in "Attendance," at http://www.baseball-statistics.com cited 18 September 2006. The attendances for the 2004–2006 seasons were printed in, respectively, "MLB Attendance Report: 2004," at http://sports.espn.go.com cited 19 September 2006, "MLB Attendance Report: 2005," at http://sports.espn.go.com cited 19 September 2006, and "MLB Attendance Report: 2006," at http://sports.espn.go.com cited 3 October 2006.

Prior to 2007, Barry Bonds had hit 734 homers and batted in 1,930 runs during his 21-year career. To achieve these results, Bonds allegedly had used various types of steroids that were supplied by his trainer Greg Anderson. In testifying to a grand jury about these matters, Bonds may have committed perjury. [National Baseball Hall of Fame Library, Cooperstown, N.Y.]

such as Barry Bonds, Gary Sheffield and Jason Giambi are constantly scrutinized in the media and then severely reprimanded and penalized by the leagfor abusing steroids and other performance-enhancing drugs, and if the gap in payrolls between small and large market clubs continues to expand, then some baseball fans will rebel and shift their support from MLB to the NBA, NFL and NHL, and perhaps to Major League Soccer.

Fourth, in 2006 the AL Devil Rays and Royals, and NL Marlins each averaged less than 20 thousand spectators per game at their home-site ballparks, which indicates that local and regional sports fans in the Tampa Bay, Kansas City and Miami areas were (and are) not passionate about their teams' performances and success. Indeed, the average attendances of the Devil Rays peaked in 1998, as did the Royals' in 1994 and Marlins' in 1993. Thus MLB and its member franchises, in conjunction with the MLBPA, need to jointly decide whether to increase the subsidies to these clubs or allow them to fold or relocate to larger and more hospitable metropolitan areas before 2010.

These four observations about the data in Table 2.1, as a group, suggest that the AL and NL teams, in total, struggled but have continued to operate and recover from the 1994–1995 work stoppage. Even so, the professional sports business, and especially MLB teams located in specific markets, will remain vulnerable to local, regional and national economic problems within the U.S., and also to global events, threats and risks.

Based on the AL's average attendances in 2004 though 2006, and the NL's in the same period, it appears that professional baseball has become more popular recently than it was during the mid-to-late 1990s to very early 2000s. That is, despite inflated prices and the payroll increases of franchises' players, millions of baseball fans decided in 2004–2006 to purchase an increasing number of tickets to regular season games and support their local teams. Nonetheless, during some seasons between 1993 and 2006 a few AL and NL clubs failed to attract a sufficient number of fans to the home games played in their respective ballparks.

To examine which teams experienced disappointing attendances in regular seasons since the early 1990s, and when, clubs with at least three consecutive years of declining average attendances are listed in column one of Table 2.2. For various reasons these ten AL and eight NL teams each drew fewer and fewer spectators per game to their ballparks across three or more seasons, which depleted their markets over a span of four or more years of performances. Next is a discussion—in chronological order—of each league's group of teams, primarily based on the data contained in Table 2.2.

Table 2.2 Teams Average Characteristics
By League and Selected Seasons, 1994–2006

Team	Season	AVGHA	AVGW%	AVGTP	AVGFCI
AL					
Angels	1994–1997	23.7	.473	9	93
	1998–2001	27.2	.481	12	115
Athletics	1993–1996	19.3	.453	10	101
Blue Jays	1994–2000	33.0	.481	14	106
Devil Rays	1998–2003	18.7	.393	15	132
Indians	1999–2003	35.7	.518	21	149
Mariners	2002–2006	37.0	.489	24	176
Orioles	1997–2003	39.4	.460	18	137
Royals	2003–2006	19.6	.396	13	118
Tigers	1993–1996	18.9	.432	10	100
	2000–2003	22.4	.375	20	161
White Sox	1993–1996	26.1	.542	12	108
NL					
Astros	2000–2003	33.6	.518	19	156
Braves	1997–2004	36.3	.611	18	148
Cardinals	2000–2003	38.1	.571	21	151
Diamondbacks	1998–2001	37.9	.527	15	119
	2002–2006	31.1	.477	17	132
Expos	1996–1999	14.7	.463	9	89
Marlins	1993–1996	29.1	.437	9	92
	1997–2000	20.5	.446	12	98
Reds	1994–1998	25.8	.522	7	82
Rockies	2000–2003	35.5	.467	15	138

Note: Columns one and two are self-explanatory. In column three is each team's regular season Average Home Attendance (AVGHA) in thousands, while column four is Average Winning Percentage (AVGW%) in decimals, column five is Average Ticket Price (AVGTP) in dollars, and column six is Average Fan Cost Index (AVGFCI) in hundreds of dollars.

Source: See "Teams," at http://www.mlb.com cited 27 September 2006, and the sources below Tables 1.2, 1.4, and 2.1.

American League

During the early-to-mid–1990s the per game attendances of the Athletics at Network Associates Park in Oakland, the Tigers at Tiger Stadium in

Detroit, and the White Sox at Comiskey Park in Chicago each decreased for three consecutive years following 1993, that is, through 1996. Although their tickets at home were reasonably priced at an average of $10 during these years, the Athletics and Tigers each finished last in divisional play in two of the four regular seasons while the White Sox won two Central Division titles. Apparently several thousands of baseball fans in the metropolitan areas of Oakland, Detroit and Chicago had decided that the players' strike in 1994–1995 was unjustified and therefore they increasingly demanded fewer tickets to watch their hometown teams play games against any AL rivals.

Besides the California Angels—who were renamed the Anaheim Angels in 1997 and had relatively weak performances in the West Division and consecutive falling home attendances during 1994–1997 and again in 1998–2001— several other AL clubs experienced at least three years of declining attendances beginning in the mid-to-late-1990s. Local baseball fans in Toronto, Baltimore, Tampa Bay and Cleveland lost interest in watching the home games of, respectively, the Blue Jays and Orioles for six straight seasons, the Devil Rays for five consecutive seasons, and the Indians for four back-to-back seasons. Because the Yankees and Red Sox dominated the AL East Division, many fans of the Blue Jays and Orioles were depressed about their teams' performances and responded by purchasing fewer tickets and attending fewer home games for half a dozen years. Interestingly, ticket prices and Fan Cost Indexes (FCIs) were significantly higher than the league average for families that enjoyed games at the SkyDome in Toronto and Oriole Park at Camden Yards in Baltimore. In turn, this caused these clubs' home attendances to decrease each season from the previous year.

The Devil Rays, meanwhile, finished last in the AL East Division each season from 1998 to 2003, and therefore the team's home attendance declined from approximately 31 thousand per game in 1998 to 13 thousand in 2003. However, because of innovative marketing programs implemented by the franchise's 32-year-old president Matt Silverman and 29-year-old general manager Andrew Friedman, the Devil Rays have begun to effectively cater to baseball fans in the Tampa Bay area. Thus in 2006, the attendance at Tropicana Field increased to approximately 17 thousand per game.[6]

Alternatively, the Indians won two Central Division titles between 1999 and 2003 but failed to win an AL pennant as the franchise did earlier in 1995 and 1997. Furthermore, during the 1999–2003 regular seasons the team charged an average price of $21 per ticket for spectators to attend its home games at Jacobs Field. It became relatively too expensive for families from the northern Ohio area to see the Indians play at home for $149 per game, which was the club's average FCI. The results was lower attendances at the

Indians' home games, which restrained the club's revenue from admissions and from sales of merchandise at Jacobs Field.[7]

During the early 2000s, the Mariners, Royals and Tigers experienced consecutive drops in home attendances for various regular seasons. On average, each club had won less than 50 percent of its games, and as a result, the hometown fans of these teams attended fewer and fewer of their games each season at, respectively, Safeco Field in Seattle, Kauffman Stadium in Kansas City, and Comerica Park in Detroit. In 2006 the Mariners finished fourth and 15 games behind the Athletics, who won the West Division, while the Royals ended the season fifth and 34 games in back of the Twins in the Central Division. The Tigers, however, were successful in 2006 and qualified for the playoffs as a wild card. After winning its first AL championship since 1984, the team was defeated in five games by the Cardinals in the World Series.

Between 1993 and 2006 inclusive, the Brewers, Rangers, Red Sox, Twins and Yankees were the five AL clubs that had not endured three or more consecutive seasons of declining home attendances. Besides the Brewers' being transferred from the AL to NL in 1998, the baseball fans who had lived in the metropolitan areas of Arlington, Texas, and Boston, Massachusetts, and of Minneapolis-St. Paul, Minnesota, and New York City were the most consistent by loyal and dedicated audiences to their home teams. In contrast, between 1993 and 2006 inclusive, the Angels, Blue Jays, Orioles and Tigers were relatively the least popular AL teams.

National League

According to Tables 2.1 and 2.2, the NL teams with the most consecutive regular season shortages in fan support were the Diamondbacks and Marlins. The former club's home attendances fell at Bank One Ballpark in Phoenix, Arizona, from approximately 44 thousand per game in 1998 to 33 thousand in 2001, and then from 39 thousand in 2002 to 25 thousand each in 2005 and 2006. Similarly the Marlins' attendances at Pro Player Stadium in southeast Florida fell from about 37 thousand per game in 1993 to 21 thousand in 1996, and then from 29 thousand per game in 1997 to 15 thousand in 2000. The Diamondbacks won three West Division titles between 1998 and 2006 and the World Series in 2001, while the Marlins qualified for the playoffs as a wild card in 1997, defeated the Cleveland Indians in seven games to win the World Series, and then played excellent baseball to win another MLB championship in 2003. However, despite these victories and titles, the baseball fans living in the Phoenix and Miami areas were not motivated to become committed customers of their home teams, and thereby they attended fewer and fewer games in consecutive years. In fact, the Diamondbacks ranked fourteenth and Marlins sixteenth among NL teams in home attendances per game in 2006.

Even though the team won the NL East Division each year, the Braves' home attendances at 50,100-seat Turner Field in Atlanta, Georgia, fell for seven consecutive seasons. Average attendances declined from almost 43 thousand per game in 1997 to about 29 thousand in 2004. Even though the club's ticket prices have been only slightly higher than the NL's average price, the Braves' excellent performances have not excited baseball fans in Atlanta and the surrounding counties. Because of the team's third-place finish in 2006, it is likely that the Braves' attendances at Turner Field with continue to flounder. In turn this suggests that the East Division's New York Mets and Philadelphia Phillies, and perhaps in future seasons the Washington Nationals, will play well enough to overtake the Braves to win—or at least contend for—a division title in 2007 and thereafter.

Besides the Diamondbacks, Marlins and Braves, the other NL teams that experienced declining attendances between 1993 and 2006 included the Astros, the Cardinals, the former Expos, the Reds and the Rockies. The mid-to-large-market Astros have improved their performances in recent seasons. Consequently in 2004–2006 the club averaged about 37 thousand per game at Minute Maid Park in Houston, Texas, versus 33 thousand per game during the 2000–2003 regular seasons. Nevertheless, since veteran player Andy Pettitte now plays for the Yankees, Jeff Bagwell has retired, and Craig Biggio may retire or be traded after the 2007 season, then baseball fans in the Houston area may not attend Astros games as they once did when the club won its division in 1997–1999 and 2001, and then finished runner-up to the Red Sox in the 2005 World Series. Because the Astros' ticket prices and other ancillary costs at its home games are relatively expensive for families with children, this means that the team must be very competitive in the NL Central Division in order to avoid returning to the years when its home attendances were well below 30 thousand per game, as they were in 1993–1997.

Second, the Cardinals have been a competitive team almost every season in the NL Central Division. Thus, local sports fans are attracted to the franchise's new ballpark in St. Louis. Because of such outstanding hitters as Albert Pujols, Scott Rolen and David Eckstein, accurate pitchers like Chris Carpenter and Walt Williams, and crafty manager Tony La Russa, the Cardinals averaged more than 42 thousand spectators per game at home in 2006 and undoubtedly will equal or increase that average in later seasons. So unlike 2000–2003 when the team's average attendance fell by six thousand per game, the sports fans in the St. Louis area and in other cities of eastern Missouri will enthusiastically support the Cardinals and the team's tradition of being a perennial contender in the Central Division.

When the Montreal Expos moved in 2005 from Canada to the nation's capital city on the U.S. east coast and were renamed the Nationals, the club's home attendances increased from 9.3 thousand per game at Montreal's Olympic Stadium to 33.6 thousand at Washington, D.C.'s RFK Stadium. When its new and modern multimillion-dollar ballpark opens in early-to-mid–2008, the Nationals are expected to attract approximately 30–35 thousand fans each game per season, which is about an average number for NL teams. Meanwhile, since 2000 the Reds and Rockies have played their home games at, respectively, Cinergy Field and then the Great American Ballpark in Cincinnati, and at Coors Field in the Denver area. At home, the Reds have averaged 27 thousand and Rockies 31 thousand per game. Given each of the club's win-loss percentages, the Reds have been the superior team and also a relatively low-cost business operation. In fact average the ticket price is more than double for a Rockies fan to attend a game at Coors Field as compared to a Reds home game. Furthermore, it costs families in Cincinnati about 40 percent less to attend a Reds game at the Great American Ballpark than it does Denver residents to observe a Rockies game at Coors Field. In other words, because of the differences in average ticket prices and FCIs, sports spectators in the Denver area are more likely to avoid a home game than are Reds fans who reside in the southeastern Ohio area.

Since 1993 the Brewers, Cubs, Dodgers, Giants, Mets, Padres, Phillies and Pirates have been the eight NL teams that did not experience three consecutive seasons of declining attendance in their home ballparks. In contrast, the least committed and most uninterested fans of NL clubs live in the cities and suburbs of Atlanta, Denver, Miami, and Phoenix. If local taxpayers do not partially finance the construction of a new baseball stadium, the Marlins will probably leave southern Florida. If they do, the club's fans may transfer their allegiances to such sports teams as the NFL Miami Dolphins, NBA Miami Heat, or NHL Florida Panthers. In future seasons the Braves, Diamondbacks and Rockies will successfully or unsuccessfully compete, but each team will continue to struggle to appeal to sports fans in their respective markets even if they are fortunate enough to occasionally win a division title and league pennant, and perhaps a World Series.

Sports Loyalty Index

During the 1990s Brand Keys Inc.'s president Dr. Robert Passikoff developed a statistic that measures and ranks how intensely baseball, football, basketball and ice hockey fans support their respective home teams relative to corresponding measurements and rankings of fans of other teams in their home market. In Passikoff's model of fan loyalty, there are four specific drivers. These drivers as variables reflect a club's pure entertainment, its authenticity, its fan bonding, and its history and tradition. Based on certain attributes, benefits and values, these drivers have expectations and professional teams that exceed the expectations have realized a higher order of fan engagement and loyalty.[8]

After surveying sports fans, Brand Keys publishes a group of statistics for teams in the various professional sports leagues, and has titled this document a Sports Loyalty Index (SLI). Table 2.3 identifies the loyalties of fans for the various clubs in professional baseball. Based on published SLIs, the table features the rankings of the top and bottom five MLB teams—including ties in ranks—for each of eight consecutive years. Given these data, the following two sections of this chapter are overviews of the top- and bottom-ranked teams in big league baseball with respect to the engagement and loyalty of their fans.

Top Ranked Teams

Across the eight seasons in Table 2.3, the most consistent and superior clubs that ranked from first through fourth on average were the New York Yankees, Houston Astros, Cleveland Indians and Boston Red Sox, while tied for fifth place were the Atlanta Braves and San Francisco Giants. Regarding the two top ranked clubs, despite an average payroll that exceeded $175 million each season, the Yankees did not win a World Series in 2001–2006. Nevertheless, their fans remained loyal during these seasons. In contrast, when they competed and won an MLB championship in 2005 and became even more exciting to watch, the Red Sox' teams bonded with the most loyal fans in MLB for two consecutive years, that is, in 2005 and 2006.

Besides the Yankees and Red Sox, the Houston Astros and Cleveland Indians are also very popular in their respective markets because they have dedicated fans. Evidently at home, these two latter big league teams play entertaining games and bond with their audiences. Also, each of them has a history and tradition that reflect positive attributes, benefits and values to the baseball fans who live in the southeast Texas and northeast Ohio areas. According to Brand Keys' SRI reports, the fans of the Astros and Indians are more avid than fans of, respectively, the NFL Texans and NBA Rockets in Houston, and the NFL Browns and NBA Cavaliers in Cleveland. There are no NHL teams in Houston or Cleveland, or an MLS club in northern Ohio. In 2006,

Table 2.3 Teams Sports Loyalty Index Rankings
Top and Bottom Five Teams, By League and Season, 1999–2006

Team	1999	2000	2001	2002	2003	2004	2005	2006
Top Five Ranks								
New York Yankees (AL)	1	2	1	2	1	1	3	3
Cleveland Indians (AL)	1	1	2	1	5	—	5	4
Houston Astros (NL)	—	3	3	3	2	2	2	2
Atlanta Braves (NL)	3	4	4	—	—	—	—	5
St. Louis Cardinals (NL)	4	—	—	—	—	—	—	5
Colorado Rockies (NL)	—	5	—	—	—	—	—	—
Boston Red Sox (AL)	—	—	—	4	—	3	1	1
Seattle Mariners (AL)	—	—	5	5	—	4	4	—
San Francisco Giants (NL)	—	—	—	—	3	5	—	—
Philadelphia Phillies (NL)	—	—	—	—	4	—	—	—
Bottom Five Ranks								
Florida Marlins (NL)	30	30	20	23	21	26	22	17
Anaheim Angels (AL)	29	29	19	20	17	23	—	—
Minnesota Twins (AL)	28	27	16	—	18	—	—	—
Montreal Expos (NL)	27	—	16	21	—	—	—	—
Los Angeles Dodgers (NL)	26	—	—	—	—	—	—	—
Tampa Bay Devil Rays (AL)	—	28	18	22	20	24	24	20
San Diego Padres (NL)	—	26	16	—	—	—	—	—
Baltimore Orioles (AL)	—	26	17	19	19	25	23	20
Chicago Cubs (NL)	—	26	—	—	—	—	—	—

Texas Rangers (AL)	—	—	—	—	—	—	22	—	16
Pittsburgh Pirates (NL)	—	—	—	—	—	—	—	21	18
Milwaukee Brewers (NL)	—	—	—	—	—	—	—	20	—
Kansas City Royals (AL)	—	—	—	—	—	—	—	—	17
Colorado Rockies (NL)	—	—	—	—	—	—	—	—	19

Note: A sports loyalty index measures the intensity with which fans support their home team(s). Based on specific attributes, benefits and values, there are four drivers—pure entertainment, authenticity, fan bonding, and history and tradition—that teams meet or exceed and which, in turn, determine an index rank that numbers from 1 to 30. In the table, teams that tied in rank are assigned the same numeric. For example, in 2000 the San Diego Padres, Baltimore Orioles, and Chicago Cubs tied for twenty-sixth place in fan loyalty. A dash (—) is entered if the team was not ranked in the top or bottom five in that MLB season. AL means American League and NL is the National League.

Source: "The Brand Keys Sports Loyalty Index," at http://www.brandkeys.com cited 18 September 2006.

meanwhile, the Houston Dynamos won an MLS title. Thus, the Dynamos represent as the fourth most popular professional sports club in southeast Texas.

Bottom Ranked Teams

Based on the SRIs for clubs in the lower portion of Table 2.3, the MLB teams that ranked at or near the bottom—that is, at 30 or in the high 20s— tended to be the Florida Marlins and then the Tampa Bay Devil Rays, Baltimore Orioles and Anaheim Angels (who were renamed Los Angeles Angels of Anaheim in 2005), and finally the Pittsburgh Pirates in 2005–2006. Given their hometown fans' lack of enthusiasm to attend home games and these clubs' poor relations with local populations, it is not surprising that the Marlins' teams were ranked between seventeenth and thirtieth inclusive during the 1999–2006 seasons and the Devil Rays from eighteenth to twenty-eighth inclusive. In contrast, the Angels have recently risen in rank, and as indicated by the hyphen, had improved above twentieth in 2005 and sixteenth in 2006, while for several reasons, the Pirates' teams in 2005 and 2006 were not very appealing to sports fans in the Pittsburgh area.

Some fans of the Orioles, however, have become outspoken about the club's failure to be more competitive during regular seasons in the AL East Division. At a home game in late September of 2006, for example, about one thousand spectators protested by staging a walkout directed at the Orioles' majority owner Peter Angelos and other investors who had purchased the franchise for $173 million in 1993, one year after Camden Yards had opened. Despite the construction of its new ballpark, which was baseball's first retro and fan-friendly facility that featured modern amenities and revenue sharing opportunities, the Orioles' home attendances have either steadily declined or been constant since the 1998 season, while the club has finished either third, fourth or fifth in its division. Moreover, the Orioles' payrolls have gradually decreased from the second highest in MLB during 1997–1999 to rank fifth, twelfth and fifteenth, and then to twenty-first in 2004, tenth in 2005, and fifteenth in 2006.

About the walkout, Angelos remarked: "Whoever joins that protest has no comprehension of what it costs to run a baseball team. When you get down to facts, putting together a team that can compete in the AL East means having a payroll between $100 million and $110 million [Orioles payroll was $72.5 million in 2006]. That money comes from the consumer, and I have chosen to keep ticket prices at a minimum [Orioles average ticket price of $22 in 2006 was sixth highest in the AL]." Anyway, to change the club's culture, Orioles executive vice president of baseball operations Mike Flanagan planned to study the franchise's problems and speak to demoralized employees, disgruntled sponsors and silent partners, and to the alienated fans who wished that Angelos would eventually sell the team. As Flanagan has stated about his role, "We want to win and I want to win. I want to be here and have [pennant] races in September that mean something and have that kind of cheering in the stands again. It's been too long."[9]

Fan Value Index

In 2006, a few journalists from *Sports Illustrated* studied some key attributes of the 30 MLB ballparks. To determine what values and experiences these venues offered to spectators at baseball games, the researchers prepared a questionnaire and solicited the opinions of sports fans. More than eight thousand people responded to the questionnaire, which included a variety of features about ballparks that were to be evaluated. These criteria included such items as the prices and accessibility of parking spaces, availability of restrooms and the quality of concessions, and other factors that made the facilities special or were disappointing to fans. After collecting and organizing the data from the questionnaires, the *Sports Illustrated* journalists published a Fan Value Index (FVI) that ranked each of the ballparks. A portion of the FVI's final results is summarized, by team, in Table 2.4. Accordingly, the table lists in columns one to five the respective ranks of the ballparks, the MLB teams that played at home in the ballpark. the names of the teams' ballparks and their capacities, and the years when the ballparks were opened for games.[10]

In 2006 these facilities offered the best to worst values for baseball fans based, on seven categories of information about the 30 ballparks — specifically average ticket prices, average cost of concessions/souvenirs, accessibility, amenities, atmosphere, neighborhood, and teams' combined on-the-field performances and star power.

Table 2.4 Home Team Ballparks
Fan Value Index Rankings by Team, 2006 Regular Season

Rank	Team	Ballpark	Capacity	Year
1	Angels	Angel Stadium	45.0	1966
2	Rockies	Coors Field	50.4	1995
3	Pirates	PNC Park	38.4	2001
4	Brewers	Miller Park	41.9	2001

(Table 2.4 continued)

Rank	Team	Ballpark	Capacity	Year
5	Rangers	Ameriquest Field	49.1	1994
6	Tigers	Comerica Park	40.9	2000
7	Indians	Jacobs Field	43.4	1994
8	White Sox	U.S. Cellular Field	40.6	1991
9	Royals	Kauffman Stadium	40.7	1973
10	Twins	HHH Metrodome	45.4	1982
11	Cardinals	Busch Stadium	46.7	2006
12	Reds	Great American Ball Park	42.2	2003
13	Orioles	Oriole Park at Camden Yards	48.8	1992
14	Giants	AT&T Park	41.5	2000
15	Phillies	Citizens Bank Park	43.6	2004
16	Diamondbacks	Chase Field	49.0	1998
17	Astros	Minute Maid Park	45.9	2000
18	Braves	Turner Field	50.0	1997
19	Yankees	Yankee Stadium	57.5	1923
20	Athletics	McAfee Coliseum	34.0	1968
21	Padres	Petco Park	42.4	2004
22	Blue Jays	Rogers Centre	50.5	1989
23	Mariners	Safeco Field	47.4	1999
24	Cubs	Wrigley Field	41.1	1914
25	Devil Rays	Tropicana Field	45.0	1990
26	Dodgers	Dodger Stadium	56.0	1962
27	Marlins	Dolphin Stadium	36.3	1987
28	Red Sox	Fenway Park	36.1	1912
29	Mets	Shea Stadium	55.6	1964
30	Nationals	RFK Stadium	56.0	1961

Note: Capacity is in thousands. Year is the date when the ballpark opened for a team with respect to a regular season.
Source: Paul Forrester, "Fan Value Index 2006: Readers Rate Which Parks Offer Best Value, Experience," at http://www.si.com cited 23 September 2006.

For example, the atmosphere at top-ranked Angel Stadium in Anaheim provided a majority of the spectators with such amenities as having close seats to the action, ability to walk around the ballpark's interior and watch games from various viewpoints, participation in a number of kid-friendly promotions, and a convenient opportunity for fans to visit Disneyland before or after an Angels game. Thus most respondents in the survey felt that the Angels franchise had treated its customers well while at games, and had charged reasonable prices for fans to be admitted into the stadium, to purchase food and beverages at the concessions, and to buy souvenirs.

Alternatively, the respondents ranked RFK Stadium in Washington, D.C., as thirtieth and last in MLB. The facility was criticized because hometown fans were feared to venture into the neighborhood surrounding the ballpark; felt that an unexciting atmosphere existed within the ballpark; complained that bland food was served at the Nationals' home games; and became depressed when the club performed poorly against its rivals in the East Division. Based on the extreme rankings of these two ballparks in the survey, apparently fans enjoyed the Angels' home games due to the memorable atmosphere and their thrilling experiences while at Angels Stadium, whereas in 2006 the Nationals' games at RFK Stadium were inferior experiences only tolerated by the team's fans because a new ballpark will be opened for the franchise sometime in 2008.

The following are some expectations about fans' values and experiences that were associated with other ballparks and which will appear in the FVIs of 2007–2009. First, the Twins, Yankees and Mets will likely increase in rank when they each begin their regular season in new but yet-to-be-named ballparks; second, besides the Nationals in Washington, D.C., modern stadiums are also desperately needed for the Athletics in Oakland (or elsewhere), the Devil Rays in Tampa Bay, and the Marlins in the Miami area; third, renovated stadiums with better atmospheres and more amenities would likely improve the rankings of the Blue Jays in Toronto, the Dodgers in Los Angeles, and the Red Sox in Boston; fourth, teams' policies of adopting competitive ticket prices and lowering vendor costs for souvenirs and food at concessions may encourage more attendance from local fans at regular season games, particularly for the teams that were ranked worse than tenth in the 2006 FVI; and fifth, more convenient, economical and efficient transportation to and from ballparks in big cities would provide fans with more value per dollar and reduce the time they need to attend games with their families and friends.

In sum, this chapter identified and discussed some problems pertaining to MLB and its teams. These, in turn, may have caused fans to temporarily or permanently abandon the sport and therefore not attend big league games or watch them on television, or to read about and discuss baseball news with other sports fans. Although MLB established higher all-time total attendances in each of the 2004–2006 regular seasons, it seems that NFL and NBA teams, and to some extent NHL and MLS clubs, have gained market share among sports fans because these leagues are less controversial than MLB. In fact, as business organizations, some of the other American sports leagues and their franchises are more sympathetic to the loyalties of their fans and communities than are baseball's marketing executives and franchise owners, the teams' coaches and players, and the MLBPA.

Based on the topics that were discussed in this chapter, Commissioner Bud Selig has overstated how popular the sport of baseball and MLB are among American sports fans, but has understated how thousands of baseball fans have become disillusioned and thus abandoned the sport. Indeed, since the 1970s–1980s there have been several owners' lockouts and players' strikes, leading to cancellation of regular season games, postseason playoffs, and a World Series. If these types of problems persist after 2007, then fans will further reject the sport and continue to lose interest in the performances and successes of teams, coaches and players in MLB.[11]

3

CONGESTED
SPORTS MARKETS

Since the beginning years and during their development as sports organizations, each of the five American-based professional leagues have increased the number of franchises and thereby expanded to cities across of North America. Between the early 1900s and 2000s the trend has been for sports leagues to penetrate consumer markets in the majority of populated regions of the United States. In turn, this expansion has resulted in a proliferation of professional teams in Major League Baseball (MLB), and in the National Basketball Association (NBA), National Football League (NFL), National Hockey League (NHL), and somewhat in Major League Soccer (MLS).[1]

During late 2006, the five leagues combined consisted of 133 clubs that played at venues in small, midsized and large metropolitan areas across the U.S. and Canada. Besides these specific sports groups, there are other leagues in each of the professional sports that have also expanded into numerous urban markets of various sizes. For example, there are clubs in AAA, AA, A and Rookie baseball leagues and in the latest American Basketball Association, the Arena Football League, the East Coast Hockey League, and minor league soccer. Consequently, most of the primary and many secondary American sports markets have one or more professional sports teams within their boundaries.

To determine if there was an optimal number of MLB sites in 2006, this chapter focuses on the locations and qualities of each sports market of the 30 teams in MLB, and discusses whether any of the other U.S. metropolitan areas and some foreign cities have the demographic characteristics and numbers of baseball fans to adequately support a new or relocating big league franchise. Specifically, Chapter 3's premise is that the overall sports market in America contains a sufficient quantity of current MLB teams, and that some areas may even have an oversupply of them.

To discuss any available data pertaining to the saturation of U.S. sports markets, and especially to those areas that host teams in professional baseball, this chapter presents this issue in five distinct sections. The first section examines the extent to which MLB has expanded in size and increased its number of teams relative to the historical growth that has occurred in four other prominent sports leagues. Then the second section of the chapter reveals which U.S. metropolitan areas host teams in the various sports and why MLB clubs in the American League (AL) and National League (NL) are located in a number of these places.

The third section provides some special characteristics about metropolitan areas that are home to the ballparks of big league teams, and contrasts how these areas vary in quality as baseball markets for regular seasons and any postseason games. The fourth section applies some descriptive statistics in order to expose the strengths and weaknesses of 15 U.S. cities as potential sites of new and/or relocating MLB teams. Finally in the fifth section, 13 foreign cities are evaluated as potential MLB markets. To support the discussion in each section, there is a table of relevant quantitative information about clubs and their market areas.

Teams in Sports Leagues

Between 1956 and 1976, the total number of professional teams that played in four sports leagues increased by 119 percent, that is, from 42 to 92, as indicated in Table 3.1. Expressing numbers as percentages and ranking the leagues from the most to least in growth, during the mid–1950s to mid–1970s the NHL had expanded by 200 percent, NBA 175 percent, NFL 133 percent, and MLB 50 percent. Because of innovations in telecommunication technologies, the expansion of television and radio networks and media markets, improvements in highway systems and airline facilities, and the economic development of central cities, suburbs and rural communities, each of these four sports leagues decided to place more and more clubs in a number of cities of various sizes across America and in Canada.

Table 3.1 Professional Sports Teams
Distribution of Teams by Years and Leagues, 1906–2006

Year	MLB	NBA	NFL	NHL	MLS	Total
1906	16	–	–	–	–	16

(Table 3.1 continued)

Year	MLB	NBA	NFL	NHL	MLS	Total
1916	16	—	—	—	—	16
1926	16	—	22	10	—	48
1936	16	—	9	8	—	33
1946	16	11	10	6	—	43
1956	16	8	12	6	—	42
1966	20	10	15	6	—	51
1976	24	22	28	18	—	92
1986	26	23	28	21	—	98
1996	28	29	30	26	10	123
2006	30	30	32	29	12	133

Note: A dash (—) means that the sports league did not exist in that year.

Source: "Major League Baseball," at http://www.mlb.com cited 9 October 2006; "National Basketball Association," at http://www.nba.com cited 9 October 2006; "National Football League," at http://www.nfl.com cited 9 October 2006; "National Hockey League," at http://www.nhl.com cited 9 October 2006; "Major League Soccer," at http://www.mls.com cited 9 October 2006.

For various economic and financial reasons, however, these leagues revised their long run strategies and became less expansionary after 1976. In other words, between 1976 and 2006 the additional sports franchises were a net of eleven NHL and eight NBA clubs, and four NFL and six MLB teams. Thus, by the late 1970s these four leagues had experienced their greatest multiyear periods of growth. Meanwhile MLS, which began operating with ten franchises in 1996, decided to change business strategies and increased its membership by two teams or 20 percent in 2005.[2]

To elaborate about the historical growth of leagues from another perspective, when the numbers of teams in each row of Table 3.1 are converted into percentages, the resulting percentage distribution of teams by year appears in Table A.3.1 of the Appendix. With respect to the results for big league baseball, the table's contents are summarized as follows.

First, MLB's share of total professional sports teams in America has gradually declined, especially since the mid-to-late 1930s. This trend will continue if one or more of the other sports leagues decide to expand into additional metropolitan areas of the U.S. Also, some of baseball's franchises in small markets may continue to struggle financially during 2008 and thereafter, so that when the league's contract with the Major League Baseball Players Association (MLBPA) expires in 2012, contraction could occur and thereby reduce MLB's proportion of the total teams below the 23 percent achieved in 2006.

Second, during the 1920s, MLB's monopoly of professional sports in America was eliminated when the NFL and NHL each organized and their clubs entered into the marketplace. Then, 20 years later, some baseball teams who had dominated their market areas were challenged because, in the mid–1940s, the NBA was formed and its franchises began to operate. And third, in 2006, four of the major sports leagues each comprised a proportion of the total teams that had varied between 21 and 24 percent inclusive. So even if MLS gradually expands during and after 2007, MLB has stabilized in its markets and its 30 teams will likely remain at approximately 20–25 percent of the total number for the next 10–15 years.

Since the early 1960s a few of MLB's expansion clubs were unsuccessful at operating in their markets and thus were forced to relocate to other metropolitan areas. First, during 11 regular seasons in the nation's capital, the Washington Senators had low attendances at their home games. As a result, in 1972 the team moved to Arlington, Texas, and was renamed the Texas Rangers. Second, after finishing the 1969 season with a win-loss record of 64–98 and placing sixth in the AL West Division, the Seattle Pilots were sold to new owners who transferred the team to Wisconsin, where it was renamed the Milwaukee Brewers. Third, after playing 28 seasons before relatively small crowds at its home ballpark, Olympic Stadium in Montreal, Quebec, MLB officials agreed to move the Expos to Washington, D.C., where the club was renamed the Washington Nationals in 2005. In short, the Senators, Pilots and Expos failed at their respective sites after one or more regular seasons. Alternatively, 11 of baseball's other expansion teams have remained at their original sites. These clubs and their home sites include the AL Angels in Anaheim, Royals in Kansas City, Mariners in Seattle, Blue Jays in Toronto, and Devil Rays in Tampa Bay. And in the NL, the six clubs are the Astros in Houston, Mets in New York, Padres in San Diego, Marlins in Miami, Rockies in Denver, and Diamondbacks in Phoenix.[3]

Due to a combination of factors, it is assumed that former baseball places such as Brooklyn or Montreal are not feasible or profitable sites for any new or relocating MLB teams. Furthermore, some small and medium sized cities have been vacated by clubs in the other professional sports leagues and are not currently home to MLB teams. For the non-baseball leagues, these include such cities as Buffalo, Rochester and Syracuse in New York, Charlotte in North Carolina, Hartford in Connecticut, and Quebec and Winnipeg in Canada. Because of their current demographics and other baseball-related factors, each of these cities is not an attractive site or viable sports market for an MLB club.

This result implies that the metropolitan areas that formerly had professional baseball, basketball, football and ice hockey teams are generally not qualified to be MLB sites. In turn, they are eliminated from being future hosts to struggling small market franchises like the Florida Marlins, Milwaukee Brewers, Pittsburgh Pirates, and/or Tampa Bay Devil Rays. Consequently, MLB franchise owners must consider a different group of areas as future sites and not those previously occupied by other sports clubs. In a nutshell, the majority of the most preferable baseball markets in North America seem to be congested with professional franchises of the various sports leagues. In part, this matter is discussed in the next section of the chapter.[4]

Sports Teams in Metropolitan Areas

To explore whether and where the saturation of sports markets exists in more detail, this portion of Chapter 3 reveals in a table how congested U.S. metropolitan areas are with respect to the presence of professional sports teams. Besides the sites of 30 MLB teams within the 26 areas that are listed in column one of Table 3.2, columns two to six depict the distribution of 105 clubs of the five sports leagues among these various areas. Not shown are a total of 28 sports teams that are not located in current MLB cities, such as the NBA Hornets of New Orleans, NFL Packers of Green Bay, NHL Oilers of Edmonton and MLS Real Salt Lake of Salt Lake City.

Table 3.2 Professional Sports Teams
Distribution by MLB Metropolitan Areas, and Leagues, 2006

Areas	MLB	NBA	NFL	NHL	MLS	Total
Atlanta	1	1	1	1	0	4
Baltimore–Towson	1	0	1	0	0	2
Boston	1	1	0	1	1	4
Chicago	2	1	1	1	1	6
Cincinnati	1	0	1	0	0	2
Cleveland	1	1	1	0	0	3
Dallas-FW-Arlington	1	1	1	1	1	5
Denver	1	1	1	1	1	5
Detroit	1	1	1	1	0	4
Houston	1	1	1	0	1	4
Kansas City	1	0	1	0	1	3
Los Angeles-Anaheim	2	2	0	2	2	8

(Table 3.2 continued)

Areas	MLB	NBA	NFL	NHL	MLS	Total
Miami	1	1	1	1	0	4
Milwaukee	1	1	0	0	0	2
Minneapolis	1	1	1	1	0	4
New York-Northern NJ	2	2	2	3	1	10
Philadelphia	1	1	1	1	0	4
Phoenix	1	1	1	1	0	4
Pittsburgh	1	0	1	1	0	3
San Diego	1	0	1	0	0	2
San Francisco–Oak.-SJ	2	1	2	0	0	5
Seattle	1	1	1	0	0	3
St. Louis	1	0	1	1	0	3
Tampa Bay	1	0	1	1	0	3
Toronto	1	1	0	1	0	3
Washington, D.C.	1	1	1	1	1	5

Note: The three abbreviated metropolitan areas are Dallas-Fort Worth-Arlington, New York-Northern New Jersey, and San Francisco–Oakland-San Jose.

Source: See the sources for Table 3.1, and "Metropolitan Areas, 1990–2000," *The World Almanac and Book of Facts* (New York, NY: World Almanac Books, 2004).

As reflected in the table, cities in the most populated metropolitan areas tend to be the home sites for more professional sports clubs than do the cities within small and medium sized areas. The former group of locations includes, for example, the New York-Northern New Jersey area with ten teams, Los Angeles-Anaheim with eight, Chicago with six, and the Dallas-Fort Worth-Arlington, Denver, San Francisco-Oakland-San Jose and Washington, D.C., areas each with five teams. In contrast, the latter group of locations consists of areas with only two clubs each. These teams are in the Baltimore-Towson market and in Cincinnati, Milwaukee and San Diego.

Interestingly, relatively high-populated areas such as Boston, Detroit and Philadelphia are each hosts to fewer professional sports teams than, for example, the smaller Dallas-Fort Worth-Arlington and Denver areas. Neither Detroit nor Philadelphia has an MLS franchise, while Boston does not contain an NFL club (the New England Patriots play at 68,000-seat Gillette Stadium in Foxboro, Massachusetts, approximately 30–40 miles east-southeast of the Boston area). Given these variances in the numbers of sports clubs within specific areas, the distribution of teams among all of the areas is primarily based on their total and relative populations and the demands of local and regional fans for each of the sports.

Regarding other aspects of the data in Table 3.2, the following are some general observations about the location, density and congestion of these sports markets with respect to the number and distribution of the 105 professional teams, and especially about the 26 areas and 30 clubs in MLB. First, given their longstanding sports histories and traditions, and their populations, economies and sports fan experiences, the metropolitan areas of Boston, Dallas-Forth Worth-Arlington, Detroit and Philadelphia are probably each capable of supporting an additional MLB team. It is highly unlikely, however, that the franchise owners of the Red Sox, Rangers, Tigers and Phillies teams will ever approve of sharing their home markets with other clubs in the same professional sport.

Second, five or approximately 20 percent of the areas in column one of Table 3.2 host at least one team in each of the sports leagues. If MLS decides to expand into areas within the south, southeast and southwest, and this soccer league's teams continue to play their regular season and postseason games during the late summer and fall months, MLS' schedule may affect the attendances of some MLB teams in their areas. These baseball franchises include the Angels, Astros, Rangers and Rockies because a portion of their Hispanic populations may decide to abandon professional baseball and become loyal soccer fans and to increasingly attend the home games of, respectively, MLS' Chivas USA, Houston Dynamo, FC Dallas and Colorado Rapids.

Third, in 2007 a new MLS club will be based in Toronto, Canada. It is unlikely, however, that the local market of baseball's Blue Jays will be diminished since Toronto is a relatively large, diverse and cosmopolitan city that has an expanding international population who are willing and able to support more than the area's three current professional sports franchises.

Fourth, there is only a minute probability of MLB ever placing a third baseball team in the Chicago, Los Angeles, or New York metropolitan areas. The owners of and investors in Chicago's Cubs and White Sox, Los Angeles' Angels and Dodgers, and New York's Mets and Yankees have enough wealth, political clout, and authority within MLB to deny the entry of another AL and/or NL team into their large, dense markets.

Fifth, when the numbers of different sports teams in each of the metropolitan areas of Table 3.2 were converted into proportions, the result is a distribution of percentages that appears in columns two through six of Table A.3.2 in the Appendix. Essentially this table reveals the relative proportions of professional baseball and then basketball, football, ice hockey and soccer teams in each of the 26 MLB metropolitan areas. Given that the total number of teams in each of the areas totaled to 100 percent, the percentages of teams per sport varied from zero to 50 percent. In fact, based on the table's contents, the proportions of teams in MLB ranged from 20 to 50 percent while the NBA's and NFL's were from zero to 50 percent, and the NHL's and MLS' from zero to 33 percent. Thus the NBA and NFL had a wider dispersion of proportions among the various metropolitan areas than did MLB and the NHL and MLS. Interestingly, this spread in percentages occurred even though there were only 21 NBA teams in 19 or 73 percent of MLB's 26 areas and despite only 25 NFL clubs in 22 or 85 percent of baseball teams' areas.

The distributions in the five columns of Table A.3.2 further indicate that some small market areas tended to have high proportions with respect to the number of current MLB teams whereas in other small market areas the percentages were relatively low. For example, MLB teams in the Baltimore-Towson, Cincinnati, Milwaukee and San Diego areas were each one-half of their total sports market, while in Cleveland, Kansas City, Pittsburgh and Tampa Bay the baseball clubs were only one-third. Alternatively, within the three largest metropolitan areas, the numbers of big league teams were 33 percent in Chicago, 25 percent in Los Angeles-Anaheim, and 20 percent in New York-Northern New Jersey. Since several of the other sports leagues' teams were also located in the three biggest and most lucrative U.S. sports markets, these different percentages suggest that the areas with relatively small populations are more congested and with MLB teams than those with million or more sports fans.

Research into the various locations of teams reveals that a number of the areas that hosted NBA, NFL, NHL and MLS clubs in 2006 did not contain an MLB franchise. The home areas of NBA teams—and listed in no specific order—were Orlando, Indianapolis, Memphis, New Orleans, San Antonio, Salt Lake City, Portland and Sacramento; home areas of NFL clubs were New Orleans, Charlotte, Green Bay, Foxboro, Buffalo, Indianapolis, Jacksonville and Nashville; home areas of NHL franchises were Buffalo, Raleigh, Columbus and Nashville in the U.S., and Montreal, Ottawa, Calgary, Toronto, Vancouver and Edmonton in Canada; and home areas of MLS teams were Columbus and Salt Lake City. Therefore during the 2006 regular seasons of four professional leagues, 22 U.S. and Canadian markets were the current homes of non–MLB clubs. Even so, a majority of these markets are inferior based on their total populations and thus not primary or even secondary areas to locate one or more big league expansion or relocating teams. Nonetheless, a few of them, such as Columbus, Nashville, Portland and San Antonio, may eventually qualify as a site for an MLB franchise.

In short, it appears that after 2007 most of the 26 metropolitan areas in Table 3.2 will each contain about the same numbers of clubs as they did in 2006. As a result, I conclude that a high proportion of current sports markets in America are saturated with professional teams. In the future, therefore, it will be necessary for MLB to search for sites in small, midsized and large U.S. and foreign metropolitan areas where big league teams are not currently located, as indicated in Tables 3.4 and 3.5.

Nevertheless, many of these areas are ranked as inferior sports places based in part on their substandard demographics and small number of local baseball fans, and on their inability or reluctance to subsidize the operation of a big league ballpark and then support am MLB franchise in the long run. Yet, if local and/or regional taxpayers and/or governments are willing and able to pay the costs for the construction of a new ballpark and upgrading the infrastructure surrounding the facility, and if wealthy local entrepreneurs or investment groups jointly assume the financial risks to become franchise owners, then MLB will be motivated to locate an existing or expansion team in one or more of these U.S. and foreign areas.

MLB Teams in Areas

In this chapter, Table 3.1 provides some sport history from the literature by designating—in ten-year increments—when 133 teams in five U.S.-based professional leagues were established. Table 3.2 depicts, as of 2006, the distribution of 105 clubs within 26 metropolitan areas. Based on the data in these two tables it was determined that the primary U.S. sports markets, for the most part, contain a fixed and sufficient number of MLB franchises. That is, the small and midsized markets are stocked with at least one baseball team while clubs located in the large markets have an incentive, and the power and wealth, to prohibit the entry of new or relocating baseball franchises into their metropolitan areas (see Table A.3.3).

In this section of the chapter, three important characteristics have been identified to partially measure and roughly evaluate the degree of congestion within 29 MLB teams' areas (excluding the AL Blue Jays in Toronto, Canada). This trio of characteristics consists of, respectively, an area's total population, its households' personal per capita income, and its number of television homes. In turn, each characteristic was ranked for the area's teams with the results reported in Table 3.3. What does the table and other demographic data and sports-specific information reveal about the conditions within each of these U.S.-based sports markets?[5]

Most Congested to
Semi-Congested Baseball Markets

Based on these areas' levels in these three characteristics, and due to the local MLB teams' home attendances, their win-loss records, and their successes at winning division and league titles, the most congested markets of big league teams are in Cincinnati, Cleveland, Denver, Kansas City, Miami, Milwaukee, Minneapolis, Pittsburgh, San Diego, Seattle and Tampa Bay. In other words, until the mid-to-late 2010s these 11 metropolitan areas—if evaluated as sports markets—each have the capacity to support only one MLB franchise. Essentially this condition means that each of these markets is deficient according to at least one of the three criteria. That is, they contain small to midsized populations, or have a relatively low proportion of homes with television sets, and/or have households with average to below-average per capita personal income levels among the areas of 14 AL and 16 NL teams.

Table 3.3 MLB Teams
Area Characteristics, by Leagues and Teams, Selected Years

Team	Population	Rank	Per Capita PI	Rank	TV Homes	Rank
American League						
Angels	12.9	2nd-t	36.9	35th-t	5.5	2nd-t
Athletics	4.1	12th-t	51.9	2nd-t	2.3	5th-t
Blue Jays	–	–	–	–	–	–
Devil Rays	2.6	20th	33.0	112th	1.7	12th
Indians	2.1	23rd	35.5	63rd	1.5	17th
Mariners	3.2	15th	41.6	15th	1.6	15th
Orioles	2.6	19th	40.8	20th	1.1	24th
Rangers	5.8	5th	37.0	44th	2.3	6th
Red Sox	4.4	10th	48.1	5th	2.2	7th
Royals	1.9	27th	35.8	60th	.9	31st
Tigers	4.3	11th	37.6	39th	1.9	11th
Twins	3.1	16th	42.0	14th	1.6	15th
White Sox	9.4	3rd-t	38.4	34th-t	3.4	3rd-t
Yankees	18.7	1st-t	45.5	8th-t	7.3	1st-t
National League						
Astros	5.2	7th	39.0	31st	1.9	10th
Braves	4.9	9th	35.0	72nd	2.0	9th
Brewers	1.5	37th	37.8	38th	.9	34th
Cardinals	2.7	18th	36.1	55th	1.2	21st

(Table 3.3 continued)

Team	Population	Rank	Per Capita PI	Rank	TV Homes	Rank
Cubs	9.4	3rd-t	38.4	34th-t	3.4	3rd-t
Diamondbacks	3.8	14th	32.5	117th	1.6	13th
Dodgers	12.9	2nd-t	36.9	35th-t	5.5	2nd-t
Giants	4.1	12th-t	51.9	2nd-t	2.3	5th-t
Marlins	5.4	6th	36.2	51st	1.5	16th
Mets	18.7	1st-t	45.5	8th-t	7.3	1st-t
Nationals	5.2	8th	49.5	4th	2.2	8th
Padres	2.9	17th	39.8	27th	1.0	27th
Phillies	5.8	4th	40.4	21st	2.9	4th
Pirates	2.3	21st	36.2	54th	1.2	22nd
Reds	1.8	25th	35.6	61st	.9	33rd
Rockies	2.3	22nd	42.5	13th	1.4	18th

Note: The metropolitan area populations in column two are reported in millions, per capita personal incomes in column four are in thousands of dollars, and the designated market area television homes in column six are in millions. The date for the area population numbers is July 1, 2005, while the year for per capita personal income is 2005, and the date of the estimates for television homes is January 1, 2007. Since populations and numbers of television homes were rounded to millions, the areas of some teams nearly tied or tied in rank, which is indicated by a t. A dash (—) for the Blue Jays indicates that metropolitan area were not available for Toronto, Canada. The Orioles' area includes Baltimore-Towson in Maryland, and the Rangers' area is Dallas-Forth Worth-Arlington in Texas. Metropolitan area characteristics are equal for the Angels and Dodgers, Athletics and Giants, White Sox and Cubs, and Yankees and Mets.

Source: "Metropolitan Areas," at http://www.census.gov cited 9 October 2006; "Personal Income and Per Capital Personal Income by Metropolitan Area, 2003–2005," at http://www.bea.gov cited 9 October 2006; "2006–2007 Local Television Households: Local Market Universe Estimates," at http://www.nielsenmedia.com cited 9 October 2006.

Furthermore, during many baseball seasons of the 1990s and early 2000s, the MLB team within each of these 11 markets was not consistently competitive in its respective division and when it qualified to compete in the playoffs, it rarely—if ever—won any recent league titles and World Series championships. As a result of this analysis, the AL Indians, Royals, Twins, Mariners and Devil Rays, and NL Reds, Rockies, Marlins, Brewers, Pirates and Padres will not be threatened for decades by the entry of another MLB team into their metropolitan areas. As of 2006 each of these teams was based in a congested sports market.

Besides these 11 teams, which each have sites within regional sports markets, there are a number of other MLB clubs that have realized benefits from one or more demographic characteristics with respect to their areas, and for various reasons have tended to excel as competitors in their divisions of the AL or NL. Therefore, they play their games at home in ballparks located within somewhat semi congested sports markets. These dozen teams include the Giants and Athletics in the San Francisco–Oakland–San Jose area, Nationals in the Washington, D.C., and Orioles in the Baltimore-Towson areas, and the Rangers in Arlington, Red Sox in Boston, Tigers in Detroit, Astros in Houston, Braves in Atlanta, Cardinals in St. Louis, Diamondbacks in Phoenix, and Phillies in Philadelphia.

Although the local markets of these 12 teams are less congested, they are not necessarily capable of supporting another MLB franchise. Some of the specific attributes of each of the clubs and/or their locations are noteworthy. For example, the metropolitan area populations and/or number of television homes are ranked at or above their league's average for the AL Athletics, Rangers, Red Sox and Tigers, and NL Astros, Braves, Giants and Phillies. Furthermore the Athletics, Red Sox, Braves and Giants are usually very competitive teams within their divisions during regular seasons. In turn, this makes it unlikely that a third team in the San Francisco–Oakland–San Jose area, or a second one in the Boston and Atlanta areas, could perform well enough each season to attract 25–30 thousand fans on average to their respective home games. Likewise the Cardinals are a dominant sports attraction in St. Louis, as are the Astros within the Houston area, and Phillies within the Philadelphia area. The Diamondbacks, meanwhile, have existed as a franchise for less than ten years and the Nationals fewer than five. Thus it is not conceivable that MLB would authorize a second team in the Atlanta, St. Louis, Houston, Philadelphia and Phoenix areas, or another club in the Washington, D.C., and Baltimore-Towson areas. In short, these are 12 teams that are located and play their home games within semi-congested sports markets. Consequently, in the future MLB will not approve of an additional expansion or relocating team within these 12 metropolitan areas.[6]

Least Congested Baseball Markets

According to the demographic criteria established in Table 3.3 and the historical attendances and performances of big league teams, in 2006 the least saturated sports markets with respect to the 30 MLB clubs were in the areas of New York, Los Angeles and Chicago. The AL and NL teams located within these markets are, respectively, the Yankees and Mets, Angels and Dodgers, and

White Sox and Cubs. There are several reasons why these six baseball clubs compete at home in the three least crowded baseball markets. First, each of the area's total population exceeds nine million and the number of television homes rank first, second and third in the nation. As a result, these three sports markets are more than able to support the home-site games of, respectively, New York's ten, Los Angeles' eight, and Chicago's six professional sports franchises.[7]

Second, the Yankees, Angels, Dodgers and White Sox are usually among the top-performing teams in their respective divisions, and thus these four clubs attract large and enthusiastic crowds to their home games even when they underperform during the regular season or in the playoffs. Furthermore the Mets in New York and Cubs in Chicago are relatively popular sports teams at home games, and also are high-valued franchises despite-not being consistent or above-average winners in their divisions in most years. And third, a proposal by MLB to place another club in one or more of these three areas would be challenged in the courts by the respective team owners and unfortunately cause local baseball fans to rebel and perhaps abandon the sport within the league's largest and most lucrative markets. Indeed, it is irrational to contemplate other big league teams playing at home in the cities or surrounding suburbs of New York, Los Angeles and Chicago.

In contrast to the data in Table 3.3, which reflect how three characteristics of the teams' metropolitan areas ranked within the U.S. during the early 2000s, an alternative method of measuring and evaluating the 25 MLB areas' population, per capita personal income and number of television homes is provided in Table A.3.3 of the Appendix. This table, which consists of five columns, denotes the relative position of these characteristics among each other rather than among all metropolitan areas across the nation. For the clubs that played at home within the same metropolitan area, such as the Cubs and White Sox, they tied in rank for each characteristic.

To summarize the results for the three characteristics, the areas in the table's column two were roughly divided into thirds. That is, the population, per capita personal income and number of television homes in the top third of the 29 teams' areas ranked from first to tenth, the middle third from eleventh to twentieth, and the bottom third from twenty-first to twenty-ninth. Since Toronto in Canada is not located within a population that is comparable to a U.S. Standard Metropolitan Statistical Area (SMSA), the Blue Jays' area was excluded from the table. Therefore, what important information—if any—does Table A.3.3 reveal about the congestion of sports markets as a group and between teams in the AL and NL?

For the distribution of the population characteristic in column three, the AL teams had four or 31 percent of their areas ranked in each of the top and bottom thirds, and five or 38 percent in the middle third. The NL, meanwhile, had six or 38 percent of their teams' areas in the top third, and five each or a total of 62 percent in the middle and bottom thirds. This distribution suggests that in proportions, more of the AL teams tended to be located in midsized areas than did the NL clubs. Alternatively, approx-imately 40 percent of the NL franchises generally operated in cities within relatively more populated areas than did the AL franchises. Furthermore, if the areas of Chicago, Los Angeles-Anaheim and New York are excluded from the upper portion of the table, then the Texas Rangers were the only other AL club that had played at home in a big metropolitan area. Even so, there is only a small to moderate misallocation of MLB teams given the ranks in population of the 25 areas.

For the distribution of per capita personal income in column four, there are greater disparities between the areas of AL and NL teams. Regarding the former group of 13 clubs, six or 46 percent of their areas had ranked in the top third, four or 31 percent in the middle third, and three or 23 percent in the bottom third of this characteristic. With respect to the latter group of 16 teams, four or 25 percent of them placed in the top third and then six or 38 percent each in the middle and bottom thirds. In other words, the households within the areas of AL teams tended to have higher incomes those who resided in the NL areas. Indeed, such midsized cities in the NL as Atlanta, Phoenix and San Diego, and smaller areas like Cincinnati, Milwaukee and Pittsburgh, each had populations that earned relatively lower incomes because of their economies and types of occupations, and also due to the education levels, skills and productivities of their labor forces (see Table A.3.4).

For the proportions and ranks of television homes in column five of Table A.3.3, this characteristic was also vastly different between the areas of AL and NL teams. That is, a total of ten or 78 percent of AL areas had ranked in the top and middle thirds while a total of 11 or 69 percent of NL areas placed in the middle and bottom thirds. In part, these leagues' allocations of television homes within the various areas were derived from the ability of households in such AL midsized cities as Detroit, Minneapolis, Oakland and Seattle to afford at least one television set. In short, the rankings of these three characteristics in Table A.3.3 confirm that MLB teams play their home games in metropolitan areas with significantly different socioeconomic attributes.

In sum, I predict that the most, semi- and least congested sports markets in MLB will each consist of about the same number of big league teams for the next 10 or more years. Moreover, if the Marlins are unable to benefit from the use of public money to finance the construction of a modern ballpark in the Miami area, their owners will be compelled to search for another city in an area to relocate the existing franchise. If so, the new site will be somewhere other than in the 26 currently occupied sports markets that are listed in Table 3.2.

In the next section of the chapter there are 15 domestic areas that are not congested with professional sports teams. Nevertheless each of them has major or minor demographic deficiencies, and/or they are economically inferior with respect to being an optimum location for hosting an expansion or relocating big league club.

Future MLB Markets

Prior to 1901, such U.S. cities as Brooklyn, Buffalo, Hartford, Indianapolis, Louisville, Providence, Syracuse, Troy and Worcester were sites for early NL teams. Besides the club in Brooklyn—which was originally nicknamed the Bridegrooms and then Superbras, but in 1901 became the Brooklyn Dodgers—the other eight franchises were canceled because of their small attendances and inferior performances at home, and also due to their cash flow problems, high amounts of debt, operating problems, and/or ownership failures. In fact, Indianapolis is the most attractive city in the group of nine since it has the essential characteristics and attributes to be a viable future location for a current or new MLB club.

In conjunction with the data contained in Table 3.3, column one of Table 3.4 lists 15 U.S. metropolitan areas that I researched and selected as being potential markets for a big league team. That is, each of these areas' total population, amount of per capita personal income, and number of television homes was used as factors, in part, to identify whether they are prospective markets for current and/or expansion big league teams. (Besides the 15 areas that are listed in Table 3.4, five other cities, the Jacksonville, Memphis, Rochester, Oklahoma City and Louisville areas, would each rank in order from sixteenth to twentieth as future baseball sites.)

Based on the characteristics in columns two, four and six of Table 3.4, and on a number of baseball articles and books that have been published in the sports literature, the three most qualified areas to place an MLB team after 2007 are Portland-Beaverton, San Antonio, and Las Vegas-Paradise. Although these areas rank first, second and third in priority, there are some disadvantages associated with each of them. For example, the Portland-Beaverton metropolitan area has average or above-average characteristics in each of the three attributes. However, the city's NBA Trailblazers are not popular among local

Table 3.4 Potential MLB Markets
Characteristics of Metropolitan Areas, Selected Years

Area	Population	Rank	Per Capita PI	Rank	TV Homes	Rank
Austin-Round Rock	1.5	38th	34.0	84th	.6	52nd
Charlotte-Gastonia-Rock Hill	1.5	36th	36.1	56th	1.0	26th
Columbus	1.7	32nd	35.2	68th	.9	32nd
Greensboro-High Point	.7	73rd	30.9	160th	.6	47th
Indianapolis	1.6	34th	36.2	52nd	1.0	25th
Las Vegas-Paradise	1.7	31st	34.8	75th	.7	43rd
Nashville	1.4	39th	36.4	48th	.9	30th
New Orleans	1.3	40th	20.7	357th	.5	54th
Norfolk-VA Beach-Newport News	1.6	33rd	33.3	107th	.7	42nd
Orlando-Kissimee	1.9	28th	31.1	154th	1.4	19th
Portland-Beaverton	2.1	24th	35.2	69th	1.1	23rd
Raleigh-Cary	1.0	51st	35.1	70th	1.0	29th
Sacramento-Yolo	2.0	26th	34.8	77th	1.3	20th
Salt Lake City-Ogden	1.1	50th	33.2	108th	.8	35th
San Antonio	1.9	29th	30.1	178th	.7	37th

Note: See Table 3.3 for descriptions of the population in column two, per capita personal income in column four, and television homes in column six. The Norfolk area includes the cities of Norfolk, Virginia Beach and Newport News. The characteristics of areas were ranked relative to those in other metropolitan areas of the U.S.

Source: "Metropolitan Areas," at http://www.census.gov cited 9 October 2006, and "2006–2007 Local Television Households: Local Market Universe Estimates," at http://www.nielsenmedia.com cited 9 October 2006.

sports fans and there is uncertainty as to whether a sufficient number of baseball fans live in the Portland-Beaverton area to adequately support an MLB club.

Unfortunately in San Antonio, the per capita personal income and number of television homes are each considerably below the group of 15's averages of, respectively, $33 thousand and 880 thousand homes. The Las Vegas-Paradise area, meanwhile, is tainted because of its reputation as the gambling capital of western America and an area whose economy is primarily dependent on the economic development and growth of the tourist industry. Anyway, these three places have demographic profiles that are each equivalent to or exceed the characteristics of MLB sites within the areas of Cincinnati, Kansas City, Milwaukee, Pittsburgh and Tampa Bay.

With respect to the remaining 12 areas listed in column one of Table 3.4, the most attractive of them as baseball sites include Indianapolis in central Indiana and Orlando in central Florida, and then Norfolk in southeast Virginia. Being located a similar number of miles from Chicago to the north, St. Louis to the west and Cincinnati to the east, Indianapolis has experienced a successful history with minor league baseball teams and national amateur athletic organizations, and the city's local sports fans are passionate about the NFL Colts and NBA Pacers. Even so, the problem is that a mid-to-large proportion of the tax money from households and businesses in Indianapolis and within Marion County would be used to build a modern major league ballpark for its new MLB team. Also, Indianapolis' metropolitan area has only a few Fortune 500 companies and multimillionaires that could afford to purchase a significant number of high-priced luxury suites, premium seats, and season tickets to the 81 home games played there each year.

Ranked after Indianapolis as a future baseball site is the Orlando area in central Florida, which has a growing population, booming commercial and residential real estate markets, a popular tourist industry because of Disney World and Sea World, and a climate with warm to hot temperatures in the spring, summer and fall, ideal for scheduling outdoor sports events. However, the failure of the Marlins to attract more sports fans from within their market to home games, and the club's inability to convince local politicians and taxpayers to subsidize the construction of a new baseball stadium in the Miami area, discourages MLB from placing a relocating or expansion team anywhere in southeast and central Florida. Finally, in the Norfolk area there are thousands of civil service and military personnel who are assigned to U.S. Navy facilities, and many of these people are baseball fans. Nonetheless, the area's total population, its per capita personal income, and its number of television homes are each average or below average with respect to the other 14 areas listed in Table 3.4. Thus Norfolk and Orlando, and then the ten areas not previously discussed in this section, are least demographically and economically developed to host a MLB club.

To complement the number counts and dollar values of Table 3.4's three characteristics—which were each ranked among all metropolitan areas in the U.S.—another way to arrange the data and then evaluate these 15 areas as potential MLB sites is to list in columns their populations, per capita personal incomes and number of television homes, and then rank each of them relative to each other, that is, from first to fifteenth. After this task was completed, areas and the ranks of their respective characteristics were organized and displayed in Table

A.3.5 of the Appendix. Accordingly, what does the latter table reveal about how qualified the 15 areas are as future locations of MLB teams?

Other than Portland-Beaverton, it is apparent that the majority of areas were inferior or unacceptable with respect to one or more of the characteristics. Indeed some areas ranked first to fifth in one or perhaps two characteristics, but then finished sixth to fifteenth in population, per capita personal income, and/or the number of television homes. These results occurred, for example, within the Charlotte-Gastonia-Rock Hill, Indianapolis, Orlando-Kissimee, and Sacramento-Yolo areas. Nevertheless, these four areas have the potential of becoming future sites since some studies have reported that such indicators as communities' rates of population and income growth, the current presence of a successful minor league baseball team and/or the headquarters of midsized or large corporations, and the willingness of local entrepreneurs and municipal governments to invest in the construction of a new multimillion dollar ballpark, are each also important factors for baseball officials to consider when evaluating the attractiveness of areas besides the three characteristics and their positions as incorporated in Tables 3.4 and A.3.4.

Based on the rankings of the characteristics in Table A.3.4, as of 2007 the three least desirable areas for a major league club were Greensboro-High Point, North Carolina, and then New Orleans and Salt Lake City-Ogden. Alternatively, there have been some articles published in the print media stating that big league baseball executives and/or some current teams and prospective franchise owners have visited and examined the merits of such areas as Portland-Beaverton and San Antonio, and even Norfolk-VA Beach-Newport News and Las Vegas-Paradise.

Since the current 26 areas that contain big league teams are congested as sports markets, and given that the majority of areas in Table 3.4 are not qualified either demographically or economically to be sites for major league teams, it will be several years before a new baseball franchise is placed in the Portland-Beaverton, San Antonio, or Las Vegas-Paradise areas. And, because the majority of U.S. metropolitan areas are saturated with professional sports teams, it will be a significant challenge for MLB owners to recommend and then unanimously approve the relocation of a current team from an inferior market. Likewise, for these and other reasons the AL and NL are unlikely to expand within America before the mid-to-late 2010s.

Global Sports Markets

In Chapter 11 of *Baseball, Inc.*, I identified and evaluated some international cities as potential sites for a relocating or new AL and/or NL team.

With the saturation of major sports markets in the U.S. since the early 2000s, there is an opportunity for MLB to assume more risks and incur marketing costs by aggressively promoting American baseball in one or more foreign cities, and then implementing a long run strategy of international expansion.

To determine a group of foreign cities that are considered to be the most and least desirable baseball markets from demographic, economic and social perspectives, Table 3.5 was prepared. As such, it contains the names and countries of 13 cities and the total populations of these cities' metropolitan areas, and how the areas ranked in size relative to each other. Since these cities have never been sites of American big league baseball teams, they are obviously not cluttered with sports franchises from any of the U.S.-based professional leagues. Furthermore, I chose each city in the table based on its sports culture and local-regional population, on its area as a home for a professional baseball franchise, and on such attributes as its growth, climate and density.[8]

Because of millions of passionate baseball fans within their populations and the availability of baseball training academies for athletes in some of the

Table 3.5 Foreign Sports Markets
Cities Ranked as Baseball Sites, Post 2006 MLB Season

Country	City	MAPOP	Rank
Mexico	Monterrey	3.7	1st
Mexico	Mexico City	22.4	2nd
Mexico	Tijuana	4.8	3rd
Puerto Rico	San Juan	2.0	4th
Dominican Republic	Santo Domingo	3.1	5th
Japan	Tokyo	36.7	6th
Taiwan	Taipei	8.1	7th
South Korea	Seoul	22.1	8th
Australia	Sydney	4.4	9th
Panama	Panama City	1.2	10th
England	London	12.5	11th
Venezuela	Caracas	3.8	12th
Cuba	Havana	2.6	113th

Note: Country in column one and City in column two are self-explanatory. MAPOP in column three is the metropolitan area population in millions. The Rank in column four was assigned based on each city's attractiveness and potential as a home site for am MLB team.

Source: "City and Area Population," at http://www.world-gazetteer.com cited 17 October 2006.

Latin American nations, MLB has an economic incentive to eventually put a team in a relatively large urban city of the Dominican Republic, Mexico, Puerto Rico and/or Venezuela. Even so, while living in these countries the big league baseball club's coaches, players and staff—particularly those who are American natives—may encounter such issues as currency devaluations, high unemployment and poverty rates in local communities, and political and social hostilities from some people and groups (see Table A.3.6).

As a result of these problems and the amount of capital expenditures needed by the team's owners to invest in a local sports stadium for at its home games, a big league franchise in Santo Domingo, Monterrey, Mexico City, San Juan, and/or Caracas would likely struggle as an ongoing business. So for a few baseball seasons, any teams based in foreign cities may require some modest financial assistance from MLB and commercial organizations in the local community, and perhaps monetary contributions from regional governments in these nations. Hopefully after a few years the club may improve its performances well enough to win one half of its games, receive more media coverage and exposure within its city and metropolitan area, expand attendances at the local home ballpark to increase the franchise's revenues, and thus survive as a sports enterprise at least in the short -run.

Given the 13 cities and distribution of their areas' populations in Table 3.5, Mexico is the most attractive foreign country to locate an MLB team after 2007. Within Mexico, the best sites for a club and its facilities are located in the areas of Monterrey and then in Mexico City and Tijuana. To justify these three places as future baseball sites, Monterrey, first of all, is Mexico's wealthiest city. It is located approximately 100 miles south-southwest of the Texas border. Everywhere in Monterrey there is modern architecture and dispersed throughout the urban area are plenty of American and international restaurants, retail stores and entertainment facilities. Besides Monterrey's conspicuous wealth and modern buildings, the city hosts the Mexican Baseball Hall of Fame, and the Mexican League's Monterrey Sultans play there in a 27-thousand-seat baseball stadium that could, if necessary, be renovated and expanded to accommodate a capacity crowd of at least 30–35 thousand fans. The Sultans' ballpark, which was built in 1990, is regarded to be the most modern baseball structure in Latin America. As reported in a recent article of the *Wall Street Journal*, "It's hard not to see the appeal of trading Canada for Latin America. The Monterrey market is convenient to a number of Texas cities and is home to 1,500 Dallas Cowboy season ticket holders. Manifestly, Latin America has plenty of budding A-Rods and millions more baseball fans. Isn't it time to give them a real chance to root for the home team?"[9]

With Monterrey being the most attractive international site, the second to fifth ranked foreign cities for a relocating or expansion MLB franchise are, respectively, in Mexico City and Tijuana, and then in San Juan and Santo Domingo. Mexico City and its surrounding metropolitan area have an immense population that supports local and popular amateur and professional Mexican baseball teams, while Tijuana is a tourist area that is very near the border that separates it from San Diego. Alternatively, San Juan and Santo Domingo are two cities where thousands of diehard sports fans root for their favorite baseball clubs and local players, and for those natives who compete on AL and NL teams. Meanwhile, because of Fidel Castro's communist regime and the current U.S. trade embargo of Cuba, Havana is not a realistic location for a big league team although it is the nearest and most convenient of the 13 cities with respect to stadiums of MLB teams in the U.S. east, midwest and southeast.

The remaining seven cities in Table 3.5 are much less attractive as MLB sites than Monterrey, Mexico City and Tijuana in Mexico, and some cities in other Latin American areas. Although each of them are situated in moderate-to-well-developed consumer markets of large and dense metropolitan areas, the cities of Tokyo, Taipei and Seoul are very distant from the coasts of North America, and their populations have distinct cultures, customs and languages relative to those in the U.S. Furthermore the London area contains some high income and competitive players on athletic teams, which include outdoor soccer leagues. English sports fans, however, are not enthusiastic or passionate about American professional baseball and the clubs in MLB.

In Sydney, or alternatively Melbourne, baseball is a popular sports activity and Australian kids, teenagers and young adults enjoy playing the game for teams in schools and organized leagues. Similar to cities in Asia, there would be high transportation costs and excessive amounts of time needed for U.S.-based teams to schedule regular season games and travel to and from baseball sites in Australia. Moreover, the sports stadiums in Australian cities are extremely inferior in capacities and amenities, especially when compared to big league ballparks in New York, Los Angeles and Chicago.

There are thousands of athletes in Venezuela who love to play baseball for fun and compete on secondary school and amateur teams, and the amateur and professional games in that nation are well attended by fans from small, midsized and large cities across the nation. Nonetheless, Venezuelan president Hugo Chavez's socialist government is controversial because he has condemned the Bush administration at the United Nations and also demonized U.S. economic and political policies in his speeches and in interviews with reporters from the national and international media. Since Chavez is a close friend of Fidel Castro and with other revolutionaries in Central and South America, it is unlikely that an MLB team could exist as a business in Venezuela for more than one or two regular seasons. Finally, locating a big league team in Panama City does not appear to be a good option since the population of that country is poor, and its nation's baseball teams no longer participate in the Caribbean Series because of inferior players, and the lack of capital that had been allocated to the sport by the Panamanian government.

As an alternative and less risky short run strategy, MLB may decide before 2010 or shortly thereafter to assemble, sponsor and operate one or more AAA, AA, A and Rookie baseball groups and affiliates within Mexico and other Latin American countries. These organizations would, in part, consist of privately owned and/or league-subsidized clubs based in relatively medium sized cities or in the metropolitan areas of Monterrey, Mexico City, Tijuana, San Juan and Santo Domingo. While playing home and away games in each of these areas, the respective minor league teams would be encouraged by MLB Commissioner Bud Selig's staff to build housing facilities for their coaches, players and staff, and to establish academies and clinics to train these nations' athletes and teach them the skills necessary to be elite professional baseball players. Although this strategy may be a costly investment in the short term for MLB franchise owners, it should ultimately increase the demand for baseball from people living in these countries, and expand the international fan base of the league and the broadcast markets for the sport across regions of the world besides North America.[10]

To conclude this section of the chapter, when wealthy foreign investors including business groups and governments commit to own and operate a baseball franchise and participate financially in the construction of a modern big league ballpark, then MLB will authorize the location of teams in cities within large international sports markets. Indeed there are a few cities in Asian and Latin American countries that have large populations of sports fans, and the necessary demographic characteristics to officially and perhaps successfully host a professional baseball club of MLB, or one, two and more minor leagues and their teams.

4

BASEBALL CONFLICTS, CONTROVERSIES, AND SCANDALS

While operating more than 100 years as a professional sports organization based in the United States Major League Baseball has frequently experienced internal and external conflicts and controversies, and also has been afflicted by different types of criminal activities, scandals and irresponsible decisions, and challenged by other kinds of ethical and social issues. Before, during and after these memorable but unfortunate events had occurred, a number of baseball fans in America and elsewhere became temporarily or permanently disillusioned with the league's commissioner and various franchise owners and their respective teams, and with one or more general managers, coaches and players, and occasionally with the Major League Baseball Players Association (MLBPA).

As a result of these matters, the popularity of baseball among sports fans has historically (and currently) declined, especially in the cities where big league clubs were located in the U.S. and Canada. Consequently during different years it is likely that a majority of MLB clubs have relinquished a portion of their market shares, and thus revenues and profits, to professional teams that play in such rival American-based sports leagues as the National Basketball Association, National Football League, and National Hockey League, and perhaps to teams in Major League Soccer.[1]

Numerous researchers have discussed in their articles and books, and in baseball magazines and trade journals, the tumultuous events that MLB has endured during its history of regular seasons and postseasons, that is, in one or from 1901 to the early 2000s. Some of the previous troubles in baseball have included, for example, such actions and activities as briberies, conspiracies, betting on games, cases of domestic violence, lockouts, strikes and the illegal purchase and consumption of cocaine, steroids and other banned substances.

Besides the deleterious social effects of these matters within the professional sports industry, baseball fans have also been aroused by the high and rising compensation of players, the increasing costs for families with children to attend regular season and postseason games at MLB ballparks, and the need to adjust to such changes as league expansion and the relocation of teams, and to the competitive imbalances that continue to exist between the small- and large-market clubs that play in various divisions of the American League (AL) and National League (NL). In short, millions of domestic and foreign baseball fans and hundreds of American communities, and the local, national and international business of MLB, have each been influenced by turmoil within and external to the sport.

According to a few recent polls, the primary issues that baseball fans are most concerned about include the exorbitant dollar amounts of players' salaries, and some of these athletes' wanton use of illegal drugs, and the increasingly higher ticket prices and other expenses for individuals and groups to attend MLB games at each of the teams' ballparks. Besides these problems, a fraction of baseball fans are also frustrated because regular season games take too many hours to finish. Although salaries, drugs, ticket prices, ballpark expenditures, and the excessive time spent to complete nine or more innings are each important issues that affect the fans' demand for professional baseball, since the mid-to-late 1800s there have been other minor and major short- and long-run problems that have emerged from the sport over the years.[2]

Based on a historical perspective, the following sections of this chapter will reveal some of the relevant and newsworthy facts about, and the implications of, various conflicts, controversies and scandals that have occurred in MLB. Then some of the more recent behavioral incidents and other troubles involving big league baseball—and not highlighted in previous chapters of the book—are discussed to determine how they have affected baseball fans and teams, and whether these issues will affect the future image of the sport and its growth and prosperity as a business in American society.

Baseball Gambling Scandals

During baseball's early history as an organization, professional baseball officials conducted investigations and frequently penalized any of the ballplayers who had violated league rules or teams' policies with respect to integrity of the game. Indeed, it was not unusual then for underworld criminals and unregulated gambling enterprises to establish relationships with professional players and make deals for them to influence the outcome of games, since these athletes had received very little compensation from franchise owners to perform for their respective baseball teams. As such, the following matters denote the types of undesirable activities and flagrant and corrupt practices that frequently occurred in the sport during the early years of baseball seasons.

Between the 1860s and late 1910s, for example, several professional baseball players from such clubs as the New York Mutuals, Louisville Grays, Chicago White Sox, St. Louis Browns, St. Louis Cardinals and Chicago Cubs illegally bet on big league games or were directly or indirectly associated with gambling interests. Specifically in 1865 and 1877 some players from the New York Mutuals and the NL Louisville Grays had accepted bribes from gamblers to intentionally lose their team's games. After baseball officials became aware of their actions, the players were either banned from the sport or temporarily suspended but then reinstated at a later date by a committee, which represented a particular group of clubs.[3]

Besides infractions by players that occurred before and during the mid-to-late 1870s, there were some violations involving others in the sport. For instance, an umpire was banned from baseball for conspiring with criminals to throw an NL game in 1882. Twenty-four years later a physician, who was working for the New York Giants, received the same penalty for offering an umpire $2,500 to cheat in games against the Chicago Cubs. Then in 1910, a big league manager and a team coach attempted to fix a number of games. Subsequently they were each banned, and so was Philadelphia Phillies owner Horace Fogel, who in 1912 publicly condemned the decisions made by umpires against his team. Furthermore, Fogel complained to the media that the NL pennant race was a crooked competition.

Another noteworthy incident happened during the 1917 World Series between the Chicago White Sox and New York Giants. Because of some players' careless and contrived mistakes made during the six games of the Series and these athletes' questionable association with groups of gamblers, the Giants' Heinie Zimmerman and Hal Chase were each suspended from professional baseball for life by a league committee. Then in 1918 there were rumors among baseball fans that the World Series was fixed by a few of the Chicago Cubs players. Accordingly this incident resulted in small crowds at Series games in Boston and Chicago and nearly caused a strike by players who asked their team owners for more of the revenues that had been generated from gate receipts during the season. In short, MLB was struggling during these years to become a reputable national sport due to gambling by players, umpires and team officials, and because of the business, international and political problems caused by World War I.

The most detestable scandal in MLB's history, however, occurred in 1919. In that year, eight Chicago White Sox players agreed to throw the World Series and lose to the Cincinnati Reds for payments of cash from gambling czar Arnold Rothstein. Although these athletes were found not quality in a criminal case—since it was not a crime then to throw baseball games—the players were banned from organized baseball for life by former judge Kenesaw Mountain Landis and who was MLB's first commissioner. Besides banishing the great "Shoeless" Joe Jackson and his seven White Sox teammates, Landis decided to also penalize other big league players for various reasons during his 25-year tenure as baseball's supreme authority. He expelled these players for such activities as accepting gifts or loans from gamblers and plotting to overthrow regular season or postseason games, and for being arrested for theft and participating in other crimes. Interestingly, Landis banned some players because they underperformed to extract more pay from their teams. Indeed these athletes loafed on the field, committed errors during some games, complained about salaries, asked to be released by the managers of their teams, and made threatening remarks to their club owners, coaches and teammates. Because of Landis' tough penalties and his successful disciplining of players, baseball's gambling problems rarely recurred until after his death in 1944.

To continue penalizing bad and irresponsible behavior, in 1947 MLB Commissioner Happy Chandler suspended Brooklyn Dodgers manager Leo Durocher for the baseball season because Durocher was seen in public with gamblers. Then during the early 1980s, MLB Commissioner Bowie Kuhn banned from baseball two well-known Hall of Famers. They were former New York Yankees outfielder Mickey Mantle and New York Giants center fielder Willie Mays. These two retired ballplayers had accepted positions to be greeters and autograph signers while they worked for a gambling casino in Atlantic City, New Jersey. To focus on Kuhn's decision and attract the sympathies of some Yankees and Giants fans, a number of newspaper sports columnists reported that Mantle and Mays had performed in the major leagues before players were earning excessively lucrative multimillion-dollar salaries. Anyway, in 1985 MLB Commissioner Peter Ueberroth reinstated Mantle and Mays so that they could voluntarily, as employees or consultants of teams, participate in and contribute to the sports industry and especially to the current and future welfare of big league baseball.

It was a few years after Ueberroth's action that the MLB commissioner's

"Shoeless" Joe Jackson played a total of 13 years for three big league teams and finished his career with a .356 batting average, which ranks as the third highest of all time. A jury acquitted Jackson in 1921 of any wrongdoing for fixing games of the 1919 World Series. He died in 1951 at the age of 63 in Greenville, South Carolina. [National Baseball Hall of Fame Library, Cooperstown, N.Y.]

After he had established a number of all-time career records during his seasons with primarily the Cincinnati Reds, Pete Rose was implicated in a gambling scandal and banned from baseball for life by former Commissioner Bart Giamatti in August 1989. [National Baseball Hall of Fame Library, Cooperstown, N.Y.]

office and lawyer John Dowd investigated Pete Rose—a former Cincinnati Reds player and manager—for illegally betting on games. Based on the testimony of his gambling partners and other evidence reported in some articles published by *Sports Illustrated*, Rose decided it would be best for him to compromise with MLB Commissioner A. Bartlett Giamatti and voluntarily agree to a lifetime ban from the sport. Even so, for many years Rose resisted pressure from baseball officials, and would not admit to being guilty of gambling. But in statements made for his 2004 book, *My Prison Without Bars*, Rose said he had bet on the Reds only to win games and volunteered to tell current MLB Commissioner Bud Selig that his statement was a fact. Despite filing applications in 1997 and 2003 for re-entry into baseball, Rose's lifetime ban has not been reconsidered by the baseball commissioner's office.[4]

In 24 years of full-time service as a player in the big leagues, Rose had a remarkable career. As of 2006, he still held several all-time regular season achievements and rankings. He placed first among players with a total of 3,562 games and 4,256 hits, with ten 200-hit seasons, 3,215 singles and 14,053 at-bats, and ranked fifth all-time with 2,165 runs scored, sixth with 5,793 total bases, tied for tenth with 15 years of batting at least .300 and twelfth with 745 consecutive games played and 1,566 walks, and tied for fourteenth because he led the league in batting average for three seasons. Nonetheless, due to his transgressions as one of baseball's greatest players, Rose will not and should never be admitted into the sport's Hall of Fame.[5]

Because of the league's restrictive rules and its severe penalties, MLB players have not been accused of betting on games and associating with gamblers to any great extent since the mid-to-late 1980s. Thus in recent years there is no evidence that this type of scandal has influenced the outcomes of regular season and postseason games, or affected the support of teams' baseball fans. Even so, if betting on sports games remains a legal activity in Nevada, it is highly unlikely that MLB will choose Las Vegas, Reno, or any other city in that state as the site for an expansion or relocating team.

Illegal Substance Abuse

Before the 1970s alcohol, although legal, was one of the primary substances that was consistently being abused by some MLB players. Generally the American public has tended to believe that excessive alcohol consumption is a weakness of individuals such as athletes in professional sports, and that MLB prevention and treatment programs to cure alcohol abuse have been available for decades for the teams' ballplayers. However, when alcohol

While pitching for the Detroit Tigers, Denny McLain won the Cy Young Award in 1968 and 1969. During his career, he reportedly engaged in bookmaking, bet heavily on horses at the racetrack, and associated with gamblers and underworld criminals. [National Baseball Hall of Fame Library, Cooperstown, N.Y.]

faded as an abusive substance in baseball during the early-to-mid–1970s, it was a few years later that illegal drugs began to emerge as a widespread social problem across North America and specifically within professional sports leagues.

The first big league player to be permanently suspended from baseball for drug use was an African American named Ferguson Jenkins, who was a very good Chicago Cubs pitcher. In early August of 1980 he was arrested in Toronto, Ontario, for the possession of cocaine. About two weeks later, MLB Commissioner Bowie Kuhn decided to ban Jenkins from the sport. Nevertheless, in September 1980 an independent arbitrator reinstated him, and in 1991, he was elected into the Baseball Hall of Fame in Cooperstown, New York. Following Jenkins' reinstatement, there were several incidents during the 1980s, 1990s and 2000s that involved the illegal abuse of drugs by some baseball players and others who were associated with the sport. Following are some prominent examples of this recurring problem in MLB.[6]

After being pressured by the media and some coaches and teammates to reveal their predicament, in 1985 several Pittsburgh Pirates players testified before a grand jury about their use of illegal substances while they were involved in professional baseball. During these so-called drug trials it was revealed that pitcher Rod Scurry had frantically searched for cocaine between innings of the Pirates' games throughout the 1980 season, while outfielder/first baseman John Milner purchased two grams of cocaine for $200 from some dealers he had met in bathrooms during home games played in Pittsburgh's Three Rivers Stadium. Besides the flagrant infractions of these two players, the team's mascot Kevin Koch purchased cocaine, and he even had the temerity to introduce some Pirates players to various drug dealers.

After seven dealers in the Pittsburgh area pleaded guilty or were convicted of selling cocaine to professional athletes, MLB Commissioner Peter Ueberroth was compelled to suspend some big league players, and that action led to their failure in the sport. For instance, Pirates slugger and first baseman Dave Parker lost his bid to be elected into the Baseball Hall of Fame, and Dale Berra, son of New York Yankees legendary catcher Yogi Berra, ruined his career while an infielder with the Pirates. Then in 1992 Rod Scurry died of a heart attack at the age of 36 in a Reno, Nevada, intensive care unit after a drug incident he had with the local police and after being admitted to the city's hospital for treatment. In the end this scandal had alienated thousands of Pirates fans, and as a result, many of them refused to continue attending the team's home and away games. However, the scandal did produce some social benefits. That is, it alerted MLB officials and team owners, sports fans and other American citizens that a substance abuse problem truly existed in baseball, and furthermore, it revealed that athletes were using drugs besides cocaine such as amphetamines, Human Growth Hormone (HGH), marijuana and steroids.

During the early 1990s another notorious incident involving illegal substances occurred when MLB Commissioner Francis Vincent permanently banned big league pitcher Steve Howe of the Los Angeles Dodgers, and formerly of the New York Yankees, from organized baseball. Indeed, Howe had six prior suspensions from the league for abusing substances, and those penalties had convinced him to plead guilty to buying cocaine from drug dealers in July 1992. Four months later, however, an arbiter reviewed the case and decided to overturn Howe's most recent suspension. In any event it became increasingly apparent to fans and observers of professional sports that some baseball players had continued to abuse different kinds of drugs despite the Pirates' well-publicized cocaine scandal of the mid-to-late 1980s.

Former Commissioner Bowie Kuhn suspended Hall of Fame pitcher Ferguson Jenkins—who won 284 games during his 19-year career in Major League Baseball and the 1971 Cy Young Award—after Jenkins was arrested because of drugs he possessed at Toronto's Exhibition Stadium in September 1980. [National Baseball Hall of Fame Library, Cooperstown, N.Y.]

Steroids

Between the mid-to-late 1990s and early 2000s it was initially hearsay and rumors, and then gradually accusations began to spread among sports fans, the media, and the general public, about how MLB players had been extensively using steroids to

In February 1986, Commissioner Peter Ueberroth suspended Pittsburgh Pirates outfielder and National League batting champion and Most Valuable Player Dave Parker from baseball for one year because of drug-related charges. [National Baseball Hall of Fame Library, Cooperstown, N.Y.]

become stronger and improve performances in order to increase their salaries and extend their careers in the sport. In a 2002 interview with an Entertainment Sports Programming Network (ESPN) sportscaster, commentator Bob Costas referred to 1994–2002 in baseball as the "Steroids Era." That is, Costas inferred that the dramatic increase in home runs that were hit by big league players during this series of seasons had occurred, in part, because of a juiced baseball and inferior pitching caused by the expansion teams, but also because of players who were abusing steroids. As evidence of what Costas had said, some MLB players began to voluntarily speak to journalists in the sports media about the drug issue as a critical problem in professional baseball.[7]

For example former San Francisco Giants pitcher Tom House admitted to a newspaper reporter that he used steroids during his big league career and that the drug had been present in baseball since the 1960s. Meanwhile, Toronto Blue Jays pitcher David Wells stated that 25 to 40 percent of all major leaguers were juiced. Then power hitter Jose Canseco said that up to 80 percent of current players had used steroids during their careers, and furthermore, he credited these drugs for his impressive performances as a batter with the Oakland Athletics, Texas Rangers, and several other clubs. Also, former San Diego Padres slugger Ken Caminiti revealed that he had won the NL Most Valuable Player Award in 1996 while on steroids. Moreover, there was suspicion that the St. Louis Cardinals' Mark McGwire and Chicago Cubs' Sammy Sosa used, respectively, such supplements as androstenedione and creatine when they vigorously competed during the late 1990s to surpass Babe Ruth's historic record of 60 home runs in a regular season. Based on their comments in the media, apparently some of these athletes had decided to expose this issue to the American public and to encourage the league and MLBPA to examine and jointly resolve it.

When they appeared before a congressional committee in 2004, some MLB athletes refused to acknowledge any steroid problems in baseball and thereby to ignore or deny what House, Wells, Canseco and Caminiti had said about players using drugs. Mark McGwire, for example, refused to admit any wrongdoing, while the Baltimore Orioles' Rafael Palmeiro testified that Canseco's statements about steroids were false. After questioning various players the committee concluded that baseball had failed to effectively confront the problems of performance-enhancing drugs, and those major leaguers who used steroids were not ideal role models to aspiring young athletes. Interestingly, in August 2005, Palmeiro tested positive for illegal substances and was suspended from playing in MLB games for ten days. A potential candidate for honors because he had clouted more than 500 home runs and batted 3,000-plus hits, Palmeiro may have ruined his opportunity to join such

Relief pitcher Steve Howe, who had saved numerous games for four teams, was suspended from baseball five times for drug and alcohol abuse. Commissioner Jay Vincent banned him in June 1992, but four months later an arbitrator overturned Howe's suspension and permitted him to continue playing in the big leagues. [National Baseball Hall of Fame Library, Cooperstown, N.Y.]

Ken Caminiti, who played a total of 15 years for three teams in the big leagues, was selected for three All-Star teams, won three Gold Gloves, and earned the 1996 National League Most Valuable Player Award. After he admitted to using steroids during his playing career, Caminiti suddenly died in 2004 at the age of 41. [National Baseball Hall of Fame Library, Cooperstown, N.Y.]

ballplayers as Joe DiMaggio, Hank Aaron, Ted Williams and other superstars in the Baseball Hall of Fame.

Regarding the use of steroids by some current professional players who are famous, the most attention and scrutiny has been focused on San Francisco Giants outfielder Barry Bonds. That is because he successfully set a MLB record by batting 73 home runs in the 2001 season, and five years later became the second all-time leader in home runs and surpassed Babe Ruth when he hit 715. In retrospect, this controversy about steroids surfaced when it was revealed that Bonds' personal trainer and an employee of Victor Conte's Bay Area Laboratory Co-operative (BALCO), Greg Anderson, had also been the trainer for two New York Yankees players, fielders Jason Giambi and Greg Sheffield. During his grand jury testimony, Giambi admitted to using steroids during his career, while Bonds said to the jury that he had used some unknown and unrecognizable lotions called the "clear" and "cream" to treat his arthritis, and which Anderson had provided him. Although Sheffield was injured but eventually started some games for the Yankees toward the end of the

2006 regular season, and in the postseason, Giambi and Bonds were productive enough to play the majority of games for their respective teams, and each hit more than 25 home runs.[8]

In 2006 a controversial book titled *Game of Shadows* was published. In it, authors Mark Fainaru-Wada and Lance Williams referred to paperwork that chronicled Barry Bonds' extensive use of several types of performance-enhancing drugs. Indeed, while they were reporters for the *San Francisco Chronicle,* Fainaru-Wada and Williams had collected their evidence about Bonds by interviewing several undisclosed sources and obtaining more than one thousand documents related to the issue. These items included affidavits from BALCO investigators and facts that were cited from grand jury testimony. According to some key information that was discussed in the book, in January 1997 Bonds had purchased androstenedione from Stan Antosh, a California biochemist. Then, in 1998 and the years thereafter, Bonds was inspired to become more muscular because of the home run competition between McGwire and Sosa. Thus Bonds received various substances from Anderson to the extent that he consumed nearly 20 pills per day and also learned how to inject himself with steroids. In one section the book states that the Giants decided not to question their superstar about the apparent change in his physical appearance because team officials feared that Bonds would become alienated and/or create a national scandal in the sport before the team's new stadium was scheduled to be opened.[9]

Subsequently, to ensure that the authors would not earn enormous profits from selling the book, Bonds sued Fainaru-Wada and Williams and also the book's publisher, Gotham Books. A few months after Judge James Warren denied Bonds' request, the lawsuit was dropped since the authors had been subpoenaed to testify about their knowledge before a grand jury. When Fainaru-Wada and Williams requested that the court excuse them from appearing before a jury, in August 2006 a district judge ordered them to comply with the subpoena and testify. If the authors refused to testify, they would be held in contempt of court and incarcerated until they decided to talk, or the grand jury term expired, or a higher ranked court moved to block the ruling. In any event, the two newspaper reporters have stated that they preferred serving time in jail as opposed to testifying and revealing the sources of their statements about Bonds in *Game of Shadows.*

On August 7, 2007, 43-year-old Barry Bonds broke Hank Aaron's record of 755 home runs during the league's 2007 regular season. Even so, it is unlikely that MLB Commissioner Bud Selig has the intention and/or support to eliminate the slugger's achievements in baseball unless a grand jury indicts Bonds and then determines without doubt that he had used steroids and/or other illegal substances to enhance his performances during regular seasons of the 1990s and 2000s. Alternatively, former U.S. Senator George Mitchell—who was appointed by Selig in May 2006 to conduct an investigation into baseball's drug problems—might uncover substantial evidence of former and/or current players who abused steroids, HGH, amphetamines, and other performance-enhancing drugs and supplements. If so, then Selig has the authority to rule that Bonds cheated and thus conclude that this great player will not be recognized by MLB as the sport's all-time home run leader and for other milestones he achieved in baseball. In short, the commissioner's decision to deny Bonds his records would be very controversial, and probably detrimental to the sport. In turn, this outcome could possibly result in one or more of the following four consequences.[10]

First, the legality of Selig's decision to reject Bonds' home run title would unquestionably be challenged by the MLBPA since, before 2002, MLB had no official policy in the collective bargaining agreements regarding the use of steroids by major and minor league players. In fact, the baseball union's lawyers had filed a grievance and argued to overturn the first steroids-related 10-day suspension of a player in June 2005 when Texas Rangers minor league pitcher Agustin Montero tried to collect $4,918 of his former salary from a contract with the team.

Second, Selig's action against Bonds would be critically analyzed by reporters and highly publicized in the media, and critiqued in detail by academics, pundits, and baseball officials within the sports industry. As a result, the big league's public goodwill, which has been gradually reestablished with baseball fans since the early-to-mid–1990s when the players' strike occurred, would be jeopardized. Certainly at risk would be MLB's recent attendance records, and the economic progress that was achieved by a memorably, entertaining and successful 2006 season.

Third, from Selig's decision MLB and one or more of its AL and NL teams would likely lose some of their market shares to other professional sports leagues and their clubs, and would also realize smaller attendances at games, lower television ratings, and negative affects on their business relationships with some investors, partners, sponsors and vendors. For sure, these three consequences will not be allowed to develop while Selig is MLB's commissioner.

And fourth, many team owners, who have significant amounts of money invested in their baseball franchises, would join to rebel against Selig if Bonds' new home run record were denied even though it was illegitimately earned. Since the commissioner's office represents the franchise owners in collective bargaining with the MLBPA, it is not realistic to assume that Selig has the evidence and power to challenge this group of 30 wealthy baseball entrepreneurs.

Because the clubs' owners and MLBPA have unanimously agreed to implement and enforce a responsible drug testing and prevention program, and Commissioner Selig has committed to rid the sport of illegal substance abuse and performance-enhancing drugs, any steroid use by current players will be frowned upon and extremely unpopular within the sport. Nonetheless, since there are no flawlessly by reliable tests to detect HGH, it may be several years before all types of steroids and performance enhancers are eliminated as a threat to the successful business and future operation of teams in big league baseball.

Labor Relations

Table 4.1 highlights a 39-year history of labor relations between groups of MLB's franchise owners and the MLBPA. As the table indicates, between 1968 and 2006 there were three lockouts initiated by owners and five strikes originated by the players' union. As a result of these eight work stoppages, some baseball fans and sports analysts, historians, and reporters have criticized the league and the union for their failure to settle differences on labor issues prior to the expiration of collective bargaining agreements and thus to compromise their differences in the best interests of baseball. Alternatively, others in the sports media and elsewhere have defended the work stoppages as necessary actions since they represented contentious issues that MLB and the union had to negotiate and resolve such as the players' pension plan, free agency and salary arbitration. Nevertheless, baseball's most recent labor relations issues and problems are very complex and threatening.

Table 4.1 MLB Labor History
By Year and Types of Negotiation, 1968–2006

Year	*History*
1968	Team owners–MLBPA sign first basic agreement for 1968–1969 regular seasons.
1970	Team owners–MLBPA concludes a preliminary agreement on a 1970–1972 contract.
1972	Players strike over pension plan and reach agreement with team owners in April.
1973	86-game lockout and tentative agreement established on three-year contract in February.

1976	Lockout in March and tentative agreement in July on four-year contract.
1980	Players strike; preliminary four-year agreement in May; free agency issue reopened.
1981	Players strike and 712 games canceled; agreement on 1981–1984 contract in July.
1985	Players strike; agreement with owners in August on 1985–1989 contract.
1990	Lockout in February; agreement in March on 1990–1993 contract.
1994	Players strike in August; team owners accept MLBPA's unconditional offer to work.
1997	Agreement in March; contract through 2000 season; MLBPA contract option in 2001.
2002	Team owners-MLBPA sign contract agreement for 2002–2006 regular seasons.
2006	Tentative agreement realized in October-November on a 2007–2011 contract.

Note: MLBPA is the Major League Baseball Players Association.

Source: Barry M. Bloom, "MLB, Union Announce New Labor Deal," at http://www.mlb.com cited 25 October 2006; "MLB Owners Unanimously Approve Labor Deal," at http://www.sportsbusinessnews.com cited 4 November 2006; Doug Pappas, "Summary of the [2002] Collective Bargaining Agreement-Analysis," at http://www.businessofbaseball.com cited 5 January 2005; "Peaceful Coexistence: Players, Owners Reach Tentative Five-Year Labor Deal," at http://www.si.com cited 24 October 2006.

Despite the approval and implementation of a Basic Collective Bargaining Agreement (BCBA) that includes the 2007–2011 MLB seasons, the frequencies and types of historical and current labor issues and their resolutions suggest that conflict, misunderstanding and tension may always exist to challenge the relationships between baseball's team owners, and the players and their union. The potential troubles in the current labor contract involve such topics as revenue sharing, the competitive balance tax, and the league's drug enforcement and prevention program. If team owners, players and the MLBPA adhere to the policies, procedures and rules as established in the 2007–2011 BCBA (hereafter abbreviated as the 2007 BCBA), it is likely that big league baseball has an opportunity to extend its prosperity many years beyond the 2007 season. Alternatively I argue that conditions may change and/or events may occur, or misinterpretation of items in the contract could arise, which would trigger dispute between the franchise owners, players, and the union during some of the seasons from 2008 to 2011.

Based on specific sections of the 2007 BCBA, there is no expectation of disagreements between owners and the MLBPA with respect to revisions that affect the debt service rule, amateur draft, draft choice compensation, current and retired players' benefit plans, minimum salary amounts and free agency. Also, there seems to be a consensus between owners and players about awarding home-field advantage in the World Series to the AL or NL based on which league's team wins the previous summer's annual all-star game, about the need to settle more than 40 legitimate grievances and disputes that have been filed by major and minor league players, and about MLB's not eliminating or merging any of the current AL or NL teams during the term of the contract.

In other words, it is anticipated that MLBPA Executive Director Donald Fehr and Commissioner Bud Selig—or their appointed representatives—will periodically meet and eventually concur if one or more of these matters require negotiation and resolution. Therefore the most controversial sections in the recent BCBA are those that specifically relate to revenue sharing, the competitive balance tax, and MLB's drug program.[11]

Revenue Sharing

The five components in the 2007 BCBA that changed from the 2002 collective bargaining agreement include revenue sharing and some amendments made to the net amounts that are to be transferred between teams; reductions of the marginal tax rates for high and low revenue clubs; eventual application of identical marginal tax rates to all teams for the first time; continuation of, and placing a cap on, the commissioner's discretionary fund; and establishing policies for club owners—who are recipients of shared revenues—to spend these funds for improving on-the-field performances within their divisions.

According to a recent study, in 2006 the 13 clubs with the largest revenue streams in MLB had shifted approximately $312 million to the 17 teams with the smallest revenue streams. The payers' amounts ranged from a high of $76 million, which was distributed by the New York Yankees, to a low of $350,000 by the Texas Rangers. In turn, the payees' amounts varied from a maximum of $33 million, which was received by the Tampa Bay Devil Rays, to a minimum of $2 million transferred to the Baltimore Orioles. Given the size of these amounts some franchise owners, such as the Yankees' George Steinbrenner, have an incentive to search for loopholes in the 2007 agreement to minimize their clubs' future obligations. For example, one well-known loophole is that a portion of the amounts that teams spend for the construction costs of new ballparks are allowed to be counted as operating expenses and thus deducted from the teams' revenue sharing liabilities (see Table A.4.1).

Besides the Yankees, another potential beneficiary of this loophole are the NL Mets. Indeed, the Mets will likely contribute some $800 million to $1 billion of its funds and/or cash reserves to the construction of a modern stadium in the New York City area. Moreover, the other 11 payers who had paid money into the revenue sharing system in 2006 may also attempt to avoid any 2007–2011 obligations by incurring operating expenses on local ballparks or for stadium construction projects. The Red Sox, for instance, may make renovations—that are categorized as necessary and very late post-construction costs—to Fenway Park in Boston, as may the Cubs to Wrigley Field in Chicago, the Mariners to Safeco Field in Seattle, and the Dodgers to Dodger Stadium in Los Angeles. If so, these clubs may become eligible for adjustments in their revenue sharing commitments.

As stated before in this section, in 2006 the franchise owners of 17 or 56 percent of MLB teams had received approximately $312 million to improve their clubs' on-the-field performances. Such improvements in performances could consist of investments in big league teams' scouting programs and/or their farm systems, building new or upgrading obsolete training facilities for ballplayers, and spending more money for modern baseball equipment and computer technology, and for any services to increase their players' skills. With respect to the amounts that were received by each of the 17 teams, the 2006 opening day payrolls of 16 or 94 percent of them exceeded their revenue sharing receipts. The differences between payrolls and receipts ranged from a high of $82 million for the NL Philadelphia Phillies to a low of $2 million for the AL Tampa Bay Devil Rays. Alternatively, the NL Florida Marlins received $31 million in revenues from other big league teams while opening the 2006 season with a payroll of only $15 million. In fact, the Marlins' owner Jeff Loria was severely criticized in the print media for trading his top performing free agents and veterans to other clubs rather than increase their salaries to retain them for the season.

Another commendable objective of MLB's revenue sharing program is for the recipient teams to improve players' on-the-field performances by spending more of the owners' money to expand their payrolls. Nevertheless, five or 29 percent of the 17 clubs' owners who received revenues each spent less than $40 million of their personal funds to improve players' salaries. As a result of this frugal its, these teams had dismal performances in MLB's 2006 regular season. To illustrate, in the AL the Devil Rays finished fourth in the East Division and the Royals fifth in the Central Division, while in the NL the Brewers ended fourth and the Pirates fifth in the Central Division, and the Rockies fifth in the West Division. However, the clubs that had the largest positive differences between their payrolls and revenue-sharing amounts performed well above average in their divisions within the AL or NL. Besides the Philadelphia Phillies' being in second place of the NL East Division, these teams included the San Diego Padres, who won the NL West Division; the Detroit Tigers, who claimed the AL championship; the Oakland Athletics, who took the AL West Division title; and the Toronto Blue Jays, who finished second in the AL East Division (see Table A.4.2).

Despite exceptional winning performances by some recipients in 2006, the Yankees, Red Sox, Cubs and any other teams that were (and will be) required to make annual revenue sharing payments in the tens of millions of dollars may rebel against distributing their funds and file protests with the commissioner and MLBPA. That is, they will insist that the payees must invest more of their own funds to improve on-the-field performances rather than rely on contributions from the high revenue franchises.

In a nutshell, there are economic incentives and operating reasons for the owners of large and midsized market teams to avoid the financial burden of making payments each year to owners of the league's low revenue clubs. Since the amounts to be transferred by some teams will likely grow in successive baseball seasons, it will be increasingly important for each of the recipient teams to expand the payrolls of players on their active rosters and make a sincere and sustained effort to become more competitive and improve on-the-field performances. In 2006, for example, the majority of clubs that had received revenue amounts performed below what was expected of them, and thus did not qualify for the AL or NL playoffs. Even though parity between teams had moderately improved because of the net transfers and marginal tax rates in the revenue sharing provision of the 2002–2006 BCBA (hereafter abbreviated as the 2002 BCBA), the owners of big city clubs will continue to seek ways to reduce their obligations of remitting more and more of their revenues into the league's central fund redistribution system (see Table A.4.3).

Competitive Balance Tax

According to the 2002 BCBA, any amounts of monies that were collected by the league from teams for this special tax had to be allocated for player benefits and/or as an input for the industry growth program, or as a contribution for the development of baseball players in foreign nations that lacked organized high school baseball activities. In contrast to the 2007 BCBA, there are four key provisions within the part of the new agreement that contains the competitive balance tax—which is referred to in baseball and by the media as a luxury tax. These four provisions are as follows.

One, most aspects of the competitive balance tax structure were extended from the 2002 to 2007 contract. That is, a team's total payroll will continue to consist of salaries and earned bonuses for all players on the 40-man roster, plus a fixed amount per team in benefits and related expenses. Furthermore, all multiyear contracts of a club's players are identified and measured at their average annual value regardless of the actual payouts to players that occurred in a specific year. Two, the marginal tax rates in 2007–2011 will be phased in and increased at specific percentages for the clubs that were over the threshold amounts for the first, second and third times. These rates are fixed at, respectively, 22.5 percent and then 30 percent and 40 percent. Three, the teams that paid a 40 percent tax rate in 2006 will also pay that percent in 2007. And four, the thresholds for tax rates are reset each year in the 2007 BCBA, to $148 million in 2007, and then $155 million in 2008, $162 million in 2009, $170 million in 2010, and $178 million in 2011.

Given these particular specifications, tax rates and threshold dollar amounts in the 2007 agreement, will the owners of such teams as the Yankees, Red Sox and Mets, and owners of other high payroll clubs be compelled to reduce their expenditures on players' salaries during and after the 2007 season in order to not exceed their competitive tax thresholds? To this question my response is, not very likely. Why? Because of free agency and the competition from teams within their divisions, I conclude that the owners of midsized and large market teams will find it advantageous for them to develop other business plans and marketing strategies to maintain their gross revenues from operations, and thus avoid reducing the payrolls of their players on the roster. Some alternative methods for clubs to generate more cash flows are the renegotiation and expansion of local and regional broadcasting agreements, increasing the total number of affiliated sponsorships and partnerships, and raising the ticket prices of seats and fees for suites at their local ballparks.

Based on the payroll amounts listed in Table 1.5 of Chapter 1 and a threshold of $136.5 million in 2006, a luxury tax of 40 percent—totaling approximately $26 million—was levied on the $198.6 million payroll (adjusted by the league to $201.5 million) of the New York Yankees for being a violator of the threshold for the fourth time. Meanwhile, in 2006 the Boston Red Sox paid $497,549 in luxury taxes. Besides the Yankees and Red Sox, there are other big league clubs that will possibly be near the lowest of the threshold amounts during many of the 2007–2011 regular seasons. The most likely teams include the Los Angeles Angels of Anaheim, the New York Mets and the Chicago White Sox. Thus it is conceivable that before 2012 the competitive balance tax will have little or no affect on 83–97 percent of MLB teams.

Moreover, since the Yankees perform at home within the sport's largest market and earn nearly $200 million each year from their broadcasting deal with the YES Network of which the club owns 38 percent—and in 2009 or 2010 is scheduled to play in a new $1 billion ballpark that will generate tens of millions in additional revenues, it is irrational to assume that major owner George Steinbrenner will maneuver to limit his club's payroll in any season to an amount that is well below the top threshold value.

Drug Program

According to a provision in the 2002 BCBA, MLB players were to be randomly tested for steroids beginning in 2003. If 2.5 percent or less of them had tested positive in 2004 and 2005, the mandatory testing of players was to be replaced by a system of survey tests. The penalty for any player who had tested positive as a first violation was enrollment and participation in a treatment program, and suspensions of 30 days to two years for any subsequent violations. However, because a number of players had tested positive while others admitted to using some kinds of pills or illegal substances at various times during their careers, the league decided to amend its drug policy twice in 2005. To be sure, MLB began to test for different types of drugs and increased the frequency of tests, and also toughened its penalties. Then after these aspects of the policy were negotiated between the commissioner, the team owners and the MLBPA, the revised policies were unanimously accepted and incorporated into the 2007 contract.

Specifically the new BCBA includes the provisions of MLB's then-current (2006–2007) drug program and extended it from the end of the 2008 baseball season to 2011. As to the contract's penalties, first-time offenders are ballplayers who abuse performance-enhancing drugs. If found guilty, they are suspended for 50 games, and second-time users for 100 games. Furthermore, the policy states that third-time violators will be banished from baseball for life. Notwithstanding the latter penalty, players who have been charged with three violations are authorized to request a hearing from a committee. If these players are successful as a result of the hearing, they could be reinstated by the commissioner.

Interestingly, the 2007 agreement has other special conditions. It specifies, for example, that any players who are guilty of consuming amphetamines will receive lesser penalties than those who use steroids. Also baseball's commissioner and team owners, in cooperation with the MLBPA, have committed to reevaluating the testing of players for synthetic HGH if a urine test is fully developed and scientifically validated. Indeed, the policy to test players for using HGH may ultimately extend from urine samples to a blood analysis if such a test is proven to be statistically accurate by a majority of scientists.[12]

An increasing number of sports fans, baseball critics and experts, and even some federal politicians have expressed their concern that MLB is too flexible and slow in testing and penalizing players for the illegal use of drugs, and therefore, the league should establish and enforce tougher penalties and more stringent standards regarding its drug program. In other words, to seriously deter teams' players from using performance-enhancing substances, MLB should consider adopting the drug policies of such a global organization as the World Anti-Doping Agency (WAA). Because of its powerful interest in protecting professional baseball players from any discriminatory actions and unfair practices by team owners, the MLBPA would undoubtedly challenge the league's efforts to implement the WAA's testing methods and penalties for drug violations committed by amateur athletes.

So until 2011, MLB's drug prevention and testing policy and its treatment program will be based on provisions specified in the 2007 contract. In turn, these provisions will be applied to detect illegal substances, and to penalize any players who test positive for drug use for the first, second and third times. Furthermore, since it appears that the U.S. Congress will be busy with national and international matters, these politicians must be more willing to trust that the big league teams will diligently test and appropriately penalize their players to comply with the 2007 BCBA.

Other Infractions

Besides the foregoing issues that essentially dealt with revenues and taxes, and labor policies and contractual agreements, historically there have been a number of specific major and minor unethical and irresponsible activities by different MLB commissioners and teams' owners, coaches and players. These types of incidents have been publicized in the media and include the following examples. First, a few baseball commissioners were biased and played favorites in governing groups in the league, and in making their investigations and decisions with respect to the structure and performance of the game. That is, some of these individuals tended to enrich certain franchise owners and certain teams, and not be equally concerned about the economic and social consequences and interests of the MLBPA and players, communities and fans.

Second, more than one of the former and/or current MLB team owners have committed unjustified, unpopular and/or illegal acts. For example, in previous years some of them colluded to temporarily suppress the growth of players' salaries, and engaged in racial and ethnic discrimination against minority ballplayers. Furthermore some owners have implicitly threatened host cities and hometown politicians, and intimidated sport fans with the relocation of their teams unless local taxpayers agreed to finance the construction of a new ballpark for them at a central site in a metropolitan area.[13]

Third, a significant number of players have committed misdeeds since the early history of the sport, when gambling and betting on games were common vices. These infractions include such recent acts as the smearing of brown sludge or pine tar on the palm of his left hand by Detroit Tigers Kenny Rogers while he pitched in game two against the St. Louis Cardinals during the 2006 World Series, and former Chicago Cubs outfielder Sammy Sosa's filling the end of his bat with cork to make it lighter, faster, and more powerful. Meanwhile various players have committed off-the-field crimes and violent acts; failed to be available for community activities and refused to allocate time to sign autographs as role models for kids; purposely avoided the media for interviews and neglected interacting with fans before and after games; and disrespected spectators at games. In total these and other incidents and altercations have been unfortunate events for baseball fans and may have discouraged local people, and especially families with children, from being interested in big league events. Most of all, these players' actions have probably diminished the goodwill of this competitive professional sport.[14]

It was during the mid–1980s that team owners jointly agreed to not bid against each other for the services of ballplayers who had qualified as free agents. The owners' intentions to collude were twofold. That is, to control the salaries of players and also to regain the power such franchises had enjoyed before the MLBPA was established in the late 1960s. As evidence of collusion by ownership groups, 26 or 56 percent of the available free agents in the players market changed clubs in 1985. Then, prior to the 1986 season, the owners decided to collude. And as expected, 29 or 87 percent of the players who had qualified as free agents remained with their original teams, and 19 or 65 percent of them only received a one-year contract from their respective clubs. Furthermore, on average the free agents who signed new contracts in 1986 received a mediocre five percent increase in their salaries from how much they had earned in the previous season. As a result of fewer free agents being demanded and signed by other clubs, the market values of players declined. Consequently, in early-to-mid–1986 the MLBPA filed a grievance against MLB for the owners' tactics to depress players' salaries. In September of 1987, an arbitrator reviewed the evidence and ruled in favor of the union.

After teams colluded once again by refusing to sign eligible free agents before the 1987 season had begun, the MLBPA filed a grievance against the league. Despite the union's submission of the grievance, most of this group of free agents decided to sign contracts with their former clubs, and as a result, players' salaries continued to gradually decline. Then, prior to the 1988 regular season, baseball's franchise owners illegally formed an information bank whereby they agreed to "deposit" the salary expectations and other data about their free agents into the bank and withdraw the statements made by other club owners about their free agents. In turn, this action compelled the MLBPA to file yet another grievance. Subsequently, an arbitrator ruled against the owners with respect to the 1987 and 1988 collusion cases and fined them a total of $100 million. Also, the arbitrator granted each of the affected players a right to seek damages from a team in court as a reward for violations that were committed by their franchise owner.

Because of arbitrators' decisions in these three cases and the economic effects of free agency, the majority of MLB players received dramatically higher salaries in 1989, and then one year later, the owners' payments to the affected players for 1990–1992 were determined to be, respectively, at least $10.5, $38 million and $64.5 million, plus an unspecified payment for punitive damages. In total, the franchise owners paid a lump sum of $280 million, which amounted to $10 million per club. The final distribution of that amount to ballplayers was made in 2005.

Finally, to settle claims made by ballplayers and the MLBPA that some free agents were conspired against by their teams in 2002 and 2003, the owners of big league clubs agreed in 2006 to make a payment of $12 million. With respect to each of these claims, the players' union decided not to file grievances while the owners refused to admit that they were guilty of collusion. Interestingly, the $12 million payment to players consisted of unspent funds that had been collected as luxury taxes from teams during 2003–2006, and which had previously been earmarked as a multimillion-dollar contribution to a reserve for players' benefits. Given the exposure and costs of these former infractions and settlements, it is unlikely that MLB franchise owners will pursue any further opportunities to collude with the intent of depressing players' salaries. Indeed it is certain that Commissioner Bud Selig and his staff of officials have become more vigilant and proactive about preventing collusion to discourage such misconduct by the teams' owners.

Besides the major and minor misdeeds by team owners, during the history of MLB there also have been numerous episodes of blatant cheating committed by players. According to a recent survey of baseball fans, the following big league players were named, in no specific order, as the sport's most significant cheaters during their careers infielder John McGraw (1891–1906), who interfered with runners by blocking, tripping and spiking them while they ran the bases. In other words, McGraw used any low and dirty tricks he could to stop runners from scoring runs; pitcher and Hall-of-Famer Gaylord Perry (1962–1983), who stood on the mound, touched his cap or sleeve, and loaded a baseball with Vaseline before throwing it to the catcher. In 1982, Perry was suspended from the big leagues; outfielder Albert Belle (1989–2000), who inserted cork in many of his bats. Eventually he was caught and suspended for seven games when one of his teammates replaced a confiscated bat of Belle's in the locker of an umpire with a bat having another player's name on it; pitcher Joe Niekro (1967–1988), who was discovered by an umpire to be using an emery board and sandpaper to doctor a baseball while on the mound. Niekro said to league officials that the board was needed to file his fingernails and the sandpaper to treat small blisters on his hand; pitcher Whitey Ford (1950–1967), who used his wedding ring to cut baseballs during innings while he pitched, planted mud pies around the mound and used them to load the baseball in his hand, and threw a gunk ball to batters by combining baby oil, turpentine and resin; outfielder Norm Cash (1958–1974), who drilled an eight-inch hole in the barrel of his bats and filled them with glue, cork and sawdust; and infielder Greg Nettles (1967–1988) and designated hitter Amos Otis (1967–1984), who inserted several substances in their bats by drilling a hole down the bats' barrels, and then stuffing cork and sawdust into the holes and sandpapering the top of the holes before adding pine tar to disguise the alteration. In short, these seven MLB players had intentionally cheated their fans and other teams, and forever tarnished their legacies as professional athletes.[15]

Other than intentionally cheating and committing mistakes, some athletes in professional baseball have established reputations for being the least likable or most disruptive players of all time. Their attitudes and behaviors, personalities and performances have created controversies among some baseball fans, owners and managers. The least likeable list includes—in no specific sequence—such current and former players as Ty Cobb (mean and racist), John Rocker (obnoxious and prejudiced), Roger Clemens (selfish and oblivious), and Ricky Henderson (self-centered and cocky). The most disruptive players are Barry Bonds (aloof and grumpy), Carl Everett (disrespectful and combative), David Wells (outspoken and disloyal), and Albert Belle (disruptive and hateful). These players were—and some still are—not well regarded or respected by many sports fans, MLB officials, and baseball reporters and pundits for their disgusting behavior and bad manners.[16]

To make sports fans feel happy about baseball, CNNSI.com's John Donovan discussed in an article some things that needed to be addressed with respect to aspects of the game. He complained, for example, about the prices of $6.50 for a hot dog and $7 for a 24-ounce cold beer at Braves' games at Turner Field in Atlanta, Georgia; professional baseball players that seem to become deaf and aloof when kids holler from their seats in the ballpark for attention and an autographed baseball; Commissioner Selig, who mentioned during the early 2000s the concept of contraction, which according to Donovan, is a dishonest, lawyerly and sleazy term; frequent and lengthy mound meetings between baseball pitchers and their managers, which are a tactic to unnecessarily stall the game, resulting in a waste of time for fans; postseason night games that start too late and last too long, and are not conveniently scheduled for kids to watch them at the ballpark or on television; an excessive number of in-stadium events before, during and after games, such as animated subway trains and car races, find-the-baseball-under-the-hats trick, and real live sausage derbies; numerous uniform changes by teams during the course of a season including black tops, sleeveless jerseys and unfamiliar hats and logos; and extreme egos and cocky attitudes of the average players who act like superstars. In other words, "Baseball faces a lot of very complicated, very adult issues in these next few weeks [July 2002]. But, you know, the problems with baseball don't end there. The game itself is a mess. Kids yawn at it. Older fans moan for the good old days," said Donovan.[17]

5

MISALLOCATION OF
FRANCHISE POWER

Within the professional sports entertainment business, Major League Baseball exists as a unique type of economic cartel. Since it expanded as an organization during the late 1990s, MLB has consisted of 30 interdependent baseball franchises. Fourteen of them participate in the American League (AL) and 16 in the National League (NL). Accordingly the owner of each franchise has been granted a legal right, and thus the authority and obligation, to operate an MLB team and maximize its profit by playing, in part, a schedule of 81 home games per season in a local ballpark within a designated geographical territory and market. Because of the different types of amenities and risks, benefits and costs associated with the particular locations of these 30 clubs—including those that are based within the same cities and metropolitan areas—there are demographic, economic and financial disparities among the various franchises in each of the leagues. Thus their power to compete as teams in divisions of the AL or NL, and to attract sports fans and generate business within their specific markets, is limited and disproportionate.[1]

Some of the economic and financial data, and also the demographic statistics about the home sites, facilities and performances of the 14 AL and 16 NL teams, are contained in the three previous chapters. Chapter 1, for example, lists in tables the distributions of the 30 clubs' average ticket prices and fan cost indexes, and their payrolls, revenues and estimated market values. In Chapter 2 there are, for a number of regular big league seasons, specific tables that reflect each of the team's characteristics such as its average attendances at home games and its ballpark's age, capacity and location as of 2006. Then in Chapter 3, there are some data in tables that denote the distribution of MLB franchises within metropolitan areas, and selected characteristics of those areas as sports markets during the early 2000s. In total, the information in these three chapters provide selected measurements of each of the teams and their markets from an operations and a business perspective.

Given the interpretation of the statistics that appear in the tables of Chapters 1–3, and then extracting the data from those tables and merging them with the contents of Chapter 4, this chapter focuses on the important criteria which in part reflect the unequal distribution of the 30 baseball teams' power, and the differences in their business environments and wealth as current franchises in MLB. As a result, this chapter will reveal these baseball organizations' opportunities and risks, and also the extent of the competitive imbalances that exist among the small, midsized and large market clubs in the AL and NL. Thus the first table in Chapter 5 provides insights about the location and quality of each big league team's metropolitan area while the second and third tables indicate, respectively, the distribution of the 30 teams' performances and the amounts and differences of their payrolls, revenues and estimated market values. Then the fourth table denotes the classifications of teams and how they had ranked based on their power as commercial enterprises within market areas and as competitors in big league baseball.

MLB Teams' Markets

A franchise owner's decision to initially establish his or her team in, or to move it from, a specific city within a metropolitan area, and thus play its home games at a given site in an assigned territory within a sports market, depends on several factors. To be sure, an area's and total population density its population growth, the number of households and these households' per capita disposable incomes, whether an area is the home to clubs in other professional sports, and how the area ranks as a television market, are each relevant factors to be considered by baseball officials and entrepreneurs when they evaluate the previous, current and future location and competitiveness of an AL or NL team.[2]

After a thorough review of information in the literature, I selected four of these factors as decision variables and incorporated them in Table 5.1. That is, an area's total population and its residents' per capita income, each area's number of homes with a television set, and its total number of professional sports teams. These are the appropriate measures used to determine the quality and infrastructure of each big league team's location as a baseball site in

2006 and how valuable it was as a sports market. Furthermore, in this table the four columns labeled Rank specifically represent the teams' relative positions among each other in the AL or NL, and not how they rated with respect to any of the non–MLB areas within the the United States.

Based on their being ranked in either first, second and/or third place with respect to population, income and/or television homes in Table 5.1 as AL and NL teams, the Yankees and Mets, and then the Angels and Dodgers, and the White Sox and Cubs each play in metropolitan areas with superior characteristics. Indeed it is a well-known fact that the three best sports markets for MLB teams are within and surrounding the New York, Los Angeles and Chicago areas, where, respectively, there exist a total of ten, eight and six professional sports franchises.

After these six big league baseball franchises, there were four other AL and NL clubs that placed at least once in a top three position of a decision variable.

Table 5.1 MLB Franchises
Distribution of Area Characteristics by
League and Team, Selected Years

Team	Population Area	Rank	Income Area	Rank	Television Homes	Rank	Teams Total	Rank
AL								
Angels	12.9	2nd	36.9	8th	5.5	2nd	8	2nd
Athletics	4.1	7th	51.9	1st	2.3	4th	5	4th-t
Blue Jays	—	—	—	—	—	—	3	9th-t
Devil Rays	2.6	11th	33.0	13th	1.7	8th	3	9th-t
Indians	2.1	12th	35.5	12th	1.5	11th	3	9th-t
Mariners	3.2	8th	41.6	5th	1.6	9th-t	3	9th-t
Orioles	2.6	10th	40.8	6th	1.1	12th	2	14th
Rangers	5.8	4th	37.0	10th	2.3	5th	5	4th-t
Red Sox	4.4	6th	48.1	2nd	2.2	6th	4	6th-t
Royals	1.9	13th	35.8	11th	.9	13th	3	9th-t
Tigers	4.3	5th	37.6	9th	1.9	7th	4	6th-t
Twins	3.1	9th	42.0	4th	1.6	9th-t	4	6th-t
White Sox	9.4	3rd	38.4	7th	3.4	3rd	6	3rd
Yankees	18.7	1st	45.5	3rd	7.3	1st	10	1st
NL								
Astros	5.2	6th	39.0	7th	1.9	8th	4	7th-t
Braves	4.9	8th	35.0	15th	2.0	7th	4	7th-t
Brewers	1.5	16th	37.8	10th	.9	15th-t	2	13th-t

Table 5.1 MLB Franchises
Distribution of Area Characteristics by
League and Team, Selected Years

Team	Population Area	Rank	Income Area	Rank	Television Homes	Rank	Teams Total	Rank
NL								
Cardinals	2.7	12th	36.1	13th	1.2	12th	3	12th
Cubs	9.4	3rd	38.4	8th	3.4	3rd	6	3rd
Diamondbacks	3.8	10th	32.5	16th	1.6	9th	4	7th-t
Dodgers	12.9	2nd	36.9	9th	5.5	2nd	8	2nd
Giants	4.1	9th	51.9	1st	2.3	5th	5	4th-t
Marlins	5.4	5th	36.2	11th	1.5	10th	4	7th-t
Mets	18.7	1st	45.5	3rd	7.3	1st	10	1st
Nationals	5.2	7th	49.5	2nd	2.2	6th	5	4th-t
Padres	2.9	11th	39.8	6th	1.0	14th	2	13th-t
Phillies	5.8	4th	40.4	5th	2.9	4th	4	7th-t
Pirates	2.3	13th	36.2	12th	1.2	13th	2	13th-t
Reds	1.8	15th	35.6	14th	.9	15th-t	2	13th-t
Rockies	2.3	14th	42.5	4th	1.4	11th	5	4th-t

Note: Each area's total population in millions is in column two, and income per capita in thousands of dollars in column four are reported for 2005, while the total number of professional sports teams in column eight is for 2006. Television homes in column six are estimates in millions for 2007. The dash (—) indicates that these characteristics are not available for the BlueJays in Toronto since Standard Metropolitan Statistical Areas (SMSAs) as geographical boundaries do not exist in Canada. The t means there is a tie in rank. AL and NL teams who play at home in the same metropolitan areas include the Angels and Dodgers in Los Angeles-Anaheim, White Sox and Cubs in Chicago, Yankees and Mets in New York, and Athletics and Giants in San Francisco-Oakland-San Jose. The Orioles' area is Baltimore-Towson, which is located in Maryland.

Source: See Tables 3.2 and 3.3 in Chapter 3.

That is, in per capita income the Athletics and Giants ranked first while the Red Sox and Nationals finished second within their respective leagues. Thus the metropolitan areas of San Francisco-Oakland-San Jose, Boston, and Washington, D.C., are each considered relatively attractive locations, and between average and large as markets for big league teams. Even so, because of the team's competition for baseball fans with the Giants and its obsolete 40-year-old ballpark, which is 43,000-seat McAfee Coliseum, the owner of the Athletics has decided to move the franchise's operations from Oakland to Fremont, California, a city that is approximately 20–25 miles from Oakland, and play at home in a yet-to-be-constructed $400 million ballpark to be named Cisco Field. Furthermore, despite its high rank in income, the nation's capital was without an MLB team between 1971, when the Senators relocated to Arlington in northeast Texas and changed their nickname to the Texas Rangers,[3] and 2005.

At the lowest end of the distribution of characteristics for the sports areas of the 30 teams listed in Table 5.1 are each of the AL clubs that ranked eleventh to thirteenth (excluding the Blue Jays in Toronto), and each of the NL teams that placed fourteenth to sixteenth in either population, income and/or number of television homes. Listed alphabetically by league, those clubs at the bottom tended to be the AL Devil Rays, Indians, Orioles and Royals, and NL Brewers, Diamondbacks, Padres, Reds and Rockies. Within these two groups, the least attractive areas that hosted big league teams in 2006 were, in the AL, Cleveland in northern Ohio for the Indians and Kansas City in western Missouri for the Royals, and in the NL, Milwaukee in southeast Wisconsin for the Brewers and Cincinnati in southwestern Ohio for the Reds. These four areas were the most unattractive in the group because they ranked near the bottom of the distributions for at least two of the three factors, and thus had the most unfavorable demographic characteristics in the table.

Regarding some of the weak factors in other low-rated areas, Tampa Bay placed eleventh in population for the Devil Rays, Miami eleventh in per capita income for the Marlins, and Pittsburgh thirteenth in television homes for the Pirates. In the NL, Atlanta ranked eighth or below in population and television homes for the Braves. And the Milwaukee, Phoenix, San Diego and Denver areas that hosted, respectively, the Brewers, Diamondbacks, Padres and Rockies placed no worse than thirteenth in at least one or two of the characteristics.

Sports markets that ranked somewhere between being superior and inferior as baseball sites included such areas in the AL as Seattle for the Mariners, Detroit for the Tigers and Minneapolis for the Twins, and in the NL as Houston for the Astros, St. Louis for the Cardinals and San Francisco for the Giants. It is apparent, therefore, that given the rankings of their characteristics these places are six medium-sized baseball markets, as are the Dallas area for the Rangers and Philadelphia area for the Phillies. Based on the robust growth of some U.S. regions' populations and incomes during the early 2000s, the characteristics of the Seattle, Houston and San Diego areas will likely improve, and thus they may become more attractive as sites for additional MLB clubs to play their home games. In contrast, some of the characteristics of other areas will be stagnant or experience small growth, especially if the number of manufacturing jobs continues to decline in such industrial cities as Cleveland, Detroit and Pittsburgh, and perhaps even in Baltimore, Philadelphia and St. Louis.

Consequently, in 2006 and later, the areas that include New York City, Chicago and Los Angeles were and will remain the dominant locations for most types of professional sports teams including those that play in MLB. Conversely, the most inferior baseball sites are and will continue to be in the areas within and surrounding relatively small cities such as Cincinnati, Kansas City and Milwaukee. Since populations, incomes, and the numbers of homes with televisions are expanding faster in some metropolitan areas of the southeast, southwest and west, the big league teams located in midsized markets as the Rangers in Dallas, Astros in Houston and Giants in San Francisco will become relatively more prosperous as business enterprises and local entertainment options, and as competitors in their respective divisions and leagues.

In other words, the specific cities and metropolitan areas that increase in size and wealth at a faster rate than what is average for the AL and NL will provide more commercial opportunities for a local MLB franchise to negotiate lucrative television and radio contracts, make business deals with sponsors, partners and vendors, and promote a team to a growing base of sports fans. Indeed, the various attributes of metropolitan areas that were contained in Table 5.1 each play a vital role in the location, development, and success or failure of the 30 existing teams in MLB. As the table depicts, there are some minor and major differences among the numbers of each characteristic for the clubs. In turn, this indicates an unequal distribution of power between the large, midsized and small markets that are current locations of professional baseball enterprises.

MLB Teams' Performances

The MLB teams who play 81 home games in their ballparks each year within large to moderately large cities are assumed to have a variety of business opportunities and important financial advantages. Likewise each of them receives a number of economic and social benefits because their metropolitan areas have superior characteristics relative to those of the clubs that are located in midsized and undersized areas. As a result, these teams' on-the-field performances in their respective divisions and leagues during regular seasons and postseasons should reflect these disparities and vary accordingly. In fact, some of the differences in teams' market sizes and locations are explained, in part, by the distribution of their home attendances in Chapter

2's Table 2.1 and by the rankings of their Sports Loyalty Indexes as depicted in Table 2.3. Since the data in these two tables represent only a few years of the big leagues, they do not indicate the complete relations and trends between variations in the characteristics of teams' markets and these clubs' performances for decades of baseball seasons.[4]

To provide a long run perspective of this relationship, Table 5.2 was developed. It shows the history of performances for the current 14 AL and 16 NL teams in MLB with respect to two significant events. That is, for a total of 102 World Series—which exclude the postseasons of 1901–1902, 1904, and 1994, when there were no World Series played—and for 105 league championships—which exclude 1994, when a players' strike caused the cancellation of the regular season and playoffs. It is important to note that the outcomes between teams in wild card games and for divisional titles are not included in the table since the consequences of these games are embedded in each of the league's championship series. Thus, performances include the results of various World Series and pennant rivalries.

Given the data about these seasons and events in the sport, Table 5.2 was primarily established to measure and relate, in part, how teams located in large, midsized and small metropolitan areas have qualified for and competed in baseball's most important games per year, and thereby have either won or failed to win previous pennants—referred to as the American League Championship Series (ALCS) and National League Championship Series (NLCS)—and then either won or finished runner-up in one or more World Series.

Table 5.2 MLB Franchises
Distribution of Performances by
League and Team, 1901–2006

Team	Seasons	World Series		Pennants	
		Wins	Runner-up	Wins	Runner-up
AL					
Angels	46	1	0	1	4
Athletics	39	4	2	6	5
Blue Jays	30	2	0	2	3
Devil Rays	9	0	0	0	0
Indians	106	2	3	5	1
Mariners	30	0	0	0	3
Orioles	53	3	4	7	2
Rangers	35	0	0	0	0

(Table 5.2 continued)

Team	Seasons	World Series		Pennants	
		Wins	Runner-up	Wins	Runner-up
AL					
Red Sox	106	6	4	11	5
Royals	38	1	1	2	4
Tigers	106	4	6	10	2
Twins	46	3	3	6	4
White Sox	106	3	2	6	2
Yankees	104	26	13	39	2
NL					
Astros	45	0	1	1	3
Braves	41	1	4	5	6
Brewers	9	0	0	0	0
Cardinals	106	10	7	17	4
Cubs	106	2	8	10	3
Diamondbacks	9	1	0	1	0
Dodgers	49	5	4	9	2
Giants	49	0	3	3	2
Marlins	14	2	0	2	0
Mets	45	2	2	4	3
Nationals	2	0	0	0	0
Padres	38	0	2	2	0
Phillies	106	1	4	5	3
Pirates	106	5	2	9	7
Reds	106	5	4	9	3
Rockies	14	0	0	0	0

Note: Seasons in column two are the number of MLB regular seasons participated in by the teams at their current sites as of 2006. The numbers of Wins in column three, Runner-up in World Series in column four, and Pennants in column five and six are self-explanatory. There was no World Series played between AL and NL teams in 1901–1902, 1904 and 1994, and no league championships in 1994.

Source: *Official Major League Baseball Fact Book 2005 Edition* (St. Louis, MO: The Sporting News, 2005).

Because of the widespread variation in the number of seasons played among the clubs in each of the leagues as reflected in column two of the table—for example, from nine for the Tampa Bay Devil Rays to 106 for the Cleveland Indians in the AL, and from two for the Washington Nationals to

106 for the Philadelphia Phillies in the NL—the relationships between the market locations of the teams and their historical performances are somewhat simplistic. Nevertheless at least the information in Table 5.2 highlights which of the current 14 AL and 16 NL franchises have been the most and least successful during their tenures in professional baseball, and whether the size and quality of their markets had been a factor directly or indirectly influencing these teams' performances.

American League

In the AL, the Yankees' clubs have dominated the two events. Indeed, that franchise has won a total of 65 World Series and pennants, and finished as a runner-up in total during 15 seasons. Except for the 1910s and 1980s, the Yankees won at least one World Series during each of the decades, and excluding the 1910s, had earned one or more victories in an ALCS. Because the club plays at home in New York City, which is the nation's and baseball's largest and most lucrative sports market, the various Yankees owners have exploited their prime location by making prudent and profitable business decisions about such tasks as the pricing of tickets at Yankee Stadium and the broadcasting of games to millions of households in the area. In turn these decisions have generated from the club's fans a vast amount of revenues, which have been invested by the franchise to attract smart general managers and experienced coaches, and to hire outstanding rookies, free agents, and veteran baseball players.[5]

Following the Yankees with 26 total wins and runner-ups in these two events are the Boston Red Sox. Despite being located for 106 seasons in one of baseball's top five markets, since 1918 the Red Sox have won only one World Series and five ALCS. However, because the Red Sox have competed in the Eastern Division and MLB had no wild card system until 1995, the Yankees' clubs have frequently overpowered Boston's best teams during the regular seasons to qualify for the AL playoffs. Nonetheless, the Red Sox are a relatively wealthy sports franchise, in part due to the team's playing its home games in Boston before hardcore baseball fans in Fenway Park.

The Chicago White Sox and Los Angeles Angels of Anaheim (previously named Los Angeles Angels and then California Angels), two other AL teams located in big cities, have not been nearly as successful as the Yankees and Red Sox in either winning or finishing runner-up in World Series and pennants. In several seasons, the Indians and Twins have outperformed the White Sox in the Central Division, while frequently the Athletics have been more competitive than the Angels in the West Division. Regarding the White Sox' and Angels' local market shares, the National Football League (NFL)

Bears and National Basketball Association (NBA) Bulls are the most prominent and popular professional sports clubs in the Chicago area. Similarly, the
NBA Los Angeles Lakers, and formerly the NFL Los Angeles Rams and
Raiders, have been the preferred teams by sports fans in America's second
largest media market.

Interestingly, two teams that play at home in midsized metropolitan
areas—that is, the 35-year-old Texas Rangers and 30-year-old Seattle
Mariners—have usually performed most seasons below the expectations of
baseball's experts. These results have occurred because the Athletics or Angels
frequently win or finish as a runner-up in the West Division. This means
that a team from the East or Central Division has usually qualified as the AL
wild card. Thus, it is a challenge for local Rangers and Mariners fans to be
passionate from season to season and support their hometown baseball clubs
even though these franchises have significantly increased their players' salaries
since the early-to-mid–1990s. Similar to the circumstances of the White Sox
in Chicago and Angels in Anaheim, perhaps the Dallas and Seattle areas are
promoted in the media as superior professional football and basketball markets rather than as the sites of popular and competitive teams in big league
baseball.

It is very unlikely that the nine-year-old Devil Rays, who are located in
the Tampa Bay area, will ever win or finish as a runner-up in the AL East
Division. That is because the franchise's market is undersized with respect to
population and income, while the club's payroll for its players, its home attendances at Tropicana Field, and its regular season performances in away games,
are inferior each year. Without the funds from revenue sharing and proceeds
from MLB's luxury tax, the Devil Rays would survive for only a few years at
their current site in western Florida. Although Tampa Bay is an attractive
city for retired senior citizens and for tourists, the area does not have a sufficient number of hardcore baseball fans who avidly root for the Devil Rays
and are willing to acquire season tickets or pay premium prices for seats to
attend the team's home games. Without a huge increase in payroll the Devil
Rays will struggle each season in their division, and especially when the club
plays its away games against such rivals as the Yankees, Red Sox, Orioles and
Blue Jays.

Excluding the very successful Yankees and moderately successful Athletics, Red Sox, Twins and Tigers, and also ignoring the performances of the
relatively unsuccessful Devil Rays, Mariners and Rangers, the remaining
seven AL teams who are either in a city of a large, medium-populated, or
undersized area each have an occasional opportunity to win their division
and/or place runner-up in an ALCS, but only a minute chance of achieving

a victory in a World Series. This analysis suggests, therefore, that the Yankees and Red Sox have prospered as champions because, in part, they play 81 of their regular season games, and some in the postseasons, before capacity crowds in ballparks at their home sites, which are located within big and lucrative metropolitan areas. In contrast to the Yankees and Red Sox, the smaller-market Athletics, Tigers and Twins are each compelled to excel and succeed for other reasons, such as the business decisions of their owners and general managers, and the experience, skills, and efforts of their coaches, scouts and players.

National League

Relative to the top-performing clubs in the AL, three of the NL's small market franchises and two of its big city teams in Table 5.2 have achieved the greatest number of total wins and runner-ups in the World Series and NLCS. These five veteran clubs and their respective first plus second place totals are the 106-year-old St. Louis Cardinals with 38, the Chicago Cubs and Pittsburgh Pirates each with 23, the Cincinnati Reds with 21, and then the 49-year-old Los Angeles Dodgers with 20. The four former teams have competed against each other and the Houston Astros in the league's Central Division since 1994, while the Dodgers joined the NL's West Division when it was established in 1969.

Since the late 1970s, the Cardinals have outperformed such division rivals as the Pirates, Reds and Cubs by winning three World Series and five pennants. Furthermore, and as denoted in Table 2.1, between the early-to-mid–1990s and 2006 the Cardinals' attendances at games played at Busch Stadium in St. Louis have exceeded the numbers of spectators that were realized by the Pirates at Forbes Field and PNC Park in Pittsburgh, by the Reds at Cinergy Field and Great American Ballpark in Cincinnati, by the Cubs at Wrigley Field in Chicago, and occasionally by the Dodgers at Dodger Stadium in Los Angeles. Despite the prior presence of the NFL Cardinals and NBA Hawks, and the current NFL Rams and NHL Blues in St. Louis, the Cardinals teams have been one of the most popular sports attractions in the eastern Missouri region for several decades.[6]

Invariably each year, the various Cardinals clubs are not seriously challenged in popularity by other professional sports teams who compete for local and area sports fans. Some MLB teams, however, are less popular because of the other sports clubs in their market areas. These, for example, include the Pirates because of the NFL Steelers and NHL Penguins, the Reds due to NFL Bengals, the Cubs because of the NHL Blackhawks, and the Dodgers on account of the Los Angeles Lakers and Clippers. In other words, St. Louis continues to be a prime location for a MLB franchise despite the area's being below the NL average in its demographic attributes.

The underperforming NL teams include the small-market Milwaukee Brewers, Arizona Diamondbacks, San Diego Padres and Colorado Rockies, and also the midsized-market Houston Astros and Philadelphia Phillies. During a combined 70 seasons in the NL, the former four teams have won a total of two World Series and three pennants, and finished runner-up in two World Series and zero NLCS. Between 1971 and 1997, however, when the Brewers played in the AL's East or Central Division, its teams played more competitively, while home attendances at Milwaukee County Stadium were higher in some seasons than at Miller Ballpark each year from 2001 to 2006. Indeed, more sports fans in Milwaukee preferred to see the Brewers challenge such clubs as the Yankees, Red Sox and Twins during the mid–1980s than watch the Brewers play against the Cubs, Expos and Mets during the early 2000s.

Regarding other aspects of teams that are located in small markets, during the early 2000s the Diamondbacks, Padres and Rockies each played in average to below average baseball areas that—among 16 NL franchises—ranked no higher than tenth in total population, fourth in household per capita income, and ninth in the number of homes with television sets. For certain, the NBA Suns in Phoenix, NFL Chargers in San Diego and NFL Broncos in Denver are each as or more popular and entertaining for local sports fans than are, respectively, the NL Diamondbacks, Padres and Rockies.

Although the 45-year-old Astros and 106-year-old Phillies each play home games at ballparks within midsized areas, during their histories in MLB the two clubs have struggled to qualify for and win a division title and then a league pennant and World Series. In fact, these two franchises have earned a total of seven wins and 11 runner-ups in various World Series and NLCS. Since the mid–1990s, sports fans in the Houston area have attended more of the Astros' regular season home games than Philadelphia's baseball fans have gone to the Phillies' home games. Nonetheless, the NBA Rockets in Houston, like the NFL Eagles, NBA 76ers and NHL Flyers in Philadelphia, have great traditions and play before large and boisterous crowds at home in their respective stadiums. Consequently, the Astros in southern Texas and Phillies in southeast Pennsylvania have not been the most popular professional sports teams in their home markets during most years.

Relative to some other NL franchises, the 41-year-old Braves, 49-year-old Giants, 14-year-old Marlins and 45-year-old Mets have each performed well-above-to-above-average in some regular seasons and postseasons, but also average-to-well-below-average in other years. Interestingly, these four teams' metropolitan areas and range from being large for the Mets in New

York, to midsized for the Braves in Atlanta and Giants in San Francisco, to small for the Marlins in Miami. With respect to a few of their home site characteristics as compared to other NL teams' areas, it is evident in Table 5.1 that the Atlanta and Miami markets each ranked relatively low in per capita income while San Francisco placed first in income and New York first in population and total number of homes with television sets. Based partially on these statistics, I am curious as to why the Giants and Mets have not won more division titles and/or finished as a runner-up in league championships and World Series. Certainly the Dodgers and Padres have been the Giants' primary competitors in the West Division, and during the 1990s and early 2000s, the Mets finished each season behind the Braves in the East Division. Even so, the Atlanta Braves and San Francisco Giants have only average power as sports teams in their respective markets, since they have won a total of one World Series and eight NLCS. The Mets, meanwhile, have above average power because they play at home in New York City. For the power rankings of these and other MLB teams, see Table 5.4 in this chapter.

A greater number of sports fans in the Miami area prefer to attend games of the NBA Heat, NFL Dolphins and/or NHL Panthers rather than those of the Marlins. Remarkably, even when this small market baseball franchise won the World Series in 1997 and again in 2003, its home attendances averaged, respectively, only 29 thousand and 16 thousand per game. During other regular seasons, while playing in the East Division, the team's attendances per game at Pro Player Stadium (formerly Joe Robbie Stadium until 1996, and renamed Dolphin Stadium in 2005) had ranged from a high of approximately 37 thousand in 1993 to a low of 10 thousand in 2002. Although Miami has experienced tremendous growth of its area's population, especially among Latinos, a significant number of the city's households earn mediocre incomes. This means that the Marlins must successfully negotiate with the municipality and/or county to share the costs necessary to construct a new ballpark, or the team's owner will be motivated to relocate his franchise to another metropolitan area.

Finally, the Washington, D.C., area is a midsized market that contains a sufficient number of households with enough income to attend games of the MLB Nationals, NFL Redskins, NBA Wizards and NHL Capitals. When the baseball club vacates RFK Stadium in 2008 or later and plays its home games in a new ballpark, the Nationals' attendances will likely increase. Furthermore the team is expected to expand its payroll and acquire better players to effectively compete against the Braves, Mets and other teams in the NL East Division. However, if the Nationals' performances at home do not meet the local fans' expectations, the club will eventually lose some of its market share to the Redskins, Wizards and/or Capitals. Consequently the Nationals must win one or more division titles and perhaps a league championship within five to ten years or be compelled to relocate when its lease expires at the club's new ballpark.

In sum, three NL teams—St. Louis Cardinals, Pittsburgh Pirates and Cincinnati Reds—each with 106-year histories, and the 49-year-old Los Angeles Dodgers, have performed above the league average because as a group they either won or finished runner-up in a total of 42 World Series and 60 NLCS. Nevertheless, the Pirates and Reds have declined in performance since the late 1970s, while the Dodgers' last victory in a World Series was in 1988. Alternatively, the small-market Milwaukee Brewers, San Diego Padres and Colorado Rockies, and midsized market Phoenix Diamondbacks and Philadelphia Phillies, seem to struggle each season to win a division championship. Lastly, the seven remaining NL teams have performed above and below their expectations in many seasons and, except for the Marlins, are each located within sports markets that will sustain their operations for several years (see Table A.5.1).

MLB Teams Payrolls, Revenues, and Estimated Values

Thus far this chapter has discussed some key elements that reflect, in part, the allocation of market power among the current 14 AL and 16 NL teams in MLB. To that end, Table 5.1 highlights the differences of each team's metropolitan area when it is measured by such variables as total population and household per capita income, and the number of homes with television sets. Also the table depicts how these areas' characteristics ranked within one league or the other. Then Table 5.2 displays a distribution of performances for the 30 MLB teams and how these performances were ranked, that is, from first to fourteenth in the AL and first to sixteenth in the NL. In that table, results were measured by each club's success or failure to win or finish runner-up in various World Series, and in competing in previous ALCS or NLCS. Based on the information in these two tables, the discussion focused on what relationships existed between the characteristics of specific market areas and their respective teams' performances. In short, demographic factors partially explain how successfully and unsuccessfully the large, midsized and small market teams have performed at their respective locations and ballparks during numerous seasons in the big leagues.

In this section of the chapter, the disparity in market power among the current 30 MLB clubs is further measured and examined. To accomplish this task, Table 5.3 was assembled. It denotes the dollar amounts that each team spent on player payrolls in 2006, the dollar amounts of these baseball organizations' total revenues in 2005, and their estimated market values in 2006 based on data from 2005. Then a distribution was established for the payroll, revenue and estimated value of the leagues' teams by ranking each of the amounts in three columns from first to fourteenth for the 14 AL clubs, and from first to sixteenth for the 16 NL clubs.[7]

Table 5.3 MLB Franchises
Distribution of Amounts by League and Team, Selected Years

Team	Payroll Amount	Rank	Revenue Amount	Rank	Value Amount	Rank
AL						
Angels	103.6	3rd	167	4th	368	4th
Athletics	62.3	11th	134	11th	234	12th
Blue Jays	71.9	8th	136	10th	286	10th
Devil Rays	35.4	14th	116	13th	209	14th
Indians	56.7	12th	150	8th	352	7th
Mariners	88.3	5th	179	3rd	428	3rd
Orioles	72.5	7th	156	6th	359	5th
Rangers	65.4	9th	153	7th	353	6th
Red Sox	120.1	2nd	206	2nd	617	2nd
Royals	47.2	13th	117	12th	239	11th
Tigers	82.3	6th	146	9th	292	9th
Twins	63.8	10th	114	14th	216	13th
White Sox	102.8	4th	157	5th	315	8th
Yankees	198.6	1st	277	1st	1026	1st
NL						
Astros	92.5	4th	173	5th	416	7th
Braves	92.4	5th	172	6th	405	9th
Brewers	56.7	13th	131	14th	235	15th
Cardinals	88.4	7th	165	8th	429	5th
Cubs	94.8	3rd	179	3rd	448	3rd
Diamondbacks	59.2	12th	145	10th-t	305	11th
Dodgers	99.1	2nd	189	2nd	482	2nd
Giants	90.8	6th	171	7th	410	8th
Marlins	14.9	16th	119	16th	226	16th
Mets	102.9	1st	195	1st	604	1st
Nationals	63.2	10th	145	10th-t	440	4th
Padres	69.7	9th	158	9th	354	10th
Phillies	88.2	8th	176	4th	424	6th

(Table 5.3 MLB continued)

Team	Payroll Amount	Rank	Revenue Amount	Rank	Value Amount	Rank
NL						
Pirates	46.8	14th	125	15th	250	14th
Reds	59.4	11th	137	13th	274	13th
Rockies	41.4	15th	145	10th-t	298	12th

Note: In column two, the payroll amounts of teams are in millions of dollars and represent opening day of the 2006 season. In column four, the teams' revenue amounts are in hundreds of millions of dollars as of the 2005 season, and these include revenue sharing receipts and payroll taxes. In column six, the value amounts of teams, also in hundreds of millions of dollars, are estimates made in 2006 based on 2005 information, and these exclude deductions for debt. The t indicates a tie in rank between teams.

Source: See Tables 1.5 and 1.6 in Chapter 1, and Michael K. Ozanian and Lesley Kump, "Steinbrenner's Tax Shelter," *Forbes* (8 May 2006), 60, 64.

When evaluated as a group, the 30 teams' payroll, revenue and value amounts reveal three important financial aspects about these MLB franchises, and furthermore about their ability to allocate resources, generate income and create wealth for the owners who had invested in these sports business enterprises. In fact, besides the metropolitan area characteristics displayed in Table 5.1 and the team performances listed in Table 5.2, the distribution of amounts in Table 5.3 are another way to disclose the absolute and relative market power of the 14 AL and 16 NL clubs in MLB as of 2006.

In a league-by-league comparison, according to Table 5.3, the AL and NL teams, respectively, averaged in payroll $83.6 and $77 million, in revenue $157.7 and $157.8 million, and in value $378 and $377 million. For the top payroll and revenue amounts of each league, the Yankees and Mets ranked first while the Red Sox and Dodgers were second. Furthermore, the AL Angels placed third in payroll and the Mariners third in revenue and value, while the NL Cubs were third within each category of amounts. In retrospect, these dollar amounts and rankings have the following implications.

First, the three AL and NL clubs with the highest payrolls—who competed at home in 81 games within their large markets—had spent money for their players in a range that varied between $2 million (New York Yankees) and $1 million (New York Mets) per win in the 2006 regular season. In contrast, the three clubs with the smallest payrolls by league were the AL Devil Rays, and then the Royals and Indians, and NL Marlins, and then, the Rockies and Pirates. For each win in 2006, these teams spent between a low of $190 thousand in payroll (Florida Marlins) to a high of $760 thousand (Kansas City Royals). Consequently, the teams located in small markets were much more efficient at converting their payroll amounts into wins than those clubs who performed at home within the most populated metropolitan areas, that is, in New York, Los Angeles and Chicago.

Second, other teams who were also efficient based on their ratios of payrolls to wins included the AL Athletics, Twins and Rangers, and NL Brewers, Diamondbacks and Reds. Alternatively, some of the inefficient clubs with high payrolls per win were the AL Mariners, Orioles and White Sox, and NL Astros, Braves and Giants. After evaluating the six teams that won their respective divisions in the 2006 season, the Athletics, Padres and Twins were much more successful and efficient at winning games per dollar spent on payroll than were the Yankees, Cardinals and Mets. Furthermore the Tigers, who were also efficient in payroll expenditures per win, won the ALCS, but then lost to the Cardinals in the World Series. In short, the relationships between teams' total payroll amounts and their regular season victories, and whether they won postseason championships, are mixed. Moreover, when teams significantly increase or decrease their payrolls from one season to the next, their performances may or may not necessarily improve or decline. These results, in part, depend on the competition from, and strategies of, other teams in their division.

Third, for the payrolls of the highest and lowest-period teams in each of the leagues, there was a $163.2 million difference between the AL Yankees and Devil Rays, and an $88 million gap between the NL Mets and Marlins. Again, if the top ranked Yankees and Mets are excluded from the analysis, the payroll differences narrowed to $84.7 million between the Red Sox and Devil Rays, and $84.2 million when comparing the payrolls of the Dodgers and Marlins. In sum, these differences reflect how dominant the payrolls of the Yankees and Mets were in 2006 among the teams in their respective leagues, and the consequences of these amounts that are noted in other tables of this chapter.

Fourth, except for the Angels, the two AL and three NL teams with the highest annual payrolls in 2006 also earned the most revenues and had the highest estimated market values. A few teams, however, had large differences in rank between payroll and revenue amounts, and also between revenue and value amounts. The former group of teams consisted of the AL Indians, Tigers and Twins, and NL Phillies and Rockies, while the latter group of clubs included the AL White Sox and NL Braves, Cardinals and Nationals. With respect to the first group of franchises, their rankings varied because these five teams may have each under- or over-compensated their players and/or generated a disproportionate amount of revenues than what was justified by the size of their payrolls. Meanwhile, for the second group of teams, the rankings of revenues and values significantly differed due to other factors such as the White Sox' 2005 World Series championship, which boosted its revenue in 2006 from 2005 to the rank of fifth; the Braves' poor performance in 2006, which placed its estimated market value at ninth; the Cardinals' new ballpark, Busch Stadium, which improved the club's estimated market value to fifth; and the Expos' franchise movement out of Montreal in 2005 and Washington, D.C.'s, decision in 2006 to build the Nationals a new stadium, which combined placed the team's rank of its estimated value to fourth.

Fifth, even when the top ranked Yankees are excluded from Table 5.3, the ranges in revenues and estimated values between the first and fourteenth AL teams are still larger than those of the first and sixteenth NL clubs. For revenue differences of teams within the AL and NL, respectively, it was $92 million and $76 million, and for estimated market values, the gap was $408 million and $378 million. When the Yankees and top ranked NL Mets are both excluded from the table, the average differences between the leagues are approximately $7 million in revenues and $31 million in estimated values are nearly zero dollars. As a result, this indicates that for various reasons the distribution of income and value among AL franchises was greater and more widespread than among clubs in the NL.

Simply put, Table 5.3 is a snapshot of the absolute and relative differences that existed among the 14 AL and 16 NL teams with respect to their amounts of payrolls, their revenues, and their estimated values. In the next portion of this chapter these distributions and disparities, and the data from previous sections, are interpreted so that each of the 30 teams is identified as being either superior, above average, average or inferior in power within its sports market and in relation to other clubs in the AL and NL. In turn, this distribution of teams will reveal the extent to which franchise power is misallocated within MLB and how these imbalances affect baseball fans and communities, and the popularity and growth of the sport in America.

MLB Teams' Power

When combined in a group there is an obvious and uneven dispersion of power among the 30 franchises in MLB, and also between teams in each of the leagues. As noted in Table 5.4, there are four distinct classifications of power. From the most to least, these four are superior, and then above average, average and inferior. Clubs were identified to be superior in power if they ranked at or near the top, or in the upper portion of the teams, for a simple majority of the variables that are listed in various columns of Tables 5.1–5.3. For the teams recognized to be above average in power, their various demo-

Table 5.4 MLB Franchises
Distribution of Power by Team and League, 2006

Superior		Above Average		Average		Inferior	
Team	*League*	*Team*	*League*	*Team*	*League*	*Team*	*League*
Yankees	AL	Angels	AL	Athletics	AL	Devil Rays	AL
Red Sox	AL	White Sox	AL	Blue Jays	AL	Royals	AL
Cubs	NL	Braves	NL	Indians	AL	Brewers	NL
Dodgers	NL	Cardinals	NL	Mariners	AL	Diamondbacks	NL
Mets	NL	Orioles	AL	Marlins	NL		
Rangers	AL	Pirates	NL				
Tigers	AL	Reds	NL				
Twins	AL	Rockies	NL				
Astros	NL						
Giants	NL						
Nationals	NL						
Padres	NL						
Phillies	NL						

Note: Each team's power ranking is based on such variables as its regular season home attendances and postseason appearances and performances, its metropolitan area characteristics, and the amounts of its payroll, revenue and estimated market value.

Source: See Tables 5.1–5.3 in this chapter.

graphic attributes, World Series and pennant results, and financial amounts of payrolls, revenues and estimated values generally ranked lower than those of the superior clubs, but higher on average than the ranks of franchises with average statistics.

If placed in the inferior column, a club ranked at or near the bottom of the AL or NL for more than one variable including its metropolitan area characteristics, postseason appearances and performances, and/or the total dollar amounts of payroll, revenue, and/or market value. For sure, there were a few teams I evaluated to be at the margin, that is, somewhere between superior and above average, above average and average, and average and inferior. In fact, a team may have been identified as average or higher according to one or two of these measurements, but was ranked as inferior because of deficiencies with respect to most of the other variables.

Table 5.4 indicates that in 2006, power among the 30 MLB teams was distributed as follows. Four or 13 percent of the clubs were ranked to be superior in power and five or 16 percent of the total as above average. Also, 13 or

44 percent of the 30 were ranked to be average in power and then eight or 27 percent as inferior. That is, nine clubs or 30 percent of the total AL and NL teams were superior or above average in power with the remaining 21 or 70 percent of them ranked as either average or inferior. These numbers and percentages across the four groups suggest that power is not equally distributed among the 30 MLB franchises and between those in each league. In fact, there were an insufficient number of superior and above average teams along with nearly half that were average, and about the expected proportion who were inferior. For why these differences in the numbers and percentages of clubs with power existed in 2006, the following reasons are cited.

Superior Power Teams

Based on the data in this and previous chapters, the Yankees, Red Sox, Cubs and Dodgers are the most powerful clubs in MLB. Besides playing their home games at sites in the nation's largest sports markets, these four franchises ranked between first and third within their respective leagues in amounts of payroll, revenue, and estimated market value. In World Series and league championship appearances, the Yankees and Red Sox placed first and second among teams in the AL while the Cubs were second and Dodgers fifth in the NL. During the 2000s, each of these four clubs had excellent attendances at their home games. To be specific, these numbers per game ranged from 37 thousand to 51 thousand for the Yankees, 31 thousand to 36 thousand for the Red Sox, 34 thousand to 39 thousand for the Cubs, and 35 thousand to 46 thousand for the Dodgers.

In power, the Yankees dominate the Mets within and adjacent to the New York area. Indeed, the Yankees franchise is the most valuable in business enterprise professional sports, not just in MLB. Within its local and regional markets, the Red Sox team is as popular among sports fans and the media as are the NBA Boston Celtics, NFL New England Patriots and NHL Boston Bruins. Since its various clubs have won six World Series and 11 ALCS, the Red Sox rank second in power among AL teams. In Chicago and its suburbs, the Cubs have a very passionate fan base and a more extensive network of business partners, sponsors, vendors, and other commercial relationships than do the White Sox, whose average home attendances, revenues and estimated market value are generally exceeded each season by those amounts for the Cubs. Although the White Sox have won three World Series, the Cubs finished runner-up in eight of their World Series and outperformed the White Sox since the early 1900s by appearing in 13 NLCS and winning 10 of them.

Finally, the Dodgers are superior in power as a franchise because they were valued at $482 million in 2006, and the club plays its home games in

Los Angeles, which is America's second largest media market. Prior to its performances in Los Angeles, the Dodgers had won two World Series and nine NLCS when the club was located in Brooklyn. Since relocating from the east to west coast in 1958, the Dodgers have won five World Series and nine NLCS in 20 total appearances. Because no NFL team has been located in the west central area of California since the Raiders and Rams left during the mid–1990s, the Dodgers and NBA Lakers are by far that market's two most prominent and lucrative sports teams. As a result, the other professional baseball, basketball, ice hockey and outdoor soccer teams that play at home in the Los Angeles area are less publicized and demanded by fans than the Dodgers and Lakers.

Above Average Power Teams

Regarding some characteristics of their metropolitan areas and in home attendances, performances and/or financial data, these five clubs were relatively superior or above average, while for other variables and relationships they ranked as average. As such, the large market Angels, White Sox and Mets, and midsized market Braves and Cardinals, are each ranked in power as an above average team in MLB. In general, the former three franchises are less respected as baseball entities in their market areas than the superior Dodgers in Los Angeles, Cubs in Chicago, and Yankees in New York. Thus, for these and other reasons, the Angels, White Sox and Mets were evaluated to be above average in power, as were the Braves and Cardinals.

Although the Angels' payroll in 2006 was the third highest in MLB, the club's home attendance, revenue, and estimated market value were each below the numbers of the Dodgers. Furthermore, the Dodgers have outperformed the Angels in winning four more World Series and eight additional league championships while located in Los Angeles. So the Angels' power in their market is not equivalent to that of the Dodgers or to the power of the three other superior clubs within their home areas.

Similarly the White Sox and Mets each qualified as being superior in a characteristic such as population, but did not place high enough in other factors to be ranked as superior teams in power based on the criteria in Tables 5.1–5.3. In other words, each of them has some deficiencies relative to their peers—who, respectively, are the Cubs and Yankees. Essentially the problems were in the amounts of payroll, revenue and estimated value for the White Sox, and in the number of its World Series appearances and victories, and NLCS won and runner-ups for the Mets. For sure, it is the presence of their hometown counterparts that partially explain why the Angels, White Sox and Mets were above average teams in power and not superior.

For various reasons, the Braves and Cardinals were also not ranked as superior big league franchises as of 2006. Although each club has been an outstanding performer at winning its division title and appearing in NLCS, they are not among the top three or four MLB franchises in market attributes or near the top in their total amounts of payroll, revenue and estimated value. Specifically the Braves have earned a victory in only one World Series and five NLCS despite the team's 14 consecutive seasons of winning a title in the East Division. Alternatively the Cardinals' payroll among NL teams was ranked seventh in 2006, while their revenue amount placed eighth and value fifth. Certainly the Cardinals' performances in the World Series and NLCS have been superior. However, because the club's metropolitan area characteristics were measured between average and below average, the Cardinals are not rated as being a superior power such as the four teams in column one of Table 5.4. In short, the five above average teams deserve their rankings relative to those clubs listed in other columns of the table.

Average Power Teams

Based on the quantities and measurements of the variables contained in Tables 5.1–5.3, in 2006 eight or 57 percent of AL, and five or 31 percent of NL franchises were evaluated to be average in market power. That is, these 13 clubs had primarily ranked—within their leagues—from fourth to eleventh (AL) or fifth to thirteenth (NL) with respect to their area characteristics and on-the-field performances, and regarding the amounts of their payroll, revenue and estimated value. In part, these ranges in ranks occurred because of differences in proportions, meaning that the AL consisted of 14 teams, in which a total of four were superior or above average and two inferior, while the NL included 16 clubs, in which a total of five were superior or above average and six inferior.

In reference to column five of Table 5.4, there were special reasons and a combination of factors for why each of the 13 teams randomly average power in MLB as of 2006. First, each of them played its home games at a ballpark within a midsized or small market that had mediocre attributes and characteristics. These teams were particularly the AL Indians, Orioles and Twins, and the NL Astros and Padres. Second, some clubs among the 13 were average in power because of their dismal performances at appearing in, winning, and/or placing runner-up in various World Series and games for a league pennant. Such weak performers, for example, included the AL Blue Jays, Mariners and Rangers, and NL Giants and Phillies. Third, some franchises within the 13 ranked as average in power due to their modest amounts of payroll and revenue, and/or estimated value. This list of teams involved the AL

Athletics and Tigers, and NL Giants and Nationals. Despite these statistics, a majority of the 13 teams had at least one measurement that was ranked as above average. To illustrate, the AL Athletics, Tigers and Twins placed high in performances, while the NL Giants, Nationals and Phillies ranked in the upper third of the distribution in an at least one or two of their metropolitan area's characteristics. And the total dollars spent on payroll and collected as revenue, and/or the estimated market value, of the AL Mariners and NL Astros exceeded the mean amounts of their competitors.

If the Athletics and Giants did not share the San Francisco-Oakland-San Jose area, then one or perhaps both of them would be ranked above average in market power. Furthermore, since 40 miles separate Baltimore, Maryland, from Washington, D.C., this is a factor that causes the Orioles and Nationals to be average organizations in their respective leagues. Thus, the clubs that likely will become above average in power before 2010 are the Athletics or Giants, and the two clubs that will probably gain power in the next three to five years after 2010 are the Orioles and Nationals. For the nine remaining franchises in column five of Table 5.4, they and their home markets are unlikely to change in power enough to enable them to join the five clubs in column three as above average.

Inferior Power Teams

Given their current locations and historical on-the-field performances, and their recent financial amounts from operating as businesses, in 2006 a total of eight or 26 percent of the big league clubs were inferior in power. Two or 25 percent of them played in the AL while six or 75 percent competed in the NL. Each of these eight baseball clubs ranked at or near the bottom of their respective leagues based on such statistics as their low attendances at home games, inability to play in and win a reasonable number of league championship series and World Series, and/or for generating substandard amounts of revenue from their performances.

Within this group of eight clubs, the Pirates and Reds each won at least two NLCS and World Series during the 1970s. Since the early 1980s, however, these two baseball organizations have faded in power within the NL because of not spending enough funds to acquire high-priced free agents and keep their superstar veteran players, neglecting to adequately increase their operating revenues, and failing to sufficiently improve their estimated market values and remain competitive in the league's Central Division.

For the other six franchises that are listed as inferior in Table 5.4, the AL Devil Rays and Royals, and the NL Brewers and Rockies, have each struggled to win regular season games within their divisions and thus to sufficiently grow their home attendances, revenues, and estimated market values. Unless they significantly increase their payrolls during 2007–2010, these four teams will likely be inferior in power for many years. Alternatively, although the Marlins have won two each NLCS and World Series, many of Miami's sports fans prefer to attend the home games of the NBA Heat, NFL Dolphins and NHL Panthers. As mentioned in previous chapters, without the construction of a new ballpark in the Miami area to add more revenues for expanding the club's payroll, the Marlins are destined to be limited in power within the NL.

Another inferior NL club, the Diamondbacks, have won one NLCS and a World Series. Nevertheless, the team has trouble competing each season for the West Division title, especially against the Giants, Padres and Dodgers, and similar to the Marlins, must co-exist with popular professional sports teams that play in the Phoenix area and who attract large numbers of fans to their home games. Based on these facts and other criteria, the Diamondbacks are below average in power as a team within the NL. Consequently, as of 2006 the Diamondbacks and seven other big league franchises were ranked to be the least powerful organizations in MLB.

In sum, this chapter revealed why a misallocation of power existed among the 30 MLB franchises in 2006. Given the distribution of metropolitan area characteristics as attributes, and of performances of teams and their various amounts of payrolls, revenues and estimated market values, there is a shortage of superior and above average clubs in big league baseball, an oversupply of those that are ranked as average, and a reasonable proportion who are inferior.

To protect their markets and wealth, undoubtedly some AL and NL franchises would voluntarily agree to collude with each other to block the entry of new or relocating MLB teams into the New York, Chicago and Los Angeles metropolitan areas. At the other end of the power rankings, the sports fans who reside in some of the midsized baseball cities, and in a majority of the small market areas, should not anticipate that their hometown clubs will be talented or lucky enough during regular seasons to win a division title, and then a league championship and World Series.

6

REFORM BASEBALL

From a business perspective, since 2004 Major League Baseball has been an especially productive, entertaining and successful organization. Indeed, the league provided a competitive schedule of professional baseball games during its regular seasons and postseasons to millions of sports fans who lived as households within urban areas and in rural regions throughout the United States and portions of Canada. In fact, during each of the three years of 2004—2006, the league established higher attendance records to regular season games, such that in 2006, more than 76 million people watched the total home and away games of MLB's 30 teams at their respective ballparks.[1]

In part, this turnout helped these franchises to earn total revenues in excess of $5 billion. Furthermore, in 2006 the league endorsed a new seven-year, $3 billion television contract with the Fox and Turner networks. Then MLB and the Major League Baseball Players Association (MLBPA) negotiated and finally signed a new six-year contractual agreement that is scheduled to expire in 2012. Numerous sports columnists and commentators have touted Commissioner Bud Selig for his leadership of the league, and have applauded the contributions of franchise owners, the MLBPA and the players for their cooperation in making baseball an increasingly popular form of entertainment and leisure activity for American sports fans and the general public.[2]

Nevertheless, baseball has not fully recovered from 1994, when a portion of its regular season, the American League Championship Series (ALCS) and National League Championship Series (NLCS), and the World Series were each canceled because of a players' strike. To verify that shortcoming, Chapters 1–5 of this book were developed. These chapters discuss a number of major and minor internal and external circumstances and problems that are current and/or potential threats to the short and long run prosperity of the game of baseball, and to the recent achievements of the teams that play in the big leagues.

Thus to improve the sport and how MLB operates as a business organization, this chapter focuses on a combination of reforms which are expressed as amendments, proposals, recommendations and/or suggestions. In total these reforms will enhance the game of baseball and make it an even more entertaining sport for fans nationwide and in foreign countries, and likewise make MLB a more efficient and profitable business organization for American League (AL) and National League (NL) officials and franchise owners, and the teams' general managers, coaches and players. Furthermore, the reforms may inspire the MLBPA to be more cooperative with its adversaries and responsible to its constituents, and to baseball fans and other stakeholders, as a result of what is proposed here and possibly implemented beyond the current regular season.

Since being permanently confirmed as baseball's ninth commissioner in the late 1990s, Allan "Bud" Selig has played a major role in the development and growth of the league. Besides reforming the sport, Selig will be most remembered by fans and the media for his efforts to cooperate with the Major League Baseball Players Association, globalize baseball, and adopt Major League Baseball drug standards. [National Baseball Hall of Fame Library, Cooperstown, N.Y.]

Depending on the reader's experiences with, and knowledge of, professional team sports, some of these reforms may seem achievable and sensible, while others may be perceived as being radical and simplistic. Even so, the specific and general changes that are put forth in the following sections of this chapter evolved from the various problems that were highlighted by the data in the various tables within Chapters 1–5. To what extent Commissioner Bud Selig and any of the teams' franchise owners, MLBPA officials and the ballplayers care about any these matters is somewhat questionable. Nonetheless, it is a premise of this book that prominent professional sports organizations such as MLB and its member clubs have financial incentives and opportunities to develop and become more successful by evaluating their business environments and markets, and how they operate as enterprises.

To be sure, the most important and fundamental good of organized baseball as an economic cartel is to ensure that 30 franchises are each maximizing their profits. Therefore, each owner or combination of owners has the authority and responsibility to establish his or her team's policies regarding such tasks as setting ticket prices to games, and to make business decisions about payroll amounts and any other matters relevant to operating independently but in cooperation with a total group of 14 AL and 16 NL franchises. Consequently, reforms are difficult and complex to develop and enforce since economic cartels like MLB frequently require collective decisions to resolve conflicts and investigate scandals. In short, this interaction means that any important proposals about league-wide matters will be overexamined and thus likely rejected unless each of the teams receives some benefits from initiating and enforcing such a policy.

This chapter is organized into five parts, and these correspond to the topics that were contained in Chapters 1–5. Within each part there is a discussion of the matters being evaluated, and then how they may be confronted and temporarily or permanently solved by such decision-makers as Commissioner Selig and his administrators, and/or the presidents of the AL and NL, one or more franchise owners, the MLBPA and players, federal and/or local government officials, and any other individuals and groups that are associated with the sport of organized baseball. Finally, the interests and preferences of fans are also key factors in implementing any reforms because they demand that MLB keep improving as an institution and as an alternative to professional basketball, football, ice hockey and outdoor soccer leagues.

Teams Prices, Costs, and Values

In retrospect the six tables in Chapter 1 provided some data about the effects of inflation, and the changes that have occurred in the amounts of average ticket prices and fan cost indexes within four U.S. professional sports leagues since the early 1990s, and more specifically about the various MLB teams' prices, costs and payrolls, and their estimated valuations. The latter topics were primarily emphasized in the chapter because they have marginally affected the market shares, and thus the revenues and profits, of baseball franchises that performed at home and away sites within small, midsized and large metropolitan areas. Because the ticket prices of seats and other costs to attend games have substantially increased for most fans and their families during the regular seasons, some AL and NL teams have failed to sufficiently expand attendances at their home ballparks. As a result, thousands of baseball fans became loyal to teams in the other professional sports.[3]

After analyzing the detailed information displayed in the various tables of Chapter 1, it is evident that since the early 1990s there has been an increasing disparity in the amounts of payrolls and estimated valuations among the majority of MLB clubs, and especially between the teams located in the smallest and largest market areas. This divergence has been a gradual but steady trend, and it means that the regular season performances of such teams as the AL Tampa Bay Devil Rays and NL Colorado Rockies will not be good enough for them to play in the postseasons. Consequently, from a financial perspective, such big city teams as the AL New York Yankees and NL Los Angeles Dodgers will continue to dominate their divisions and therefore be contenders each season to compete in most games and qualify for their league's playoffs.

Reforms

Accordingly, because of general inflation and to meet local demand, ticket prices should always be established by each of the teams and not the cartel. In other words, the pricing of tickets for ballpark seats is a responsibility of the franchise owners and not the commissioner or AL and NL administrations. Eventually the differences between the average ticket prices of small, midsized and large market teams will stabilize and no longer be a major contributing factor to the wide variation in revenues and fan cost indexes between teams in each of the leagues. If any of organized baseball's owners are greedy and overprice seats in their home ballparks, the fans in local markets will penalize these owners by reducing their attend once at regular season games whether they are played in Tampa Bay, Denver, New York or Los Angeles. So in the future, MLB's franchise owners should be more conscientious when they set ticket prices to games. Moreover, it would be counterproductive for Commissioner Selig or the leagues' officials to interfere with teams' ticket pricing policies.

Alternatively, franchise owners should more frequently and intensely monitor the prices charged by vendors so that spectators are not gouged by the prices for food and beer, soft drinks, hot dogs, caps and other products that are sold during games at the home ballparks. That is, teams must aggressively negotiate with their vendors and provide incentives for them to raise or lower the prices for these and other items based on the local area's inflation rate so that a reasonable percentage return can be earned. Only if absolutely necessary should teams establish price ceilings or similar controls on specific products to protect spectators from being abused when they buy goods and/or services from vendors while at home games. Indeed, more cups of beer and soft drinks will be demanded at $5 each than $6. In short, these are costs that influence attendance and therefore must be determined between each franchise and its respective vendors.

Regarding any problems caused by the increasing differences in payrolls between clubs within the AL and NL, there are a few options that should be evaluated and discussed by franchise owners and the MLBPA before the current collective bargaining agreement expires in 2012. One option is for MLB to simply increase the luxury tax rates on payrolls by some equitable percent over a number of baseball seasons and/or lower the various monetary thresholds so that teams are taxed if their payrolls exceed these smaller amounts. According to this reform, more clubs than the Yankees would pay a luxury tax each season based on the values of their payrolls.

As a result, owners of the high payroll clubs will be reluctant to overbid for free agents and signing veterans—who are playing beyond their prime years—to contract extensions that are not based on improvements in their performances. So if the owners of the Yankees, Red Sox, and other large market teams continue to expand their payrolls by excessive amounts during 2007 to 2012, then a salary cap should be proposed and openly negotiated between franchise owners and the MLBPA. Otherwise, such payroll disparities will further diminish the opportunities for each of the small, and some midsized, teams to compete for and win a division title.

Another worthwhile option is for MLB to further expand revenue sharing amounts from the big to small market teams by reallocating a higher percentage of funds that are generated locally from broadcast rights and ticket sales. The additional amounts of money to be redistributed would primarily come from MLB teams in Chicago, Los Angeles and New York, and provided to those franchises with revenues that are below average relative to their divisional competitors. However, there must be a straightforward and verifiable system whereby the recipients of these funds must be required to invest in player development programs and show progress in improving the on-the-field performances of their teams. Thus any of the recipient franchise owners who violate the system's requirements will be penalized in some manner by the league and placed on probation with respect to receiving future revenue payments.

A third option to be offered as a reform is for MLB to impose a significantly higher luxury tax on specific teams and also an increase in revenues shared from them during the years of the next collective bargaining contract. Although this is a drastic measure that several big city clubs would immediately challenge, it may result in more parity within a few seasons among teams within the AL and NL and gradually narrow the differences in their payrolls and net revenues. Furthermore, the estimated valuations and sales prices of small market franchises would improve at a faster rate and allow these clubs to sell more debt securities and expand their recruitment of better and more productive baseball players. However, a revolt by the teams located in Chicago, Los Angeles and New York could happen if this reform were implemented. In turn, this would severely subvert relations between owners of certain teams, and the MLBPA and players.

In the end some combination of these options, prescribed as reforms, will be necessary for the group of 30 MLB teams to become as popular, successful, and equal in parity as the 32 in the National Football League (NFL). Indeed that result will occur when such clubs as the Devil Rays, Indians and Mariners, and Nationals, Pirates and Rockies, each have a realistic opportunity in any season to win, respectively, the AL East, Central and West Divisions, and NL East, Central and West Divisions. Based on the evidence thus far in approving and initiating reforms about ticket prices and vendors' costs, and about redistributing more revenues to equalize payrolls and estimated valuations, these opportunities are unlikely to become realities for several years despite improvements in the relationship between Commissioner Selig and the 14 AL and 16 NL franchise owners, and the MLBPA and teams' players.

Sports Fans Abandon Baseball

After analyzing the problems associated with the 30 teams' prices, costs and values in Chapter 1, the next topics of concern that have affected organized baseball were discussed in Chapter 2. That is, since the early-to-mid–1980s there has been a steady but noticeable erosion of baseball's fan base, particularly among the households within urban areas and families who live in rural areas across the U.S. Due to teams' higher ticket prices and the increase in costs associated with viewing regular season games in local ballparks, and because of some demographic, economic and social reasons, a few segments of America's population have decided not to participate in or attend amateur and professional baseball games, and to forego being lifelong fans of the sport or any of the major league teams. Most importantly, these groups include African American kids and teenage athletes, single white females who are less than 21 years old, and married adult women between the ages of 25 and 45. As a result of this failure, MLB's share of the nation's sports market has declined as more and more people change their loyalties to become interested in the success of NFL and NBA clubs, and in the games played between Major League Soccer (MLS) teams.[4]

Specifically, in Chapter 2 there is a table of numbers that indicate some recent trends in the 30 big league teams' total and average home attendances, their average winning percentages, and in their ticket prices and fan cost indexes. Furthermore, two other tables in the chapter report such facts as first, how some MLB teams ranked in loyalty among their fans during eight seasons, and second, which ballparks were the most and least fun for spectators. Accordingly the data in the chapter's four tables expose some favorable and unfavorable aspects about the 30 MLB franchises from sport fans' perspectives, and especially about certain AL and NL clubs that ranked as the best and worst in relation to expanding or contracting the numbers of their local, regional and national fans. Given the information in Chapter 2, what reforms might be developed and initiated by organized baseball to revive the sport among various households and other types of groups in America?

Reforms

To attract baseball fans and entertain them for the long run, and ensure that they are loyal and enthusiastic about the sport, the AL, NL and their member teams, and the MLBPA must jointly invest additional resources into various consumer surveys and marketing studies, and then contribute funds into more grass-roots programs and urban projects. Based on the contents of Chapter 2, these types of investments must be allocated for promoting baseball to specific groups of the population including African American kids, teenagers and young adults who live in inner cities, pre-adult and adult women, and Latino households within large and midsized metropolitan areas. If these programs and projects of MLB and the MLBPA are not successful at convincing these groups to be sports fans, then some of the teams in other sports leagues will be a more attractive option for them to love and support. For sure, African Americans of all ages have become more involved with basketball and football activities, while girls and women are becoming increasingly fascinated with professional football and Latinos with soccer leagues. In other words, big league baseball needs to extend its fan base beyond white, middle-aged males, who proportionately are not the fastest-growing demographic segment of the U.S. population.

It is especially important that the small market baseball teams that are located in such metropolitan areas as Cleveland, Minneapolis and Pittsburgh try to expand by diversifying their primary groups of fans. Historically, the middle-aged white males in these areas have tended to shift from rooting for the Indians, Twins and Pirates to the Browns and Cavaliers in Cleveland, Timberwolves and Vikings in Minneapolis, and Steelers and Penguins in Pittsburgh. Rather than continue to rely on proceeds from the luxury tax and revenue sharing, these and other baseball clubs should continually invest their resources in order to find innovative ways to better advertise and promote themselves locally to African Americans, and to women of all races and ages. Likewise, the teams that play at home in big cities must continue to sell discounted tickets and special packages for weekend games and series to minorities and families with two or more children. In fact, some of these teams could offer special deals by occasionally providing vehicles and subsidizing other modes of transportation for poor and disadvantaged families to use so they can attend games in the evenings and on weekends.

According to the eight years of Sports Loyalty Indexes (SLIs), which are listed in Table 2.3 of Chapter 2, people of both genders and all ages and racial groups within the areas of Tampa Bay, Baltimore-Towson and Miami are needed as dedicated fans of, respectively, the Devil Rays, Orioles and Marlins. So to increase their popularity as sports organizations, each of these teams may adopt a variety of reforms. That is, they should seriously consider such actions as changing their uniform styles, improving on-the-field performances with better and more charismatic players, becoming more involved with kids and teenagers within their local communities, investing in unique and effective promotion and marketing programs, and attempting new pricing strategies for tickets, beer and soft drinks, and food, merchandise and baseball memorabilia sold at the ballpark.

If for some reason those methods do not succeed, then more risky measures could be implemented to stimulate local fans' interest in baseball. That is, the MLB franchises with inferior SLI scores may need to reorganize by changing their ownership groups and/or general managers, executive staff and coaches. Moreover, the big league clubs that ranked low in popularity with fans in their local markets should also study and imitate the programs and projects of the MLB teams who were ranked at or near the top of the SLIs during the early 2000s. Among that group were the Boston Red Sox, Cleveland Indians, Houston Astros and New York Yankees. As another suggestion, the Devil Rays in Tampa Bay might imitate the programs successfully used by the NFL Buccaneers, the Orioles in Baltimore the projects of the NFL Ravens, and the Marlins in Miami the activities of the NFL Dolphins and NBA Heat. To be sure, the best way of appealing to their current and potential fans is for the Devil Rays, Orioles and Marlins to win division titles and league championships, and a future World Series.

In order to inspire fans and motivate them to attend one or more regular season home games, an important element is that all sports teams must provide a friendly and enjoyable atmosphere for fans who buy tickets ballparks. According to Table 2.4 in Chapter 2, spectators did not have fun and a good experience during the 2006 MLB season while watching games at several ballparks, including RFK Stadium in Washington, D.C., Shea Stadium in New York and Fenway Park in Boston. In contrast, spectators enjoyed memorable experiences at Angel Stadium in Anaheim, Coors Field in Denver and PNC Park in Pittsburgh. Since they ranked at the bottom of the Fan Value Index for the 2006 season, the Nationals, Mets and Red Sox each have some problems associated with their home ballparks. Some issues will be eliminated for the Nationals and Mets when these clubs move from their obsolete ballparks and play home games in new stadiums. However, for the Red Sox it may be necessary to change some features of Fenway Park so that it provides spectators with more entertainment value per dollar spent. Such strategies might include special discounts on tickets for families and other groups, price reductions for beer and other beverages and food sold during games, improvements in parking facilities, and other things that reward and give benefits to fans. As such, whatever activities and methods worked to entertain fans of the Angels, Rockies and Pirates at their ballparks may be worthwhile to also adopt at the home games of the three lowest-ranked clubs in the Fan Value Index.

Congested Sports Markets

As noted in Chapter 3, it was revealed that in 2006 the most prominent market areas in the U.S. were saturated with professional sports teams from a combination of the specific leagues. To show which areas had been occupied and by what clubs, the chapter provides in different tables an assortment of data relative to when and where these different franchises were established. Specifically the contents of one table included the distribution of teams in each sport by years, and another table denoted the distribution of areas that contained one or more MLB, NBA, NFL, NHL and/or MLS clubs. Then other tables listed some inequalities in the characteristics of baseball markets among the 13 AL (excluding the Toronto Blue Jays) and 16 NL teams, and also ranked 15 areas in the U.S. and 13 in foreign nations as potential sites for the homes of big league franchises.[5]

In short, an analysis of the data in Chapter 3 revealed to what extent U.S. sports markets are congested with professional teams and if any metropolitan areas in America and elsewhere had the demographic characteristics to be future locations of expansion and relocating MLB clubs. Thus the following proposals and/or recommendations are provided to avoid the further saturation and any deterioration of baseball markets within the U.S., to increase the availability and quality of big league teams, and to make the sport more entertaining and popular among MLB fans across the world.

Reforms

To alleviate the problem of there being a non-optimal number of teams in any of the U.S. sports markets, one option that baseball officials should consider is to simply fold one to three of the most inferior clubs in both the AL and NL. Identified as a policy of "contraction" by Commissioner Bud Selig during the early 2000s, his proposal was immediately denounced by the MLBPA for being controversial, radical and unnecessary. Nevertheless, eliminating a few franchises in each of the leagues and allocating their ballplayers to other major and perhaps minor league clubs, or releasing them, would increase the competitiveness of games because there would be better pitchers and hitters on the remaining clubs. However, for this reform to be recommended and implemented in the future, MLB owners and the MLBPA must reevaluate their positions on other related issues that affect teams and players, such as arbitration, free agency, pension rights and minimum salaries.

If the previous option is not feasible as a strategy to reduce the saturation of teams in particular metropolitan areas, then franchise owners and the baseball players' union might compromise and decide to merge at least two of the teams in one or more divisions of the AL and NL. This action contemplates that two of the least competitive clubs could be merged, with the excess players becoming free agents or being released to play baseball in the minor leagues and for teams in Asia, Europe and Latin America. Realistically, this is a complicated and far-fetched reform because a merger of this type requires important decisions to be made about several sensitive matters, including which of the teams to consolidate, how to determine the estimated valuation of the newly formed franchise, what amount of compensation must be provided to the former owners, and in what market area will the merged team be located. Indeed, it is very unlikely that either "contraction" or consolidation will be approved as ways to relieve the overabundance of MLB teams within and across baseball's current total of 26 metropolitan areas.

Since the elimination and/or merger of any of the 30 big league clubs each have a remote possibility of being implemented, there is another option for MLB. It is whether to authorize any club currently located within a very disadvantageous area, struggling to compete with its divisional rivals and attract local fans, to move elsewhere. In other words, the league should permit the franchise to shift to any site within an area that is known to be a potentially profitable baseball market, and where other professional teams in the NBA, NFL, NHL, and perhaps MLS may or may not be located.

Because they were listed and ranked in Table 3.4 of Chapter 3, the metropolitan areas with the most satisfactory characteristics included Portland-Beaverton, San Antonio and Las Vegas-Paradise, and then Indianapolis, Orlando and Norfolk-Virginia Beach-Newport News. Although each of these areas had minor deficiencies with respect to their home population, per capita personal income and/or number of television homes, they emerged from my research to be satisfactory as future sites for an MLB team during the years 2010–2015. Besides Las Vegas and Norfolk, two other areas where there are no current teams of the five professional leagues—and thus uncluttered as sports markets—are Austin-Round Rock in Texas and Greensboro-High Point in North Carolina.

After this option is approved and aggressively implemented, hopefully the MLB teams that had moved to better sports markets would be motivated to improve their operations and be more successful on the field and as business enterprises. A critical issue, however, is that relocation to any of these occupied or unoccupied sports markets would depend on whether taxpayers within the areas will agree to partially or wholly fund the construction of a new multimillion-dollar ballpark that meets MLB standards. As reported in articles of the baseball literature, prospective ownership groups and some governments from Las Vegas, Norfolk and San Antonio, and other midsized cities and metropolitan areas have expressed an interest in contributing to the funding of a new stadium for a big league team if they were chosen as a future site.

As an alternative to adding more big league baseball teams to undersaturated areas within the U.S., MLB should evaluate other consumer markets and then decide whether to move a current or new club into a midsized or large city of a foreign nation, but preferably not Canada. Indeed, this reform provides a number of economic and social benefits that would greatly boost the popularity of professional baseball and the league's teams to sports fans across the world. Although the NFL continues to sponsor a few clubs that play a schedule of regular season games and postseasons in Western European nations, MLB has an excellent opportunity to place one or more teams in international cities where soccer and then baseball are the most traditional and beloved sports for athletes to participate in and for local people to support.

Table 3.5 in Chapter 3 contains a list of 13 foreign cities and the recent populations of their metropolitan areas. According to some demographic statistics and sport-specific factors, the best locations for a MLB club are sites in Monterrey, Mexico, and Mexico City, and then in Tijuana, Mexico, and San Juan, Puerto Rico. Within each of these four areas there are several thousands of hardcore baseball fans who would enjoy attending the home games played by a local big league club.

Certainly there are many business risks and costs, and other significant problems to overcome, for the owners, coaches and players of any MLB teams that exist in these areas. Besides politics and government instability, and currency devaluation, economic recession and price deflation and inflation, these issues include first, whether there are a sufficient number of individuals and/or groups in the local areas willing and able to invest in, own and operate a big league franchise; second, whether the area's households and commercial organizations have the financial capability to afford paying $20 or more for a ticket to single games and at least $25–$100 in additional costs for products at the ballpark; third, whether taxpayers and/or governments will contribute millions to construct a new stadium or renovate an existing minor league ballpark; and fourth, whether baseball players born in the U.S. can be persuaded to spend nine or more months each season to live with their families in a foreign nation.

Regarding opportunities for MLB to play in two other international markets that are listed in column two of Table 3.5, Havana in Cuba will be an attractive city for a big league team when Fidel Castro and his government are removed from power. And despite Venezuelan president Hugo Chavez's behavior and socialist policies, Caracas is a city of baseball addicts and a potential but unlikely site for hosting an MLB club. Therefore, to adopt a global strategy and avoid congested sports markets in areas of the U.S., American baseball in one or more of these foreign nations may succeed if the AL and/or NL decide in the future to expand the sport beyond small, mid-sized and large metropolitan areas in North America.

Finally, any reforms that include a combination of contraction, expansion, merger and relocation must be revisited by MLB if professional baseball continues to decline as one of the favorite sports for Americans. In short, the saturation of sports markets in most of the primary areas within the U.S.

suggests that other strategies should be explored to grow the attendances, revenues and profits of AL and NL teams and increase the incomes of their owners, coaches and players.

Baseball Conflicts, Controversies, and Scandals

The group of proposals to be discussed next in this section were derived from a few of the historical and current conflicts, controversies and scandals that have involved some of MLB's commissioners, franchise owners and the MLBPA, and/or the teams' coaches and players. As reflected in Chapter 4, these matters include gambling and the betting on big league games during the late 1800s and early-to-mid–1900s, the abuse of illegal substances and performance-enhancing drugs by professional baseball players, previous labor relations issues between owners and the MLBPA, and various incidents of unethical behavior, cheating and misdeeds instigated and undertaken by MLB coaches and players. Indeed, these and other problems have damaged baseball's image and popularity with its fans and the general public, negatively affected the reputations of some teams and players, and delayed the sport's mission of expanding its business.[6]

To be sure, each of the professional sports in America have always contained instigators and troublemakers, athletes who have become involved with minor and major criminal activities, commit acts of personal and/or domestic violence, and otherwise seem to engage in self-destructive behavior and unfortunate incidents. For these kinds of situations to be minimized, MLB and its member teams have adopted and enforced various policies, procedures and rules that are meant to deter and penalize such practices. Commissioners Kenesaw Mountain Landis and Bart Giamatti, for example, decided to ban a number of ballplayers for life from the sport, an effective way of reducing but not totally eliminating betting on games by those actively participating in MLB. Although that type of crime has become extremely rare or unexposed in recent decades among players in professional baseball, other and perhaps worse problems have emerged that need to be further investigated and dealt with in a forceful manner by Commissioner Selig and the AL and NL presidents, and especially by each of the franchise owners and the MLBPA.

In fact the most recent controversy that has been exploited in the news and disturbed sports fans is the consumption and/or injection of performance-enhancing drugs and steroids by former superstars like Jose Canseco, Mark McGwire and Rafael Palmiero, and by such current ballplayers as Gary

Sheffield, Jason Giambi, and Barry Bonds. After many years of stonewalling or ignoring that ballplayers were abusing drugs, MLB changed its policies during the early 2000s and adopted a drug testing program, but initially imposed relatively lenient penalties with loopholes to punish those who had failed the tests. Recently, these penalties were toughened and expanded.

Reforms

It is recommended, therefore, that any future reforms regarding the use of illegal drugs—to be implemented by the league in cooperation with the MLBPA—should include the following provisions. That is, sponsoring and investing in more programs to counsel and educate players and their families about the health consequences of using these substances; adopting more frequent, random and up-to-date testing of players before, during and after regular seasons; providing special assistance to MLB's foreign players who have language barriers to clearly understand teams' rules; and if necessary, significantly increasing the penalties for first, second and third time violators. As a final proposal, Commissioner Selig's staff and the 30 MLB franchises should each establish an ethics office staffed with personnel who communicate with each other any information regarding the development of new kinds of medications and/or procedures that disguise or conceal drugs and other substances within humans bodies Underground laboratories and licensed and unlicensed businesses manufacture and distribute these "stealth" products for profit, and thus exploit big league players.

Because of its recent collective bargaining agreement with the MLBPA, MLB will not experience a strike or lockout through 2012. Therefore any ambiguities in the contact about revenue sharing and the competitive balance tax, and about the programs and penalties for drug abuse and other violations of the league and teams' rules, are issues that will not likely be amended until after the agreement expires. Some problems, however, may develop before 2012. If so, hopefully the owners and players will compromise, settle their differences and revise the contract. Nevertheless, if teams' attendances and revenues continue to increase as they did in 2006, then no work stoppages will occur.

Alternatively, if the federal government or a grand jury obtains documents that indicate the widespread use of drugs by big league ballplayers, or the U.S. economy slides into a recession and consumers unfortunately decide to decrease their expenditures on leisure activities, some franchise owners may be motivated to cut their teams' payrolls, release or trade veteran players who have expensive multiyear contracts, and explicitly refuse to sign free agents who seek large increases in their salaries. If this scenario occurs, then the

MLBPA would challenge baseball's owners in court or request arbitration. To avoid a confrontation, the leagues' administrators and team owners should jointly develop a well-thought-out and detailed contingency plan. When completed, the plan could serve as a blueprint to prepare this group of sports entrepreneurs for how to manage any unexpected calamities during the remaining life of the current contract and future collective bargaining agreements.

Undoubtedly a fraction of MLB teams' players will intentionally cheat and make other wrong behavioral decisions before, during and after games. Although a majority of these situations are embarrassing and unfortunate for the

One year after a grand jury indicted eight White Sox players for conspiring to fix the 1919 World Series, Major League Baseball's first commissioner, Judge Kenesaw Mountain Landis, banned these players—who included centerfielder "Shoeless" Joe Jackson—from baseball for life. [National Baseball Hall of Fame Library, Cooperstown, N.Y.]

players and for baseball, they generally will not have long run implications. In a specific section of Chapter 4, some of these incidents involved players who, for example, had smeared substances on baseballs while pitching and hitters who used cork to reduce the weight of their bats.

But when franchise owners colluded to lessen players' salaries during the 1980s and early 1990s, MLB had to write rules that would prohibit further collusion. As a recommendation intended to discourage this type of unlawful practice from happening again, the leagues need to be more vigilant and audit teams' revenue sources, payroll distributions and suspicious receipts and expenditures in order to prevent and detect any collusive behav-

During his career in baseball, Jose Canseco played for seven Major League Baseball teams and in total had hit 462 homers and batted in 1,407 runs, and in 1988 won the American League Most Valuable Player Award. Published in 2005, Canseco's book *Juiced* revealed to what extent illegal substances had been abused in baseball. [National Baseball Hall of Fame Library, Cooperstown, N.Y.]

ior between a few owners and among the group of them. This is an important reform to benefit baseball's future popularity, growth and business operations, and to preserve the mutual trust and partnership that owners and players have developed in recent years as exemplified by the approval of a new labor agreement in 2006.

Misallocation of Franchise Power

As measured in Chapter 5, within the MLB cartel there are vast differences in power among the 14 AL and 16 NL franchises, specifically with respect to their historical performances and market areas' characteristics, and to their payrolls, revenues and estimated valuations. To determine how much these criteria varied among the 30 teams during the early 1990s to 2000s, three tables of data were prepared. In turn, each of the tables contains a set of numbers and/or dollar values that designate how this information ranked per team relative to other member clubs within the AL and NL. Importantly, the purpose of organizing and evaluating this demographic, geographic and economic data was to indicate which of the professional teams have the superior, above average, average and least power as competitors in their respective divisions and leagues, and as business enterprises in MLB.

Table 5.1 contains the distributions and ranks of each team's metropolitan area characteristics. That is, the areas' population, income per capita and number of homes with televisions, and the total number of professional sports clubs. Table 5.2 displays each of the team's total seasons at its home site, and the numbers of wins and runners-up in World Series and AL or NL championship series. Then Table 5.3 lists the 30 teams' payrolls, revenues and valuations for selected years, and ranks each of these amounts from first to fourteenth in the AL and first to sixteenth in the NL. Following a discussion of those tables and topics, Table 5.4 concludes the chapter by ranking the teams in power as superior, above average, average or inferior.[7]

Reforms

Based on the variables and amounts entered in the tables of Chapter 5, from a power perspective there are extreme inequalities between many of the teams in each league and across them. To redistribute that power and thus create more parity within the two groups of teams, some reforms have been proposed and discussed in previous sections of this chapter. For example, Commissioner Selig and franchise owners may eventually decide to reallocate additional revenues from the large to small market franchises. Furthermore, the thresholds of teams' payrolls could be reduced. This policy means that increased amounts of luxury taxes would be collected from these organizations and then redistributed from the high to low payroll clubs, who in turn must agree to spend the millions of dollars they receive in taxes from the league to improve their player development programs.

Although it would be controversial, another reform is for MLB to permit one or more of the inferior AL and/or NL clubs to move into a different market, and perhaps into an area adjacent to the cities of Chicago, Los Angeles, and/or New York City. For a final but realistic proposal to amend and rearrange the power structure within MLB, there will be increasing pressure from some franchise owners for MLB to establish a hard cap on the amounts of teams' payrolls for each regular season, and to adjust these amounts periodically because of natural differences in metropolitan areas' demographic, geographic and economic conditions.

Anyway, as discussed in sections of this and prior chapters, the reasons, specifications and consequences, and time periods for implementing some or all of these reforms, or various combinations of them, need to be thoroughly studied by a joint committee that consists of Commissioner Selig, team owners, representatives of the MLBPA, baseball business and financial consultants, and sports economists. For their task, the group must determine quantitatively and qualitatively whether it is in the long run interests of baseball to shift additional revenues and luxury tax receipts from one or more of the superior and perhaps above average franchises to those that are inferior, to set payroll caps and floors for each of the clubs, and to liberalize the movement of teams by freeing them to relocate to larger and more lucrative metropolitan areas within the U.S. or in foreign nations. As a result of these reforms, which are intended to reallocate power between a few or even many of the teams over a number of years, it is expected that inferior franchises would appreciate in power while the Yankees, Red Sox, Cubs and Dodgers, and maybe the Mets, White Sox and Angels, would each voluntarily forego a portion of their current cash flows and future revenues to improve the long run competitiveness, prosperity and entertainment value of MLB.

During the reallocation process over a number of seasons, the Devil Rays, Royals and Brewers, and the other five inferior teams that are listed in column seven of Table 5.4, will improve in performances within their respective divisions because they will have received more funds to hire outstanding free agents and rehire veteran players, and to invest in player development programs including baseball academies in some Latin American and Asian countries. If that experimental reform does not succeed, then MLB should consider more drastic ways to increase the parity between clubs in the AL and

NL. Such actions could consist of realigning clubs within the six divisions, of eliminating some teams and/or merging them, and of moving clubs into larger market areas within the U.S. and in international cities.

Summary of Reforms

For sure, each proposal and recommendation discussed within the previous five sections of this chapter has short and long run advantages and disadvantages to be considered, and economic and financial consequences to be estimated, by MLB's decision makers. In other words, these reforms will vary with respect to being realistic and cost effective for baseball's franchise owners and their teams, and for the MLBPA. Furthermore, there are some important implications that will likely affect the 30 clubs' home markets and sports fans, and local and regional businesses and governments.

The increasing differences between the relative amounts of revenues and payrolls of the 14 AL and 16 NL franchises have created conspicuous inequities in their capabilities to perform on the field within the East, Central and West Divisions and across the sport's regular seasons. Indeed, the four superior and five above average clubs that were ranked in Table 5.4 have more commercial opportunities and better local conditions to be successful than each of the 21 teams classified as average or inferior. So it behooves Commissioner Selig and his administration to be leaders and coordinate plans and policies with various team owners and the MLBPA, and jointly decide whether adopting one or more of the reforms discussed in this chapter are in the best or worst long run interests of baseball and MLB.

In conclusion, these groups of baseball officials must take into account the prices, costs and values as discussed in Chapter 1, sports fans who abandon baseball as depicted in Chapter 2, congestion of sports markets as derived in Chapter 3, the conflicts, controversies and scandals as detailed in Chapter 4, and the misallocation of franchises' power as examined in Chapter 5. Therefore it is the premise of this book that such topics as these will determine if MLB succeeds by expanding its market share and thus prevents various teams from the NBA, NFL, NHL and MLS of becoming the most dominant business enterprises and superpowers within the U.S. professional sports industry during the early-to-middle years of the twenty-first century.

APPENDIX

Table A.1.1 Teams Home Attendances
By Leagues and Regular Seasons, 1993–2006

Team	1993	1994	1995	1996	1997	1998	1999	2000	2001	2002	2003	2004	2005	2006
AL														
Angels	2.0	1.5	1.7	1.8	1.7	2.5	2.2	2.0	2.0	2.3	3.0	3.3	3.4	3.4
Athletics	2.0	1.3	1.1	1.1	1.2	1.2	1.4	1.7	2.1	2.1	2.2	2.2	2.1	1.9
Blue Jays	4.0	2.9	2.8	2.5	2.5	2.4	2.1	1.8	1.9	1.6	1.8	1.9	1.9	2.3
Brewers	1.6	1.2	1.0	1.3	1.4	—	—	—	—	—	—	—	—	—
Devil Rays	—	—	—	—	—	2.5	1.7	1.5	1.2	1.0	1.0	1.2	1.1	1.3
Indians	2.1	2.0	2.8	3.3	3.4	3.4	3.4	3.4	3.1	2.6	1.7	1.8	1.9	2.0
Mariners	2.0	1.1	1.6	2.7	3.1	1.4	3.1	3.5	3.5	3.2	2.9	2.6	2.4	2.1
Orioles	3.6	2.5	3.0	3.6	3.7	3.6	3.4	3.2	3.0	2.6	2.4	2.7	2.6	2.1
Rangers	2.2	2.5	1.9	2.8	2.9	2.9	2.7	2.8	2.8	2.3	2.1	2.5	2.4	2.3
Red Sox	2.4	1.7	2.1	2.3	2.2	2.3	2.4	2.5	2.6	2.6	2.7	2.8	2.8	2.9
Royals	1.9	1.4	1.2	1.4	1.5	1.5	1.5	1.6	1.5	1.3	1.7	1.6	1.3	1.3
Tigers	1.9	1.1	1.1	1.1	1.3	1.4	2.0	2.5	1.9	1.5	1.3	1.9	2.0	2.5
Twins	2.0	1.3	1.0	1.4	1.4	1.1	1.2	1.0	1.7	1.9	1.9	1.8	2.0	2.2
White Sox	2.5	1.6	1.6	1.6	1.8	1.3	1.3	1.9	1.7	1.6	1.9	1.9	2.3	2.9
Yankees	2.4	1.6	1.7	2.2	2.5	2.9	3.2	3.2	3.2	3.4	3.4	3.7	4.0	4.2
NL														
Astros	2.0	1.5	1.3	1.9	2.0	2.4	2.7	3.0	2.9	2.5	2.4	3.0	2.7	3.0
Braves	3.8	2.5	2.5	2.9	3.4	3.3	3.2	3.2	2.8	2.6	2.4	2.3	2.5	2.5
Brewers	—	—	—	—	—	1.8	1.7	1.5	2.8	1.9	1.7	2.0	2.2	2.3
Cardinals	2.8	1.8	1.7	2.6	2.3	3.1	3.2	3.3	3.1	3.0	2.9	3.0	3.4	3.4
Cubs	2.6	1.8	1.9	2.2	2.1	2.6	2.8	2.7	2.7	2.7	2.9	3.1	3.1	3.1
Diamondbacks	—	—	—	—	—	3.6	3.0	2.9	2.7	3.1	2.8	2.5	2.0	2.0
Dodgers	3.1	2.2	2.7	3.1	3.3	3.0	3.0	3.0	3.0	3.1	3.1	3.4	3.6	3.7
Expos	1.6	1.2	1.3	1.6	1.4	.9	.7	.9	.6	.8	1.0	.7	—	—

Team	1993	1994	1995	1996	1997	1998	1999	2000	2001	2002	2003	2004	2005	2006
Giants	2.6	1.7	1.2	1.4	1.6	1.9	2.0	3.3	3.3	3.2	3.2	3.2	3.1	3.1
Marlins	3.0	1.9	1.7	1.7	2.3	1.7	1.3	1.2	1.2	.8	1.3	1.7	1.8	1.1
Mets	1.8	1.1	1.2	1.5	1.7	2.2	2.7	2.7	2.6	2.8	2.1	2.3	2.7	3.3
Nationals	—	—	—	—	—	—	—	—	—	—	—	—	2.7	2.1
Padres	1.3	.9	1.0	2.1	2.0	2.5	2.5	2.4	2.3	2.2	2.0	3.0	2.8	2.6
Phillies	3.1	2.2	2.0	1.8	1.4	1.7	1.8	1.6	1.7	1.6	2.2	3.2	2.6	2.7
Pirates	1.6	1.2	.9	1.3	1.6	1.5	1.6	1.7	2.4	1.7	1.6	1.5	1.7	1.8
Reds	2.4	1.9	1.8	1.8	1.7	1.7	2.0	2.6	1.8	1.8	2.3	2.2	1.9	2.1
Rockies	—	—	3.3	3.8	3.8	3.7	3.2	3.2	3.1	2.7	2.3	2.3	1.9	2.1
MLB Average	2.5	1.7	1.8	2.1	2.2	2.3	2.3	2.4	2.4	2.3	2.3	2.4	2.4	2.5

Note: Attendances are reported in millions. The dash (—) indicates a MLB team did not exist at the site during that season.
Source: "MLB Attendance Report," at http://www.sports.espn.go.com cited 3 October 2006.

Table A.1.2 MLB Teams Average Ticket Prices
High and Low Prices, by League and Regular Season, 1993–2006

Team	1993	1994	1995	1996	1997	1998	1999	2000	2001	2002	2003	2004	2005	2006
AL														
Angels	8	8	8	9	11	13	13	11	11	15	16	16	17	18
Brewers	9	9	9	9	9	—	—	—	—	—	—	—	—	—
Devil Rays	—	—	—	—	—	15	15	12	16	15	14	16	13	17
Indians	8	12	12	14	15	17	18	20	22	22	22	20	21	21
Mariners	7	9	9	11	13	14	19	23	22	24	24	24	24	24
Red Sox	11	13	13	15	17	20	24	28	34	39	38	40	44	46
Royals	9	10	10	9	9	10	11	11	12	12	12	13	13	13
Twins	9	9	9	10	8	8	8	9	10	11	13	14	16	17
White Sox	11	12	12	14	13	14	15	14	18	18	22	21	25	26

(Table A.1.2 continued)

Team	1993	1994	1995	1996	1997	1998	1999	2000	2001	2002	2003	2004	2005	2006
AL														
Yankees	**13**	**14**	**15**	**14**	**18**	**20**	23	25	24	24	24	24	27	28
AL Average	9	10	11	11	12	14	15	17	18	18	19	19	21	22
NL														
Braves	9	12	12	**13**	17	**17**	**19**	19	20	20	17	17	17	17
Cubs	**11**	**13**	**13**	**13**	14	14	17	17	21	**24**	**24**	**28**	**32**	**34**
Expos	8	8	8	9	**8**	9	9	**10**	9	**9**	**10**	**10**	–	–
Mets	10	10	10	11	13	16	**19**	**24**	**22**	22	23	23	23	25
Reds	7	7	7	7	**8**	**8**	9	**10**	15	16	18	18	17	17
Rockies	7	7	10	10	12	15	15	16	15	15	15	15	**14**	**14**
NL Average	8	9	9	10	11	12	14	15	16	17	18	18	21	21
MLB Average	9	10	10	11	12	13	15	16	17	18	19	19	21	21

Note: Ticket prices are rounded into dollars. Those in bold were the highest and lowest prices in the league for that season. The dash (–) indicates that the team did not exist in the AL or NL during the year.

Source: See the sources below Table 1.2 of Chapter 1.

Table A.1.3 MLB Fan Costs Per Game
By Product Type and Regular Season, 1993–2006

Product	1993	1994	1995	1996	1997	1998	1999	2000	2001	2002	2003	2004	2005	2006
Adult T	9.73	10.60	10.73	11.32	12.39	13.66	15.00	16.81	17.64	18.30	19.01	19.82	21.17	22.21
Child T	–	–	–	–	–	–	14.54	16.29	17.20	17.95	18.86	19.67	20.97	22.00

	1993	1994	1995	1996	1997	1998	1999	2000	2001	2002	2003	2004	2005	2006
Beer	3.09	3.22	3.27	3.51	3.68	3.84	3.98	4.20	4.67	4.82	5.08	5.17	5.34	5.42
Soda	1.39	1.57	1.64	1.81	1.81	1.98	2.03	2.26	2.24	2.45	2.61	2.66	2.84	3.07
Hot Dog	1.78	1.74	1.80	1.89	1.97	2.15	2.42	2.51	2.57	2.72	2.97	3.05	3.23	3.31
Parking	5.76	6.01	6.10	6.31	6.38	6.78	7.15	7.38	9.23	8.79	9.98	10.28	11.05	11.41
Program	2.91	3.08	3.00	3.20	3.27	3.64	3.88	3.64	4.26	4.13	4.25	3.98	4.06	3.89
Cap	11.01	11.08	11.13	11.62	11.14	11.09	10.99	12.04	12.30	12.67	12.25	12.65	13.01	13.62

Note: Adult T is the price of one each Adult Ticket in dollars and Child T is the price of one each Child Ticket in dollars. A dash (—) means that Team Marketing Report did not estimate the price of child tickets for that year. The values in the table are the average dollars per product and not the total fan cost. See Table 1.4 in Chapter 1 for the fan cost indexes of each team by year.

Source: "Major League Baseball," at http://www.teammarketing.com cited 10 September 2006.

Table A.1.4 MLB Teams Fan Cost Indexes

High and Low Indexes, by League and Regular Season, 1993–2006

Team AL	1993	1994	1995	1996	1997	1998	1999	2000	2001	2002	2003	2004	2005	2006
Angels	84	**90**	90	92	101	113	121	117	**110**	**113**	130	133	125	134
Athletics	99	100	101	104	94	98	92	94	120	124	139	145	152	170
Brewers	91	87	**86**	**85**	94	—	—	—	—	—	—	—	—	—
Mariners	85	95	95	106	118	125	136	**179**	180	173	175	173	172	186
Red Sox	100	102	112	117	129	144	160	168	**209**	**228**	**238**	**263**	**276**	**287**
Royals	86	98	98	96	**85**	**96**	110	100	119	**113**	112	**120**	**120**	**120**
Twins	**82**	**90**	97	100	97	97	97	102	130	121	127	131	146	149
White Sox	97	106	110	**118**	115	120	123	122	138	159	159	160	188	191
Yankees	**113**	**115**	**118**	**134**	**148**	**166**		174	178	178	182	183	193	208
AL Average	94	100	101	109	119	125	125	134	144	148	155	157	163	169

(Table A.1.4 continued)

Team	1993	1994	1995	1996	1997	1998	1999	2000	2001	2002	2003	2004	2005	2006
NL														
Braves	97	113	**113**	**121**	**135**	**134**	144	160	156	155	154	144	145	145
Brewers	–	–	–	–	–	97	95	100	124	130	128	124	**130**	**131**
Cubs	**103**	**108**	112	116	121	120	134	135	166	181	172	194	210	219
Expos	86	82	86	90	86	93	87	**88**	76	**84**	**100**	**108**	–	–
Giants	87	100	102	**121**	110	108	110	161	163	169	178	184	191	201
Mets	86	91	91	104	114	132	**154**	**175**	**175**	177	**182**	186	186	207
Reds	77	79	**81**	**81**	**82**	**89**	96	104	129	127	140	140	145	156
NL Average	87	91	93	100	104	110	117	129	137	141	146	153	164	172
MLB Average	90	95	97	102	106	115	121	132	140	145	150	155	163	171

Note: The FCIs are rounded into dollars. Those in bold were the highest and lowest of the teams in that season. The dash (—) indicates that a team did not exist at that location during the year.
Source: See the source below Table 1.4 of Chapter 1.

Table A.1.5 MLB Team Payrolls Per Win
By Leagues and Regular Seasons, 2000–2006

Team	2000	2001	2002	2003	2004	2005	2006
AL							
Anaheim Angels	.66	.65	.63	1.03	1.25	1.02	1.16
Baltimore Orioles	.93	1.22	.93	1.01	.72	1.09	1.03
Boston Red Sox	.88	1.39	1.25	1.14	1.32	1.22	1.39
Chicago White Sox	.37	.75	.70	.73	.77	.73	1.14
Cleveland Indians	.87	1.04	1.05	.78	.53	.43	.72
Detroit Tigers	.69	.77	1.02	1.28	.81	.96	.97
Kansas City Royals	.34	.55	.84	.54	.77	.62	.76
Minnesota Twins	.24	.32	.44	.63	.59	.67	.66
New York Yankees	1.09	1.20	1.34	1.67	1.86	2.18	2.04
Oakland Athletics	.33	.38	.39	.53	.66	.66	.66
Seattle Mariners	.65	.68	.94	1.02	1.29	1.02	1.13
Tampa Bay Devil Rays	.88	.82	.65	.43	.34	.39	.58
Texas Rangers	.81	1.18	1.51	1.45	.88	.63	.81
Toronto Blue Jays	.65	.92	.88	.68	.75	.57	.82
AL Average	.67	.84	.89	.92	.89	.87	.99
NL							
Atlanta Braves	.92	1.07	.93	.96	.82	.95	1.16
Arizona Diamondbacks	.90	.92	1.11	.99	1.34	.78	.77
Chicago Cubs	.91	.82	1.10	.95	1.13	.96	.43
Cincinnati Reds	.49	.66	.57	.73	.61	.67	.74
Colorado Rockies	.77	.93	.71	.90	1.02	.48	.54
Florida Marlins	.27	.50	.55	.61	.60	.67	.19
Houston Astros	.69	.71	.79	.83	.89	.85	1.12
Los Angeles Dodgers	1.03	1.34	1.12	1.33	1.09	1.23	1.12
Milwaukee Brewers	.50	.68	.88	.63	.44	.52	.75
Montreal Expos	.40	.51	.44	.56	.58	—	—
New York Mets	.87	1.13	1.37	1.70	1.45	1.25	1.06
Philadelphia Phillies	.70	.54	.76	.83	1.13	1.07	1.03
Pittsburgh Pirates	.48	.75	.65	.70	.45	.44	.69
San Diego Padres	.71	.48	.61	.79	.75	.80	.79
San Francisco Giants	.51	.75	.86	.89	.90	1.11	1.19
St. Louis Cardinals	.72	.81	.76	1.09	.88	.87	1.06

(Table A.15 continued)

Team	2000	2001	2002	2003	2004	2005	2006
NL							
Washington Nationals	—	—	—	—	—	.77	.89
NL Average	.67	.78	.82	.90	.88	.83	.85
MLB Average	.67	.80	.85	.91	.89	.85	.92

Note: The tabled values are each team's total payroll in dollars divided by the number of wins during each of five regular seasons. In the 2000 regular season, for example, the Anaheim Angels spent approximately $660 thousand for each win. To further interpret the entries in the table, the teams with lower numbers were more efficient, when performances were expressed in dollars per victory, than were the clubs with higher numbers. The dash (—) means that no MLB team existed in Montreal in 2005 and 2006, and in Washington, D.C., in 2000–2004.

Source: See the source below Table 1.3 of Chapter 1.

Table A.2.1 Customer Loyalty Awards
By Professional Sport Leagues and Seasons, 1999–2006

League	1999	2000	2001	2002	2003	2004	2005	2006
MLB	G	NA	G	G	G	G-t	NA	B
NBA	NA	NA	NA	NA	NA	NA	NA	S
NFL	NA	G	NA	NA	NA	G-t	G	G
NHL	NA	NA	NA	NA	NA	NA	NA	NA

Note: The awards are earned by the professional sports leagues whose brands demonstrate the highest levels of loyalty and consumer engagement. The winners are identified with a G for Gold, S for Silver, or B for Bronze. The NA means No Award and t indicates a tie between the leagues. There were no silver or bronze Customer Loyalty Awards given before 2006 or any awards prior to 1999.

Source: "Brandweek Customer Loyalty Awards Powered by Brand Keys," at http://www. brandkeys.com cited 16 January 2007.

Table A.2.2 World Series Television Ratings
By Year and Network, 1993–2006

Year	Network	Rating%	Number of Homes	Share%
1993	CBS	17.3	19.2	30
1994	—	—	—	—
1995	ABC—NBC	19.5	21.7	33
1996	FOX	17.4	19.4	29
1997	NBC	16.8	18.7	29

(Table A.2.2 continued)

Year	Network	Rating%	Number of Homes	Share%
1998	FOX	14.1	15.7	24
1999	NBC	16.0	17.8	26
2000	FOX	12.4	13.8	21
2001	FOX	15.7	17.5	25
2002	FOX	11.9	13.3	20
2003	FOX	12.8	14.3	22
2004	FOX	15.8	17.6	25
2005	FOX	11.1	12.4	19
2006	FOX	10.1	11.3	17

Note: Network in column two is self-explanatory. Rating% in column three is the percentage of United States television households who had tuned in to the World Series that year and each rating point equals 1,1114,000 homes. The Number of Homes in column four is in millions. Share% in column five is the percentage of households who had watched the World Series among those homes with televisions in use at the time. The dash (—) indicates television ratings were not recorded in 1994 because of a players' strike and no World Series being played in MLB.

Source: "Sign of the Times: World Series TV Ratings Plunge Again to Record Low," at http://www.si.com cited 30 October 2006, and "Tuning Out: Fans to Pay Price For Declining Postseason Ratings," at http://www.si.com cited 24 October 2006.

Table A.3.1 Professional Sports Teams
Percent of Teams, by Years and Leagues, 1906–2006

Year	%MLB	%NBA	%NFL	%NHL	%MLS	%Total
1906	100	0	0	0	0	100
1916	100	0	0	0	0	100
1926	33	0	46	21	0	100
1936	48	0	27	25	0	100
1946	37	26	23	14	0	100
1956	38	19	29	14	0	100
1966	39	20	29	12	0	100
1976	26	24	30	20	0	100
1986	26	23	29	22	0	100
1996	23	24	24	21	8	100
2006	23	23	24	21	9	100

Note: Columns two through six denote each of the sports league's number of teams expressed as a percentage of the total teams during each year. Some percentages were marginally rounded to equal a total of 100 percent for each of the years.

Source: See the source below Table 3.1 of Chapter 3.

Table A.3.2 Professional Sports Teams
By MLB Metropolitan Areas and Sports Leagues, 2006

Areas	%MLB	%NBA	%NFL	%NHL	%MLS	%Total
Atlanta	25	25	25	25	0	100
Baltimore–Towson	50	0	50	0	0	100
Boston	25	25	0	25	25	100
Chicago	33	17	17	17	17	100
Cincinnati	50	0	50	0	0	100
Cleveland	33	33	33	0	0	100
Dallas-FW-Arlington	20	20	20	20	20	100
Denver	20	20	20	20	20	100
Detroit	20	20	20	20	20	100
Houston	25	25	25	0	25	100
Kansas City	33	0	33	0	33	100
Los Angeles-Anaheim	25	25	0	25	25	100
Miami	25	25	25	25	0	100
Milwaukee	50	50	0	0	0	100
Minneapolis	25	25	25	25	0	100
New York-Northern NJ	20	20	20	30	10	100
Philadelphia	25	25	25	25	0	100
Phoenix	25	25	25	25	0	100
Pittsburgh	33	0	33	33	0	100
San Diego	50	0	50	0	0	100
San Francisco-Oak.-SJ	40	20	40	0	0	100
Seattle	33	33	33	0	0	100
St. Louis	33	0	33	33	0	100
Tampa Bay	33	0	33	33	0	100
Toronto	33	33	0	33	0	100
Washington D.C.	29	14	29	14	14	100

Note: The three abbreviated metropolitan areas are Dallas-Fort Worth-Arlington, New York-Northern New Jersey, and San Francisco-Oakland-San Jose. Because some of the percentages were rounded, a few totals of specific areas may equal 99 or 101 percent.

Source: See the source below Table 3.2 of Chapter 3.

Table A.3.3 MLB Teams
Area Characteristics, Ranked by Team, Selected Years

Team	Area	Population	Per Capita PI	TV Homes
AL				
Angels	Los Angeles-Anaheim	2nd-t	16th-t	3rd-t
Athletics	San Francisco-Oak.-SJ	15th-t	1st-t	8th-t
Blue Jays	NA	—	—	—
Devil Rays	Tampa Bay	23rd	28th	16th
Indians	Cleveland	26th	26th	21st

(Table A.3.3 continued)

Team AL	Area	Population	Per Capita PI	TV Homes
Mariners	Seattle	18th	9th	18th
Orioles	Baltimore–Towson	22nd	10th	25th
Rangers	Dallas–FW–Arlington	8th	20th	10th
Red Sox	Boston	13th	4th	11th
Royals	Kansas City	27th	24th	27th
Tigers	Detroit	14th	19th	15th
Twins	Minneapolis	19th	8th	18th
White Sox	Chicago	3rd-t	14th-t	5th-t
Yankees	New York–Northern NJ	1st-t	5th-t	1st-t

Team NL	Area	Population	Per Capita PI	TV Homes
Astros	Houston	10th	13th	14th
Braves	Atlanta	12th	27th	13th
Brewers	Milwaukee	29th	18th	29th
Cardinals	St. Louis	21st	23rd	23rd
Cubs	Chicago	3rd-t	14th-t	5th-t
Diamondbacks	Phoenix	17th	29th	17th
Dodgers	Los Angeles–Anaheim	2nd-t	16th-t	3rd-t
Giants	San Francisco–Oak.–SJ	15th-t	1st-t	8th-t
Marlins	Miami	9th	21st	20th
Mets	New York–Northern NJ	1st-t	5th-t	1st-t
Nationals	Washington D.C.	11th	3rd	12th
Padres	San Diego	20th	12th	26th
Phillies	Philadelphia	7th	11th	7th
Pirates	Pittsburgh	24th	22nd	24th
Reds	Cincinnati	28th	25th	28th
Rockies	Denver	25th	7th	22nd

Note: Based on 13 AL and 16 NL clubs, the areas' three characteristics were each ranked from first to twenty-ninth. Since the Toronto area is not an SMSA, NA means Not Available and the dash (—) indicates unranked. The t denotes a tie in rank between two teams. The note below Table 3.3 defines each of the characteristics and identifies the abbreviated areas.

Source: See the source below Table 3.3 of Chapter 3.

Table A.3.4 MLB Teams
City Characteristics, by Team, 2002

Team AL	City	Square Miles	Population	Employment
Angels	Anaheim	48	332	164
Athletics	Oakland	56	402	182

(Table A.3.4 continued)

Team	City	Square Miles	Population	Employment
AL				
Blue Jays	Toronto	243	2481	1409
Devil Rays	Tampa Bay	112	315	185
Indians	Cleveland	77	467	180
Mariners	Seattle	83	570	331
Orioles	Baltimore	80	638	269
Rangers	Arlington	95	349	189
Red Sox	Boston	48	589	295
Royals	Kansas City	313	443	247
Tigers	Detroit	138	925	336
Twins	Minneapolis	54	375	209
White Sox	Chicago	227	2886	1221
Yankees	New York	303	8084	3453
NL				
Astros	Houston	579	2009	1004
Braves	Atlanta	131	424	219
Brewers	Milwaukee	96	590	247
Cardinals	St. Louis	61	338	145
Cubs	Chicago	227	2886	1221
Diamondbacks	Phoenix	474	1371	774
Dodgers	Los Angeles	469	3798	1739
Giants	San Francisco	46	764	391
Marlins	Miami	35	374	173
Mets	New York	303	8084	3453
Nationals	Washington D.C.	61	570	284
Padres	San Diego	324	1259	643
Phillies	Philadelphia	135	1492	628
Pirates	Pittsburgh	55	327	159
Reds	Cincinnati	78	323	161
Rockies	Denver	153	560	279

Note: The cities' populations and numbers of employed in 2002 are each reported in thousands.

Source: "100 Most Populous U.S. Cities," The World Almanac and Book of Facts 2004 (New York: World Almanac Books, 2004), 327–336; "Statistics Canada, Canada's National Statistics Agency," at http://www.statcan.ca cited 23 January 2007.

Table A.3.5 Potential MLB Markets
Metropolitan Area Characteristics, Ranked by Area, Selected Years

Area	Population	Rank	Per Capita PI	Rank	TV Homes	Rank
Austin-Round Rock	1.5	10th	34.0	9th	.6	14th
Charlotte-Gastonia-						
Rock Hill	1.5	9th	36.1	3rd	1.0	5th
Columbus	1.7	6th	35.2	4th	.9	8th
Greensboro-High Point	.7	15th	30.9	13th	.6	13th
Indianapolis	1.6	8th	36.2	2nd	1.0	4th
Las Vegas-Paradise	1.7	5th	34.8	7th	.7	12th
Nashville	1.4	11th	36.4	1st	.9	7th
New Orleans	1.3	12th	20.7	15th	.5	15th
Norfolk-VA Beach-						
Newport News	1.6	7th	33.3	10th	.7	11th
Orlando-Kissimee	1.9	3rd	31.1	12th	1.4	1st
Portland-Beaverton	2.1	1st	35.2	5th	1.1	3rd
Raleigh-Cary	1.0	14th	35.1	6th	1.0	6th
Sacramento-Yolo	2.0	2nd	34.8	8th	1.3	2nd
Salt Lake City-Ogden	1.1	13th	33.2	11th	.8	9th
San Antonio	1.9	4th	30.1	14th	.7	10th

Note: The note below Table 3.3 defines Population, Per Capita Personal Income, and Television (TV) Homes. Population and TV Homes were rounded to millions, and Per Capita PI to thousands of dollars. Due to rounding, the ranks of each characteristic in columns three, five and seven were assigned and correspond to those in Table 3.4 even though the numbers and values among some of the areas were equal, such as the Population in Austin-Round Rock and Charlotte-Gastonia-Rock Hill. Thus, there were no ties in areas' ranks for each of the characteristics.

Source: See the source below Table 3.4 of Chapter 3.

Table A.3.6 Principal Agglomerations
Ranked by Total Population of Agglomerations, January 2006

Country	City	Population	World Rank
Japan	Tokyo	34.2	1st
Mexico	Mexico City	22.8	2nd
South Korea	Seoul	22.3	3rd
United Kingdom	London	12.0	21st
Taiwan	Taipei	6.9	43rd
Venezuela	Caracas	4.7	64th
Australia	Sydney	4.3	71st
Mexico	Monterrey	3.9	78th
Dominican Republic	Santo Domingo	3.0	122nd
Puerto Rico	San Juan	2.8	133rd

(Table A.3.6 continued)

Country	City	Population	World Rank
Cuba	Havana	2.3	161st
Mexico	Tijuana	1.7	237th
Panama	Panama City	1.2	347th

Note: The populations of principal agglomerations, which are reported in millions, include a central city and neighboring communities linked to it by continuous built-up areas or commuters. The columns titled Country, City and World Rank are self-explanatory.

Source: "The Principal Agglomerations of the World," at http://www.citypopulation.de cited 17 October 2006.

Table A.4.1 MLB Teams
Revenues Shared, by Team, 2001–2003, 2006

Team	2001	2002	2003	2006	Total
AL					
Angels	9.5	(1.3)	1.8	(11.0)	(1.0)
Athletics	10.5	9.2	11.7	19.0	50.4
Blue Jays	9.8	13.6	18.7	31.0	73.1
Devil Rays	12.3	14.7	20.4	33.0	80.4
Indians	(13.2)	(10.6)	(4.8)	6.0	(22.6)
Mariners	(18.7)	(19.8)	(31.0)	(25.0)	(94.5)
Orioles	(6.8)	(5.3)	.2	2.0	(9.9)
Rangers	(8.7)	(8.2)	(7.1)	(.3)	(24.3)
Red Sox	(16.4)	(17.8)	(38.6)	(52.0)	(124.8)
Royals	15.9	16.6	19.0	30.0	81.5
Tigers	5.1	11.6	16.7	25.0	58.4
Twins	19.0	12.9	17.2	22.0	71.1
White Sox	(4.2)	(3.8)	(4.8)	(18.0)	(30.8)
Yankees	(26.5)	(26.6)	(52.6)	(76.0)	(181.7)
NL					
Astros	(5.1)	(4.3)	1.1	(11.0)	(19.3)
Braves	(10.6)	(9.7)	(11.2)	(10.0)	(41.5)
Brewers	1.7	8.5	16.5	24.0	50.7
Cardinals	(8.2)	(8.3)	(9.2)	(19.0)	(44.7)
Cubs	(6.5)	(8.2)	(16.7)	(32.0)	(63.4)
Diamondbacks	(4.4)	(3.2)	1.4	13.0	6.8
Dodgers	(9.1)	(9.2)	(9.4)	(20.0)	(47.7)
Expos	28.5	28.4	29.5	–	86.4
Giants	(6.3)	(9.6)	(12.9)	(14.0)	(42.8)
Marlins	18.5	20.9	21.0	31.0	91.4
Mets	(15.6)	(17.3)	(21.4)	(24.0)	(78.3)

(Table A.4.1 continued)

Team	2001	2002	2003	2006	Total
NL					
Nationals	—	—	—	3.9	3.9
Padres	8.6	6.2	13.2	5.7	33.8
Phillies	11.7	9.8	9.0	5.8	36.3
Pirates	1.7	6.4	13.2	25.0	46.3
Reds	13.4	9.8	6.4	16.0	45.6
Rockies	(6.0)	(5.1)	2.4	16.0	7.3

Note: Payment amounts, in millions of dollars, are in parentheses during the years. A dash (—) means that the team did not exist in the NL. Revenues shared were not reported for 2004–2005.

Source: "2001 Team-by-Team Revenues and Expenses Forecast," at http://www.usa today.com cited 24 January 2007; "Revenue Sharing (by the Numbers)," at http://www. sportsbusinessnews.com cited 5 October 2004; Howard Bloom, "The Good News a New MLB Labor Accord," at http://www.sportsbusinessnews.com cited 24 October 2006.

Table A.4.2 MLB Teams
Differences in Revenues Shared and Payrolls, by Team, 2006

Team	Revenues Shared	Payrolls	Differences	Win Percentages
AL				
Athletics	19.0	62.2	(43.2)	.574
Blue Jays	31.0	71.9	(40.9)	.537
Devil Rays	33.0	35.4	(2.4)	.377
Indians	6.0	56.0	(50.0)	.481
Orioles	2.0	72.5	(70.5)	.432
Royals	30.0	47.2	(17.2)	.383
Tigers	25.0	82.6	(57.6)	.586
Twins	22.0	63.3	(41.3)	.593
AL Average	21.0	61.3	(40.3)	.495
NL				
Brewers	24.0	57.5	(33.5)	.463
Diamondbacks	13.0	59.6	(46.6)	.469
Marlins	31.0	14.9	16.1	.481
Nationals	3.9	63.1	(59.2)	.438
Padres	5.7	69.8	(64.1)	.543
Phillies	5.8	88.2	(82.4)	.525
Pirates	25.0	46.7	(21.7)	.414
Reds	16.0	60.9	(44.9)	.494
Rockies	16.0	41.2	(25.2)	.469

(Table A.4.2 continued)

Team NL	Revenues Shared	Payrolls	Differences	Win Percentages
NL Average	15.6	55.7	(40.1)	.477
MLB Average	18.1	58.3	(40.2)	.486

Note: Revenues shared, payrolls and differences are in thousands of dollars and win percentages are each team's number of wins divided by total games, and expressed in decimals.

Source: Howard Bloom, "The Good News a New MLB Labor Accord," at http://www.sportsbusinessnews.com cited 24 October 2006.

Table A.4.3 MLB Players Salaries
Minimum and Average Salary, by Year, 1990(2006

Year	Minimum	%CH	Average	%CH
1990	100	—	578.9	—
1991	100	0	891.1	53
1992	109	9	1084.4	21
1993	109	0	1120.2	3
1994	109	0	1188.6	6
1995	109	0	1071.0	(9)
1996	109	0	1176.9	9
1997	150	37	1383.5	17
1998	170	13	1441.4	4
1999	200	17	1720.0	19
2000	200	0	1988.0	15
2001	200	0	2264.4	13
2002	200	0	2383.2	5
2003	300	50	2555.4	7
2004	300	0	2490.0	(3)
2005	316	5	2589.6	4
2006	327	3	2866.5	10

Note: The %CH is the annual percentage changes in the minimum and average salaries of MLB players. The dash (—) indicates that the percentage changes are not applicable in 1990. The percentage changes in parentheses means a decline in the averages in 1995 and 2004.

Source: "Decline is First Since 1965," at http://www.sports.espn.go.com cited 5 January 2005; "2006 Salaries," at http://www.sportsline.com cited 23 January 2007; "Who Wants to be a Millionaire?" at http://www.cnnsi.com cited 5 April 2001; "The Baseball Archive," at http://www.baseball1.com cited 30 December 2004; "Year in Review," at http://www.baseball-almanac.com cited 25 January 2007.

Table A.5.1 MLB Teams
Final Winning Percentages, by League and Seasons, 1993–2006

Team	1993	1994	1995	1996	1997	1998	1999	2000	2001	2002	2003	2004	2005	2006
AL														
Angels	.438	.409	.538	.435	.519	.525	.432	.506	.463	.611	.475	.568	.586	.549
Athletics	.420	.447	.465	.481	.401	.457	.537	.565	.630	.636	.593	.562	.543	.574
Blue Jays	.586	.478	.389	.457	.469	.543	.519	.512	.494	.481	.531	.416	.494	.537
Brewers	.426	.461	.451	.494	.484	—	—	—	—	—	—	—	—	–
Devil Rays	—	—	—	—	—	.389	.426	.429	.383	.342	.389	.435	.414	.377
Indians	.469	.584	.694	.615	.534	.549	.599	.556	.562	.457	.420	.494	.574	.481
Mariners	.506	.438	.545	.528	.556	.472	.488	.562	.716	.574	.574	.389	.426	.481
Orioles	.525	.563	.493	.543	.605	.488	.481	.457	.391	.414	.438	.481	.457	.432
Rangers	.531	.456	.514	.556	.475	.543	.586	.438	.451	.444	.438	.549	.488	.494
Red Sox	.494	.470	.597	.525	.481	.568	.580	.525	.509	.574	.586	.605	.586	.531
Royals	.519	.557	.486	.466	.416	.447	.398	.475	.401	.383	.512	.358	.346	.383
Tigers	.525	.461	.417	.327	.488	.401	.429	.488	.407	.342	.265	.444	.438	.586
Twins	.438	.469	.389	.481	.420	.432	.394	.426	.525	.584	.556	.568	.512	.593
White Sox	.580	.593	.472	.525	.497	.494	.466	.586	.512	.500	.531	.512	.611	.556
Yankees	.543	.619	.549	.568	.593	.704	.605	.540	.594	.640	.623	.623	.586	.599
NL														
Astros	.525	.574	.528	.506	.519	.630	.599	.444	.574	.519	.537	.568	.549	.506
Braves	.642	.596	.625	.593	.623	.654	.636	.586	.543	.631	.623	.593	.556	.488
Brewers	—	—	—	—	—	.457	.460	.451	.420	.346	.420	.416	.500	.463
Cardinals	.537	.465	.434	.543	.451	.512	.466	.586	.574	.599	.525	.648	.617	.516
Cubs	.519	.434	.507	.469	.420	.552	.414	.401	.543	.414	.543	.549	.488	.407
Diamondbacks	—	—	—	—	—	.401	.617	.525	.568	.605	.519	.315	.475	.469
Dodgers	.500	.509	.542	.556	.543	.512	.475	.531	.531	.568	.525	.574	.438	.543
Expos	.580	.649	.458	.543	.481	.401	.420	.414	.420	.512	.512	.414	—	–

(Table A.5.1 continued)

Team	1993	1994	1995	1996	1997	1998	1999	2000	2001	2002	2003	2004	2005	2006
AL														
Giants	.636	.478	.465	.420	.556	.546	.531	.599	.556	.590	.621	.562	.463	.472
Marlins	.395	.443	.469	.494	.568	.333	.395	.491	.469	.488	.562	.512	.512	.481
Mets	.364	.487	.479	.438	.543	.543	.595	.580	.506	.466	.410	.438	.512	.599
Nationals	—	—	—	—	—	—	—	—	—	—	—	—	.500	.438
Padres	.377	.402	.486	.562	.469	.605	.457	.469	.488	.407	.395	.537	.506	.543
Phillies	.599	.470	.479	.414	.420	.463	.475	.401	.531	.497	.531	.531	.543	.525
Pirates	.463	.465	.403	.451	.488	.426	.484	.426	.383	.447	.463	.447	.414	.414
Reds	.451	.579	.590	.500	.469	.475	.589	.525	.407	.481	.426	.469	.451	.494
Rockies	.414	.453	.535	.512	.512	.475	.444	.506	.451	.451	.457	.420	.414	.469

Note: The winning percentages are in decimals and self-explanatory. A dash (—) indicates that a team did not exist in the league that season.

Source: "Teams History," at http://www.mlb.com cited 17 January 2007.

CHAPTER NOTES

Introduction

1. For their favorite sport to watch from being interested in the sports news, the survey revealed that 14 percent of adults who responded had watched baseball very/somewhat closely and 12 percent not very/not at all closely. These statistics are reported in "Americans to Rest of World: Soccer Not Really Our Thing," *Pew Research Center* (14 June 2006), 1–10. Other information about sports fans' loyalty and passion for baseball and MLB teams are Tim Dahlberg, "Column: Fan Loyalty Stretches Only So Far," at http://www.netscape.com, cited 19 April 2006; Paul Forrester, "Fan Value Index 2006: Readers Rate Which Parks Offer Best Value, Experience," at http://www.si.com, cited 23 September 2006; "National Survey Ranks Baseball Fans," at http://forums.nyyfans.com, cited 24 September 2006; Don Walker, "Wanted: Younger Fans," at http://www.jsonline.com, cited 25 September 2006.

2. These and other facts are further examined throughout the chapters in *Baseball in Crisis*, and also are discussed in Gary Gillette, "MLB Not as Popular as it Once Was," at http://www.sportsbusinessnews.com, cited 6 August 2006. For some articles that relate to current and future problems in baseball, see Mark Hyman, "The Racial Gap in the Grandstands," *BusinessWeek* (2 October 2006), 78–79; John Kuenster, "Fans Offer Six Ways to Improve Game at the Major League Level," *Baseball Digest* (December 2006), 17–19; John

Donovan, "Negotiate This: Baseball Has Lots of Problems That Need Fixing, Too," at http://www.cnnsi.com, cited 27 October 2006; "Poll: MLB Too Soft on Steroids," at http://www.si.com, cited 25 April 2006; Jon Weisman, "Tuning Out: Fans to Pay Price For Declining Postseason Ratings," at http://www.si.com, cited 24 October 2006.

3. See such publications as the *Official Major League Baseball Fact Book 2005 Edition* (St. Louis, MO: The Sporting News, 2005); Bill James, *The New Bill James Historical Baseball Abstract* (New York: Free Press, 2003); Jonah Keri and James Click, *Baseball Between the Numbers* (New York: Basic Books, 2006); Alan Schwarz and Peter Gammons, *The Numbers Game: Baseball's Lifelong Fascination with Statistics* (New York: St. Martin's Griffin, 2004).

4. The books referenced in the Literature Review include Gerald W. Scully, *The Business of Major League Baseball* (Chicago, IL: University of Chicago Press, 1989); Andrew Zimbalist, *Baseball and Billions: A Probing Look Inside the Big Business of Our National Pastime* (New York: Basic Books, 1992); Paul M. Sommers, ed., *Diamonds Are Forever: The Business of Baseball* (Washington, D.C.: The Brookings Institution, 1992); Daniel R. Marburger, ed., *Stee-Rike Four! What's Wrong With the Business of Baseball?* (Westport, CT: Praeger, 1997); Bob Costas, *Fair Ball: A Fan's Case for Baseball* (New York: Broadway Books, 2001); Andrew Zimbalist, *In the Best Interests of Baseball? The Revolutionary Reign*

of Bud Selig (Hoboken, NJ: Wiley, 2006); Frank P. Jozsa, Jr., *Baseball, Inc.: The National Pastime as Big Business* (Jefferson, NC: McFarland, 2006).

5. Ticket prices, ballpark costs, and teams' valuations are discussed partially in such articles as Jeffrey L. Seglin, "Who Has the Right to Playoff Tickets?" *Charlotte Observer* (8 October 2006), 3D; Chris Isidore, "Baseball Ticket Prices: Supply, Not Millionaires," at http://cnnmoney.com, cited 15 April 2006; "Major League Baseball," at http://www.team marketing.com, cited 10 September 2006; "Forbes Financial 2004 Valuation For MLB Franchise," at http://www.sportsbusiness news.com, cited 5 October 2004.

6. See Tim Keown, "Changing the Culture," *Wall Street Journal* (16–17 September 2006), R7; Peter Barzilai and John Follaco, "What's the Problem With Baseball?" at http://www.usatoday.com, cited 15 September 2006; "The Battle of the Sexes — Fifty Million Women Avidly Follow Professional Sports," at http://www.arbitron.com, cited 24 September 2006; "Sports Loyalty Index," at http://www.brandkeys.com, cited 17 September 2006.

7. There are numerous publications about professional sports markets, the locations of MLB clubs, and the sites of big league ballparks. For example, see "Ballparks," at http://www.ballparks.com, cited 15 December 2006; Murray Chass, "Baseball in D.C., They Have a Name But No Money," at http://www.sportsbusinessnews.com, cited 30 November 2004; Frank P. Jozsa, Jr. and John J. Guthrie, Jr., *Relocating Teams and Expanding Leagues in Professional Sports: How the Major Leagues Respond to Market Conditions* (Westport, CT: Quorum, 1999); "Three Clubs Set Example With Private Ballpark Funding," at http://www.si.com, cited 15 November 2006.

8. The types of activities and events that have contributed to baseball fans' dissatisfaction with MLB and some its teams and their players are reported in John Moores, "When Push Comes to Shove: Union Hurts Baseball," *Wall Street Journal* (12 July 2005), D8; Joshua Prager, "Baseball's Dirty Open Secret," *Wall Street Journal* (26 October 2006), D6; "Feds Close to Getting Proof of Steroid Use in Baseball," at http://www.si.com, cited 30 December 2006; "Major League Baseball Scandals," at http://en.wikipedia.org, cited 30 October 2006.

9. For information about the distribution of power among the 30 big league teams, see Howard Bloom, "Major League Baseball — the Haves vs. the Have Nots," at http://www.sportsbusinessnews.com, cited 14 December 2006; "Is the 2006 World Series All About Parity?" at http://www.sportsbusinessnews.com, cited 24 October 2006; "MLB Teams: 2005 Valuations," at http://www.forbes.com, cited 12 September 2006; "Yankees Luxury Tax — Their Bill Comes Due," at http://www.sportsbusinessnews.com, cited 23 December 2006.

10. For various types of proposed reforms, see such Internet sources as "An Open Letter to Baseball Fans From Commissioner Allan H. (Bud) Selig," at http://www.mlb.com, cited 19 September 2006; Hal Bodley, "Baseball Officials Announce Tougher Steroids Policy," at http://www.usatoday.com, cited 27 October 2006; "MLB Owners Unanimously Approve Labor Deal," at http://www.sportsbusinessnews.com, cited 4 November 2006; "Players, Owners Settle Collusion Claim," at http://www.si.com, cited 7 November 2006. Five prominent sports books that, in part, provide strategies for reforming big league baseball are Scott Barzilla, *Checks and Imbalances: Competitive Disparity in Major League Baseball* (Jefferson, NC: McFarland, 2002); Roger G. Noll, ed., *Government and the Sports Business: Studies in the Regulation of Economic Activity* (Washington, D.C.: The Brookings Institution, 1974); James Quirk and Rodney D. Fort, *Pay Dirt: The Business of Professional Team Sports* (Princeton, NJ: Princeton University Press, 1992); George Will, *Bunts: Curt Flood, Camden Yards, Pete Rose and Other Reflections on Baseball* (New York: Scribner, 1999); Andrew Zimbalist, *May the Best Team Win: Baseball Economics and Public Policy* (Washington, D.C.: The Brookings Institution, 2003).

Chapter 1

1. Some prominent books that discuss the history of MLB and the business operations and managerial strategies of professional baseball franchises are Frank P. Jozsa, Jr., *Baseball, Inc.: The National Pastime as Big Business* (Jefferson, NC: McFarland, 2006); Albert Theodore Powers, *The Business of Baseball* (Jefferson, NC: McFarland, 2003); Andrew Zimbalist, *Baseball and Billions: A Probing Look Inside the Big Business of Our National Pastime* (New York: Basic Books,

1992); James Quirk and Rodney D. Fort, *Pay Dirt: The Business of Professional Team Sports* (Princeton, NJ: Princeton University Press, 1992).

2. For other readings about the availability of tickets and various ticket prices of MLB teams, see "Baseball Ticket Prices Up 5.4 Percent," *Charlotte Observer* (4 April 2006), 2C; Russell Adams, "The New Price of Loyalty," *Wall Street Journal* (4–5 March 2006), P1, P3; "MLB Ticket Prices Going Up For 2006," at http://www.sportsbusinessnews.com, cited 4 April 2006; Chris Isidore, "Baseball Ticket Prices: Supply, Not Millionaires," at http://cnnmoney.com, cited 15 April 2006; Jeffrey L. Seglin, "Who Has the Right to Playoff Tickets?" *Charlotte Observer* (8 October 2006): 3D.

3. Consumer price indexes are reported in the "Table Containing History of CPI-U U.S.," at http://www.bls.gov, cited 11 September 2006, and in *The World Almanac and Book of Facts* (New York: World Almanac Books, 1950–2005). The Gross Domestic Product Deflator by year is available in "What Was the GDP Then?" at http://www.en.net, cited 11 September 2006.

4. The issue of parity among clubs in the American and National Leagues of Major League Baseball is a topic in several titles. These include Scott Brazilla, *Checks and Imbalances: Competitive Disparity in Major League Baseball* (Jefferson, NC: McFarland, 2002); Gerald W. Scully, *The Business of Major League Baseball* (Chicago, IL: University of Chicago Press, 1989); Bob Costas, *Fair Ball: A Fan's Case for Baseball* (New York: Broadway Books, 2001); Roger G. Noll, ed., *Government and the Sports Business: Studies in the Regulation of Economic Activity* (Washington, D.C.: The Brookings Institution, 1974); Paul M. Sommers, ed., *Diamonds Are Forever: The Business of Baseball* (Washington, D.C.: The Brookings Institution, 1992).

5. On pages 72–84 of *Baseball, Inc.*, an essay titled "Major League Players' Salaries and Team Payrolls" includes two sections, one each about an evaluation of players' salaries and an analysis of team payrolls. The author concludes: "...most of the small-market teams in the AL and NL lack the operating revenues to successfully hire high-priced free agents and to resign their most valuable veteran players." Furthermore, "...the league will bargain with the MLBPA [Major League Baseball Players Association] about a salary

cap, greater revenue sharing from high-to low-payroll franchises, and/or an increase in the luxury tax rate."

6. The valuation of professional baseball teams is based, in part, on such factors as the franchise's brand recognition, current stadium deal, operating income per season, ownership of one or more regional sports networks, home attendances, number of season ticket holders, amount of debt, and its market's total population, growth in population, and income per capita. For more details about baseball finance and wealth, see Michael K. Ozanian, "Selective Accounting," *Forbes* (14 December 1998), 124–134; "Forbes Financial 2004 Valuation For MLB Franchise," at http://www.sportsbusinessnews.com, cited 5 October 2004; "MLB Teams: 2005 Valuations," at http://www.forbes.com, cited 12 September 2006; Mike Bauman, "A Great Year For the Grand Old Game," at http://www.mlb.com, cited 27 December 2005.

7. Some articles that discuss sports fans and their problems with MLB are Howard Bloom, "The Yankees Lose and So Do Their Fans," at http://www.sportsbusinessnews.com, cited 6 October 2006; Jerry Crasnick, "It Really Does 'Suck' to Be a Baltimore Orioles Fan These Days," at http://www.sportsbusinessnews.com, cited 21 September 2006; Tim Dahlberg, "Column: Fan Loyalty Stretches Only So Far," at http://www.netscape.com, cited 19 April 2006; "Fans Conflicted About Bonds," at http://www.usatoday.com, cited 14 March 2006; Spencer Fordin, "Orioles Fans Have Had Enough," at http://www.sportsbusinessnews.com, cited 22 September 2006; "National Survey Ranks Baseball Fans," at http://forums.nyyfans.com, cited 24 September 2006; Don Walker, "Wanted: Younger Fans," at http://www.jsonline.com, cited 25 September 2006.

Chapter 2

1. For some demographic, economic, and financial statistics on spectator sports, including professional sports leagues and markets, see Kelli D. Washington and Richard K. Miller, *The 2004 Entertainment, Media & Advertising Market Research Handbook, Sixth Edition* (Norcross, GA: Richard K. Miller & Associates, Inc., 2004).

2. Various results from surveys, polls, and other research about baseball and MLB fans are reported in Peter Barzilai and John Fol-

laco, "What's the Problem with Baseball?" at http://www.usatoday.com, cited 15 September 2006; "Major League Baseball Properties Selects Scarborough Sports Marketing For Consumer and Fan Research Services," at http://www.arbitron.com, cited 24 September 2006; "Americans to Rest of World: Soccer Not Really Our Thing," *Pew Research Center* (14 June 2006), 1–10; Mark Hyman, "The Racial Gap in the Grandstands," *BusinessWeek* (2 October 2006), 78–79; Gary Gillette, "MLB Not as Popular as it Once Was," at http://www.sportsbusinessnews.com, cited 6 August 2006.

3. See "National Survey Ranks Baseball Fans," at http://forums.nyyfans.com, cited 24 September 2006, and Don Walker, "Wanted: Younger Fans," at http://www.jsonline.com, cited 25 September 2006.

4. To learn why African Americans have abandoned baseball for other team sports and activities, see two articles by Paul Doyle and Matt Egan: "The Diamond Doesn't Cut It for African American Kids Anymore," at http://www.sportsbusinessnews.com, cited 17 September 2006; and "In Harford, a Look at the Challenges Youth Baseball is Facing," at http://www.sportsbusinessnews.com, cited 17 September 2006.

5. During the period 1998 to 2002, MLB baseball was one of the most popular sports for women who were 18 years old and older. These and other facts about female sports fans are contained in "The Battle of the Sexes — Fifty Million Women Avidly Follow Professional Sports," at http://www.arbitron.com, cited 24 September 2006.

6. "A young Harvard grad fresh from Wall Street aims to overcome the Devil Rays' history of failure." This leader's skills and strategies are discussed in Tim Keown, "Changing the Culture," *Wall Street Journal* (16–17 September 2006), R7.

7. Team Marketing Report, which is based in Chicago, Illinois, publishes each year the average ticket prices and fan cost indexes of teams in the professional sports leagues. See the company's web site at http://www.teammarketing.com for these values. For some controversies about ticket prices, see Howard Bloom, "The Yankees Lose and So Do Their Fans," at http://www.sportsbusinessnews.com, cited 6 October 2006, and Russell Adams, "Baseball-Playoff Seats Get Harder to Score," *Wall Street Journal* (27 September 2006), D1, D3.

8. In a message to the author, Robert Passikoff described the construction and derivation of a sports loyalty index as "...a combination of psychological inquiry and casual path analyses that is a four-factor solution. The drivers describe how a fan will look at a category, will compare offerings (in this case, teams) and how they will positively behave toward them (viewership and/or attendance and/or purchase of licensed merchandise." Passikoff's syndicated report is available at "Sports Loyalty Index," at http://www.brandkeys.com, cited 17 September 2006.

9. See Spencer Fordin, "Orioles Fans Have Had Enough," at http://www.sportsbusinessnews.com, cited 22 September 2006; Jerry Crasnick, "It Really Does 'Suck' to Be a Baltimore Orioles Fan These Days," at http://www.sportsbusinessnews.com, cited 21 September 2006; Howard Bloom, "Baltimore Orioles Fans — When Not Enough Is Too Much," at http://www.sportsbusinessnews.com, cited 26 September 2006.

10. Accordingly, a fan value index determines which MLB ballparks offer the best value for the money spent by fans attending games, rather than the best experience overall. In 2005, it was *Sports Illustrated* journalists and not fans that decided which teams' ballparks had provided the most and least values, and best and worst experiences, during MLB's regular season. For index results, see Paul Forrester, "Fan Value Index 2006: Readers Rate Which Parks Offer Best Value, Experience," at http://www.si.com, cited 23 September 2006.

11. For information about the recent performance of MLB's commissioner, see Jack O'Connell, "Selig Receives Business Honor," at http://www.mlb.com, cited 22 December 2006; "Selig Plans to Retire When Contract Ends in 2009," at http://www.si.com, cited 1 December 2006; Barry M. Bloom, "MLB Owners Approve Latest National TV Agreements," at http://www.sportsbusinessnews.com, cited 17 November 2006; Mike Bauman, "A Great Year for the Grand Old Game," at http://www.mlb.com, cited 27 December 2005.

Chapter 3

1. For information about previous and future league expansions and team relocations in one or more of the professional sports leagues, see Frank P. Jozsa, Jr. and John J.

Guthrie, Jr., *Relocating Teams and Expanding Leagues in Professional Sports: How the Major Leagues Respond to Market Conditions* (Westport, CT: Quorum, 1999); Frank P. Jozsa, Jr., *American Sports Empire: How the Leagues Breed Success* (Westport, CT: Praeger, 2003); idem, *Big Sports, Big Business: A Century of Expansions, Mergers, and Reorganizations* (Westport, CT: Praeger, 2006); Roger G. Noll, ed., *Government and the Sports Business: Studies in the Regulation of Economic Activity* (Washington, D.C.: The Brookings Institution, 1974); Kenneth M. Jennings, *Balls and Strikes: The Money Game in Professional Baseball* (Westport, CT: Praeger, 1990); Gerald W. Scully, *The Business of Major League Baseball* (Chicago, IL: University of Chicago Press, 1989); Andrew Zimbalist, *Baseball and Billions: A Probing Look Inside the Big Business of Our National Pastime* (New York: Basic Books, 1992).

2. Besides the literature that is listed in Note 1 for this chapter, the histories of each professional sports league and their teams are posted on worldwide web sites. These sites for Major League Baseball and the National Basketball Association, National Football League, National Hockey League and Major League Soccer are, respectively, mlb.com, nba.com, nfl.com, nhl.com and mlsnet.com.

3. There are 4 various sources that reveal statistics and the performances of MLB teams and players during various regular seasons and postseasons. For example, see the *Official Major League Baseball Fact Book 2005 Edition* (St. Louis, MO: The Sporting News, 2005); *The World Almanac and Book of Facts* (New York: World Almanac Books, 1950–2005); Bill James, *The New Bill James Historical Baseball Abstract* (New York: Free Press, 2003); Alan Schwarz and Peter Gammons, *The Numbers Game: Baseball's Lifelong Fascination With Statistics* (New York: St. Martin's Griffin, 2004). For aspects of the social and historical development and environment of baseball in America, see Peter Carino, ed. *Baseball/Literature/Culture: Essays, 1995–2003* (Jefferson, NC: McFarland, 2003); John Helyar, *Lords of the Realm: The Real History of Baseball* (New York: Ballantine, 1994); David Q. Voight, *American Baseball: From Gentlemen's Sport to the Commissioner System* (Norman: University of Oklahoma Press, 1966).

4. The ownership histories and many attendance records, and the radio and television incomes of franchises in professional baseball,

football, basketball and ice hockey to the early 1990s, are contained in James Quirk and Rodney D. Fort, *Pay Dirt: The Business of Professional Team Sports* (Princeton, NJ: Princeton University Press, 1992). In fact, this book was used by the author to determine when clubs were canceled and sold, and why they had moved to other cities within metropolitan areas.

5. Since provinces and not counties or metropolitan areas are designated in Canada, the demographic characteristics of Toronto were not included in Table 3.3. If evaluated, however, Toronto is a midsized sports market with respect to population, per capita personal income, and number of television homes. That is, the city's characteristics are relatively comparable to those in the Houston, Texas, and San Francisco–Oakland–San Jose, California, areas.

6. When MLB chose to move the Expos from Montreal to Washington, D.C., in 2005, Baltimore Orioles owner Peter Angelos threatened to challenge the relocation of the club into a nearby city and hinted that he would file a lawsuit against the league, if necessary, to protect his investment and territorial rights within his geographical sports market. This threat and other controversial aspects about the relocation issue are discussed in Ed Waldman, "Baseball in D.C., Mr. Angelos Goes to Visit Mr. Selig," at http://www.sportsbusiness news.com, cited 8 October 2004; Jon Morgan, "Baseball in D.C., Camden Yards May Cost More," at http://www.sportsbusiness news.com, cited 29 September 2004; Barry M. Bloom, "MLB Selects D.C. For Expos," at http://www.mlb.com, cited 30 September 2004; Murray Chass, "Baseball in D.C., They Have a Name But No Money," at http://www. sportsbusinessnews.com, cited 30 November 2004. For some recent readings about the feelings of Orioles fans and their relationships with Angelos, see Howard Bloom, "Baltimore Orioles Fans — When Not Enough is Too Much," at http://www.sportsbusinessnews. com, cited 26 September 2006; Jerry Crasnick, "It Really Does 'Suck' to be a Baltimore Orioles Fan These Days," at http://www.sports businessnews.com, cited 21 September 2006; Spencer Fordin, "Orioles Fans Have Had Enough," at http://www.sportsbusinessnews. com, cited 22 September 2006.

7. Besides some MLB clubs, a few teams in former professional baseball leagues have been located within these three large U.S.

markets. These leagues include the Early National League (1876–1900), American Association (1882–1891), Union Association (1884), Players League (1890), and Federal League (1914–1915). See *Pay Dirt*, 378–391.

8. The book's essay 11, which is titled "Global Business Strategies and Markets," discusses the global expansion of MLB. Indeed, these foreign cities were listed as potential sites in Frank P. Jozsa, Jr., *Baseball, Inc.: The National Pastime as Big Business* (Jefferson, NC: McFarland, 2006). Also, the international strategies of big league baseball and the other U.S.-based professional sports leagues are analyzed in Frank P. Jozsa, Jr., *Sports Capitalism: The Foreign Business of American Professional Leagues* (Aldershot, England: Ashgate, 2004).

9. See *Baseball, Inc.*, 110.

10. The impact of international baseball players on MLB teams and within local American communities has been profound. For this topic, see Mark Hyman, "The Racial Gap in the Grandstands," *BusinessWeek* (2 October 2006), 78–79; "Globalization of Baseball," *The Boston Globe* (27 March 1998), F3–F8; "The Wide World of Baseball: Foreign-Born Players Are Filling Major League Rosters," *Baseball Digest* (February 2003), 30–39; John Donovan, "Globalization of the Grand Old Game Hits All-Time High," at http://www.cnnsi.com, cited 17 July 2003; "29.2 Percent of Major League Baseball Players Born Outside the United States," at http://www.mlb.com, cited 12 April 2005. Also, a well-researched report about international players in the big leagues is Stuart Anderson and L. Brian Andrew, *Coming to America: Immigrants, Baseball and the Contributions of Foreign-Born Players to America's Pastime* (Arlington, VA: National Foundation for American Policy, October 2006).

Chapter 4

1. For how sports fans rate the entertainment value of baseball and the other professional sports, see "Americans to Rest of World: Soccer Not Really Our Thing," *Pew Research Center* (14 June 2006), 1–10; Peter Barzilai and John Follaco, "What's the Problem with Baseball?" at http://www.usatoday.com, cited 15 September 2006; Tim Dahlberg, "Column: Fan Loyalty Stretches Only So Far," at http://www.netscape.com, cited 19 April 2006; Jerry Crasnick, "Is MLB Held

to a Higher Standard?" at http://www.sports businessnews.com, cited 7 August 2006.

2. Information about baseball's history, and the sport's business opportunities and problems, are included in such books as Frank P. Jozsa, Jr., *Baseball, Inc.: The National Pastime as Big Business* (Jefferson, NC: McFarland, 2006); Scott Barzilla, *Checks and Imbalances: Competitive Disparity in Major League Baseball* (Jefferson, NC: McFarland, 2002); Andrew Zimbalist, *May the Best Team Win: Baseball Economics and Public Policy* (Washington, D.C.: The Brookings Institution, 2003); Roger G. Noll, ed., *Government and the Sports Business: Studies in the Regulation of Economic Activity* (Washington, D.C.: The Brookings Institution, 1974).

3. Various articles have been published in the literature about the betting and gambling on games by MLB players. Some of them are, for example, "Major League Baseball Scandals," at http://en.wikipedia.org, cited 30 October 2006; "List of Major League Baseball Figures That Have Been Banned for Life," at http://www.answers.com, cited 30 October 2006; Brooks Marlin, "Major League Baseball's 'Permanently Ineligible' List (Thing)," at http://everything2.com, cited 30 October 2006.

4. See Pete Rose and Rick Hill, *My Prison Without Bars* (New York: Rodale Books, 2004); George F. Will, *Bunts: Curt Flood, Camden Yards, Pete Rose and Other Reflections on Baseball* (New York: Scribner, 1999); Michael Sokolove, *Hustle: The Myth, Life, and Lies of Pete Rose* (New York: Simon and Schuster, 2005); James Reston, *Collision at Home Plate: The Lives of Pete Rose and Bart Giamatti* (Lincoln, NE: Bison Books, 1997).

5. A number of statistics about former and/or current baseball players' performances are contained in *Official Major League Baseball Fact Book 2005 Edition* (St. Louis, MO: The Sporting News, 2005); *The World Almanac and Book of Facts* (New York: World Almanac Books, 1950–2005); Bill James, *The New Bill James Historical Baseball Abstract* (New York: Free Press, 2003).

6. Some readings about baseball scandals include the previously cited "Major League Baseball Scandals," "List of Major League Figures That Have Been Banned for Life," and "Major League Baseball's 'Permanently Ineligible' List (Thing)."

7. For more information about the steroids issue, see "Steroids in Baseball," at http://

www.answers.com, cited 30 October 2006; "Juicy Controversy," at http://www.si.com, cited 26 December 2005; "Behavior Modification. Glavine: Amphetamine Testing Changing Culture," at http://www.si.com, cited 29 September 2006; "An Open Letter to Baseball Fans from Commissioner Allan H. (Bud) Selig," at http://www.mlb.com, cited 19 September 2006.

8. Baseball fans and most experts have mixed views about Barry Bonds and why he used illegal substances. For example, read "Proof That Baseball Fans Could Care Less If the Players Are Juiced," at http://www.sportsbusinessnews.com, cited 20 October 2006; "Poll: MLB Too Soft on Steroids," at http://www.si.com, cited 25 April 2006; Kyle Wingfield, "'Roid Outrage: '80s Stars Got Muscled Out of Cooperstown," *Wall Street Journal* (17 January 2006), D8; Ben Walker, "Poll: Half of Fans Rooting Against Bonds," at http://www.capecodonline.com, cited 21 October 2006.

9. See Mark Fainaru-Wada and Lance Williams, *Game of Shadows: Barry Bonds, BALCO, and the Steroids Scandal That Rocked Professional Sports* (New York: Gotham Books, 2006). Besides Bonds, other baseball players implicated in the book are Jason and Jeremy Giambi and Gary Sheffield, and such professional athletes as track stars Marion Jones and Tim Montgomery and former NFL linebacker Bill Romanowski.

10. Despite their differences, Commissioner Bud Selig and MLBPA Executive Director Don Fehr intend to cooperate to rid baseball of illegal drugs. See Hal Bodley, "Baseball Officials Announce Tougher Steroids Policy," at http://www.usatoday. com, cited 27 October 2006; "AP: Players Could Scrap New Drug Policy," at http:// www.mlb.com, cited 9 May 2006; Jason Stark, "MLBPA, Sen. Mitchell at Odds Over Former Player Interviews," at http://www. sportbusinessnews.com, cited 6 June 2006. For other articles about the roles of Selig and Fehr in the investigation of steroids, see Howard Bloom, "Senator Mitchell — There Is No Gas in His Engine I," at http://www. sportsbusinessnews.com, cited 4 December 2006; "Paper Defends Right to Confidentiality," at http://www.si.com, cited 4 December 2006; Howard Bloom, "Senator Mitchell — There Is No Gas in His Engine II," at http:// www.sportsbusinessnews.com, cited 5 December 2006.

11. For details about the 2002–2006 and/ or 2007–2011 BCBAs, see "MLB Owners Unanimously Approve Labor Deal," at http:// www.sportsbusinessnews.com, cited 4 November 2006; Howard Bloom, "Inside the Latest MLB CBA," at http://www.sports businessnews.com, cited 27 October 2006; Barry M. Bloom, "MLB, Union Announce New Labor Deal," at http://www.mlb.com, cited 25 October 2006; "MLB, MLBPA Reach Five-Year Labor Accord," at http:// www.sportsbusinessnews.com, cited 25 October 2006; Doug Pappas, "Summary of the [2002] Collective Bargaining Agreement-Analysis," at http://www.businessofbaseball. com, cited 5 January 2005.

12. Dr. Gary Wadler, an internist on WADA's prohibited list and its methods committee, says MLB should start testing its players for HGH. See Darren Rovell, "Baseball Needs to Wake Up to HGH," at http://www. sportsbusinessnews.com, cited 8 June 2006.

13. The collusion cases involving baseball franchise owners are, in part, discussed in "The 1980s," at http://www.cbaforfans.com, cited 30 October 2006; "The 1990s," at http: //www.cbaforfans.com, cited 30 October 2006; "Players, Owners Settle Collusion Claim," at http://www.si.com, cited 7 November 2006.

14. Two articles that discuss the negative effects of player misbehavior and conduct in MLB are John Moores, "When Push Comes to Shove: Union Hurts Baseball," *Wall Street Journal* (12 July 2005), D8, and Joshua Prager, "Baseball's Dirty Open Secret," *Wall Street Journal* (26 October 2006), D6.

15. Also, former MLB players who had received votes as cheaters in a poll of baseball fans were George Brett (1973–1993), Preacher Roe (1938–1954), Rick Honeycutt (1977– 1997), Don Sutton (1966–1988), and Kevin Gross (1983–1997). See "Biggest Cheaters in Baseball," at http://www.espn.com, cited 6 November 2006.

16. See "The Readers' List: Least Likeable Ballplayers," at http://www.espn.com, cited 10 November 2006, and "Readers: Most Disruptive Players," at http://www.espn.com, cited 10 November 2006.

17. According to the author of the article, other issues that involve players, umpires, games and/or ballparks that need to be addressed by MLB officials are players chewing and spitting tobacco, interminably long-lasting games, the climbing of fences and railings

by players to catch fly balls within ballparks, excessive umpire warnings for pitchers not to throw inside to batters, and short porches in the outfields of ballparks. These problems were discussed in John Donovan, "Negotiate This: Baseball Has Lots of Other Problems That Need Fixing, Too," at http://www.si.com, cited 27 October 2006.

Chapter 5

1. For the economic theories and business strategies of cartels, see Michael R. Baye, *Managerial Economics and Business Strategies,* Fifth Edition (New York: McGraw-Hill Irwin, 2006), and Paul G. Keat and Philip K.Y. Young, *Managerial Economics: Economic Tools for Today's Decision Makers* (Upper Saddle River, NJ: Pearson Prentice Hall, 2006). Three intriguing books about the history, business and operation of MLB, which were authored by sports economists, are Roger G. Noll, ed., *Government and the Sports Business: Studies in the Regulation of Economic Activity* (Washington, D.C.: The Brookings Institution, 1974); James Quirk and Rodney D. Fort, *Pay Dirt: The Business of Professional Team Sports* (Princeton, NJ: Princeton University Press, 1992); Frank P. Jozsa, Jr., *Baseball, Inc.: The National Pastime as Big Business* (Jefferson, NC: McFarland, 2006).

2. More information about MLB teams and their home markets is available in Scott Brazilla, *Checks and Imbalances: Competitive Disparity in Major League Baseball* (Jefferson, NC: McFarland, 2002), and Frank P. Jozsa, Jr. and John J. Guthrie, Jr., *Relocating Teams and Expanding Leagues in Professional Sports: How the Major Leagues Respond to Market Conditions* (Westport, CT: Quorum, 1999).

3. The Oakland baseball franchise and Cisco Company signed a business, marketing and technology agreement whereby the club will "build the world's most technologically sophisticated baseball park in Fremont, California to serve as the home of the A's." For more details about this agreement, see "Cisco and Athletics Announce Cisco Field," at http://www.sportsbusinessnews.com, cited 15 November 2006.

4. There are different methods and statistics that measure how loyal fans are to the brands of sports teams. Some suggested readings about this topic include "The Brand Keys Sports Loyalty Index," at http://www.brandkeys.com, cited 18 September 2006;

"Sports Loyalty Systems (SLS) Launches an Interesting Sports Branding Program," at http://www.sportsbusinessnews.com, cited 29 July 2005, and Sebastian Shapiro, *The Most Valuable Brands in Sports: The 2002 Report* (New York: FutureBrand, 2002).

5. During the 1910s, the Yankees had seven different managers and thus did not consistently win championships until after Babe Ruth joined the team in 1920. Similarly, from 1980 to 1990 inclusive, six managers coached Yankees teams, and during this period, the club won one AL pennant but was defeated in the 1981 World Series by the Los Angeles Dodgers. The performances of MLB franchises for the 1901–2003 regular seasons and postseasons are contained in the *Official Major League Baseball Fact Book 2005 Edition* (St. Louis, MO: The Sporting News, 2005).

6. The new baseball stadium for the Cardinals in St. Louis replaces the original 49,625-seat Busch Stadium, which was built in 1966. For descriptions of all MLB ballparks, see "Ballparks," at http://www.ballparks.com, cited 15 December 2006, and the league's web site "Major League Baseball," at http://www.mlb.com, cited 9 October 2006.

7. Financial information about big league teams is reported in several publications. A few of these sources are Michael K. Ozanian, "Selective Accounting," *Forbes* (14 December 1998), 124–134; "Baseball Payrolls List by Team," at http://sportsillustrated.netscape.cnn.com, cited 6 April 2006; "Forbes Financial 2004 Valuation for MLB Franchise," at http://www.sportsbusinessnews.com, cited 5 October 2004; "MLB Cash Flows," at http://www.baseballguru.com cited 9 November 2004.

Chapter 6

1. For articles about the attendances, revenues, and/or other matters related to the business of MLB and its teams in 2006, see Stefan Fatsis and Peter Keating, "Getting Into the Game," *Wall Street Journal* (16–17 September 2006), R1, R3; "Stealing Bases, Not Jobs," *Wall Street Journal* (20 October 2006), W13; Adam Thompson, "Fox Roots, Roots, Roots for Long Series and Right Teams in Baseball Playoffs," *Wall Street Journal* (25 September 2006), B1, B5; Tim Lemke, "Major League Baseball Enjoys Winning Season," at http://www.sportsbusinessnews.com, cited 24 July 2006; Howard Bloom, "In

2006 — What a Year for MLB and Bud Selig," at http://www.sportsbusinessnews.com, cited 28 December 2006; "Crowd Pleaser: MLB Sets Attendance Record," at http://www.si.com, cited 1 October 2006.

2. Baseball's new collective bargaining agreement is discussed in Mike Bauman, "Baseball Labor Peace in Our Time, Great For the Game," http://www.sportsbusiness-news.com, cited 27 December 2006; Jon Heyman, "Selig Finally Appreciated For His Work as Commissioner," at http://www.si.com, cited 6 January 2007; "MLB, MLBPA Reach Five-Year Labor Accord," at http://www.sportsbusinessnews.com, cited 25 October 2006.

3. MLB teams' prices, costs, and values are topics in Chapter 1. Some readings include "Baseball Ticket Prices Up 5.4 Percent," *Charlotte Observer* (4 April 2006), 2C; "Forbes Financial 2004 Valuation For MLB Franchise," at http://www.sportsbusiness-news.com, cited 5 October 2004; "Average Salary Climbs 9 Percent to Nearly $2.7 Million," at http://www.si.com, cited 21 December 2006.

4. Chapter 2, for the most part, analyzes when and why MLB fans have abandoned the sport. For example, see Terry Armour, "What Happened to the Black Baseball Fans?" *Chicago Tribune* (30 August 2002), 1; Sam Walker, "Strike Averted, Baseball Teams Try to Woo Fans," *Wall Street Journal* (3 September 2002), B1–B2; Peter Barzilai and John Follaco, "What's the Problem with Baseball?" at http://www.usatoday.com, cited 15 September 2006; Don Walker, "Wanted: Younger Fans," at http://www.jsonline.com, cited 25 September 2006.

5. MLB strategies that focus on congested sports markets within the U.S. and/or international expansion were highlighted in Justin Catansos, "Baseball Should Go Where the Money Is." *BusinessWeek* (29 June 1998), 131; Sean McAdam, "Baseball OKs Contraction," *Charlotte Observer* (7 November 2001), 1C, 5C; "Globalization of Baseball," *The Boston Globe* (27 March 1998), F3–F8; Barry M.

Bloom, "MLB Selects D.C. For Expos," at http://www.mlb.com, cited 30 September 2004.

6. There are a variety of readings about prior and current problems in big league baseball. See John Moores, "When Push Comes to Shove: Union Hurts Baseball," *Wall Street Journal* (12 July 2005), D8; Joshua Prager, "Baseball's Dirty Open Secret," *Wall Street Journal* (26 October 2006), D6; Michael L. Walden, "Has Baseball Struck Out? Money, Markets, and Competition," *Carolina Journal* (September 2002), 23; "Biggest Cheaters in Baseball," at http://www.espn.com, cited 6 November 2006; Tim Dahlberg, "Column: Fan Loyalty Stretches Only So Far," at http://www.netscape.com, cited 19 April 2006; John Donovan, "Negotiate This: Baseball Has Lots of Problems That Need Fixing, Too," at http://www.cnnsi.com, cited 27 October 2006; Spencer Fordin, "Orioles Fans Have Had Enough," at http://www.sportsbusinessnews.com, cited 22 September 2006; "Sign of the Times: World Series TV Ratings Plunge Again to Record Low," at http://www.si.com, cited 30 October 2006; Jon Weisman, "Tuning Out: Fans to Pay Price For Declining Postseason Ratings," at http://www.si.com, cited 24 October 2006.

7. The misallocation of franchises and differences in their business and economic power as sports enterprises are reflected in Frank P. Jozsa, Jr., "Major League Players' Salaries and Team Payrolls," in Frank P. Jozsa, Jr., *Baseball, Inc.: The National Pastime as Big Business*, 74–82; Michael K. Ozanian and Lesley Stump, "Steinbrenner's Tax Shelter," *Forbes* (8 May 2006), 60, 64; Paul M. Sommers, "Ticket Prices and Player Salaries in Major League Baseball," *Journal of Recreational Mathematics* (Winter 1994), 274–276; "The Brand Keys Sports Loyalty Index," at http://www.brandkeys.com, cited 18 September 2006; "MLB Cash Flows," at http://www.baseballguru.com, cited 9 November 2004; "Yankees Luxury Tax — Their Bill Comes Due," at http://www.sportsbusinessnews.com, cited 23 December 2006.

BIBLIOGRAPHY

Articles

Adams, Russell. "Baseball-Playoff Seats Get Harder to Score." *Wall Street Journal* (27 September 2006): D1, D3.
_____. "Here Come the Technocrats." *Wall Street Journal* (16–17 September 2006): R7.
_____. "The New Price of Loyalty." *Wall Street Journal* (4–5 March 2006): P1, P3.
_____. "So Long to the Suite Life." *Wall Street Journal* (17 February 2007): P1, P4.
"Americans to Rest of World: Soccer Not Really Our Thing." *Pew Research Center* (14 June 2006): 1–10.
Armour, Terry. "What Happened to the Black Baseball Fans?" *Chicago Tribune* (30 August 2002): 1.
Baade, R., and R. Dye. "The Impact of Stadiums and Professional Sports on Metropolitan Area Development." In *Growth and Change* (1990): 1–14.
"Baseball Needs a Firm Hand." *BusinessWeek* (26 May 1997): 182.
"Baseball Ticket Prices Up 5.4 Percent." *Charlotte Observer* (4 April 2006): 2C.
"Baseball Wants Blacks Back." *Toronto Star* (14 July 2004): C4.
"Baseball's Pitch for Diversity: America's Game Is Scoring with Minority Vendors." *Ebony* (July 2004): 118–120.
Begley, Sharon. "A New Study Shows How Baseball Myths Can Hurt the Game." *Wall Street Journal* (16 February 2007): B1.
Blum, Ronald. "Cash Flow: Baseball Wants Some." *The Daily News* (15 July 2000): 1C, 3C.
Catansos, Justin. "Baseball Should Go Where the Money Is." *BusinessWeek* (29 June 1998): 131.
Chass, Murray. "What if We Had a Permanent Commissioner?" *New York Times* (12 February 2005): 86.
"Cheating Not Limited to Putting Cork in Bat." *USA Today* (5 June 2003): 3C.
Connors, Philip. "Baseball: Agony and Ecstasy in Minnesota." *Wall Street Journal* (23 July 2001): A13.
Dumcius, Gintautas. "Lawmakers Push Bill Imposing Steroid Sanctions." *Wall Street Journal* (24 May 2005): D4.
Fatsis, Stefan, and Peter Keating. "Getting Into the Game." *Wall Street Journal* (16–17 September 2006): R1, R3.

"Globalization of Baseball." *The Boston Globe* (27 March 1998): F3–F8.

"House Act Aimed at Contraction." *Charlotte Observer* (15 November 2001): 5C.

Hyman, Mark. "The Racial Gap in the Grandstands." *BusinessWeek* (2 October 2006): 78–79.

_____. "Steroid Scandal? Pass the Peanuts." *BusinessWeek* (20 December 2004): 44.

Jozsa, Frank P., Jr. "Major League Players' Salaries and Team Payrolls." In Frank P. Jozsa, Jr. *Baseball, Inc.: The National Pastime as Big Business*, 74–82.

Keown, Tim. "Changing the Culture." *Wall Street Journal* (16–17 September 2006): R7.

Kornheiser, Tony. "Baseball's Union Wields a Big Bat." *The Washington Post* (3 March 2004): D1.

Kuenster, John. "Fans Offer Six Ways to Improve Game at the Major League Level." *Baseball Digest* (December 2004): 17–19.

Lamme, Jacob F. "The Twelve Year Rain Delay: Why a Change in Leadership Will Benefit the Game of Baseball." *Albany Law Review* (Fall 2004): 155–182.

Lowry, Tom, et. al. "For the Love of the Game — and Cheap Seats." *BusinessWeek* (28 May 2001): 46–47.

Martin, Justin. "Can Baseball Make It in Mexico?" *Fortune* (30 September 1996): 32–33.

McAdam, Sean. "Baseball OKs Contraction." *Charlotte Observer* (7 November 2001): 1C, 5C.

McGraw, D. "Playing the Stadium Game." *U.S. News & World Report* (3 June 1996): 46.

"Metropolitan Areas, 1990–2000." *The World Almanac and Book of Facts 2004* (New York: World Almanac Books, 2004): 375.

Moores, John. "When Push Comes to Shove: Union Hurts Baseball." *Wall Street Journal* (12 July 2005): D8.

Morell, John. "How Much for Tickets? You Need a Scorecard." *New York Times* (8 June 2003): 3–4.

O'Connell, Vanessa. "Baseball Strike Might Shut Out Teams with Soft Brand Status." *Wall Street Journal* (23 August 2002): A11.

"100 Most Populous Cities." *The World Almanac and Book of Facts 2004* (New York: World Almanac Books, 2004): 327–336.

Ozanian, Michael K. "Selective Accounting." *Forbes* (14 December 1998): 124–134.

Ozanian, Michael K., and Kurt Badenhausen. "Baseball Going Broke? Don't Believe It." *Wall Street Journal* (27 July 2000): A22.

Ozanian, Michael K., and Lesley Kump. "Steinbrenner's Tax Shelter." *Forbes* (8 May 2006): 60, 64.

Prager, Joshua. "Baseball's Dirty Open Secret." *Wall Street Journal* (26 October 2006): D6.

"Record-Breaking Major League Baseball Remains Timeless." *MediaWeek* (18 October 2004): S3.

Seglin, Jeffrey L. "Who Has the Right to Playoff Tickets?" *Charlotte Observer* (8 October 2006): 3D.

Sommers, Paul M. "Ticket Prices and Player Salaries in Major League Baseball." *Journal of Recreational Mathematics* (Winter 1994): 274–276.

"Sports Work Stoppages." *Charlotte Observer* (25 October 1998): 6H.

"Stealing Bases, Not Jobs." *Wall Street Journal* (20 October 2006): W13.

Steinberg, Brian, and Suzanne Vranica. "Sticking with the National Pastime." *Wall Street Journal* (30 March 2005): B3.

Steinbreder, John. "The Owners." *Sports Illustrated* (13 September 1993): 64–87.

St. John, Allen. "Praising Pitcher's Parks." *Wall Street Journal* (13 October 2006): W4.

Thompson, Adam. "Fox Roots, Roots, Roots for Long Series and Right Teams in Baseball Playoffs." *Wall Street Journal* (25 September 2006): B1, B5.

_____. "Is Baseball Drugs Ruling a Fourth-Amendment Foul?" *Wall Street Journal* (16 January 2007): B1, B2.

Thomaselli, Rich. "Baseball Tries Makeover." *Advertising Age* (3 February 2003): 3–4.

Thurow, Roger. "Thrown for a Curve: On the Field, Baseball Is Integrated, for Fans It's a Different Story." *Wall Street Journal* (28 August 1998): A1.

Walden, Michael L. "Has Baseball Struck Out? Money, Markets, and Competition." *Carolina Journal* (September 2002): 23.

Walker, Sam. "Strike Averted, Baseball Teams Try to Woo Fans." *Wall Street Journal* (3 September 2002): B1–B2.

Weinbach, Jon. "When Players Don't Pay." *Wall Street Journal* (17 June 2005): W1, W8.

"The Wide World of Baseball: Foreign-Born Players Are Filling Major League Rosters." *Baseball Digest* (February 2003): 30–39.

Will, George. "Baseball Thrives Despite Intense, Unjust Criticism." *Charlotte Observer* (3 April 2005): 3P.

Wingfield, Kyle. "'Roid Outrage: '80s Stars Got Muscled Out of Cooperstown." *Wall Street Journal* (17 January 2006): D8.

Zimbalist, Andrew. "Why 'Yer Out!' Is a Bad Call for Baseball." *BusinessWeek* (12 November 2001): 120.

Books

Aaseng, N. *The Locker Room Mirror: How Sports Reflect Society*. New York: Walker & Company, 1993.

Barzilla, Scott. *Checks and Imbalances: Competitive Disparity in Major League Baseball*. Jefferson, NC: McFarland, 2002.

_____. *The State of Baseball Management: Decision-Making in the Best and Worst Teams, 1993–2003*. Jefferson, NC: McFarland, 2004.

Baye, Michael R. *Managerial Economics and Business Strategy*. Fifth Edition. New York: McGraw-Hill Irwin, 2006.

Bradbury, J.C. *The Baseball Economist: The Real Game Exposed*. New York: Dutton Adult, 2007.

Burk, Robert F. *Much More Than a Game: Players, Owners, and American Baseball Since 1921*. Chapel Hill: University of North Carolina Press, 2001.

Cagan, J., and N. deMause. *Field of Schemes*. Monroe, ME: Common Courage Press, 1998.

Callahan, D. *The Cheating Culture: Why More Americans Are Doing Wrong to Get Ahead*. New York: Harcourt, 2004.

Carino, Peter, ed. *Baseball/Literature/Culture: Essays, 1995–2001*. Jefferson, NC: McFarland, 2003.

Coakley, J. *Sport in Society: Issues and Controversies*. Boston, MA: Irwin-McGraw-Hill, 1998.

Costas, Bob. *Fair Ball: A Fan's Case for Baseball*. New York: Broadway Books, 2001.

Cull, Robert J. *Rumors of Baseball's Demise: How the Balance of Competition Swung and the Critics Missed*. Jefferson, NC: McFarland, 2006.

Delaney, K., and R. Eckstein. *Public Dollars, Private Stadiums*. New Brunswick, NJ: Rutgers University Press, 2003.

Fainaru-Wada, Mark, and Lance Williams. *Game of Shadows: Barry Bonds, BALCO, and the Steroids Scandal That Rocked Professional Sports*. New York: Gotham Books, 2006.

Finley, Peter, and Laura Finley. *The Sports Industry's War on Athletes*. Westport, CT: Praeger, 2006.

Helyar, John. *Lords of the Realm: The Real History of Baseball*. New York: Ballantine, 1994.

James, Bill. *The New Bill James Historical Baseball Abstract*. New York: Free Press, 2003.

Jennings, Kenneth M. *Balls and Strikes: The Money Game in Professional Baseball*. Westport, CT: Praeger, 1990.

Jozsa, Frank P., Jr. *American Sports Empire: How the Leagues Breed Success*. Westport, CT: Praeger, 2003.

_____. *Baseball, Inc.: The National Pastime as Big Business.* Jefferson, NC: McFarland, 2006.

_____. *Big Sports, Big Business: A Century of Expansions, Mergers, and Reorganizations.* Westport, CT: Praeger, 2006.

_____. *Sports Capitalism: The Foreign Business of American Professional Leagues.* Aldershot, England: Ashgate, 2004.

Jozsa, Frank P., Jr., and John J. Guthrie, Jr. *Relocating Teams and Expanding Leagues in Professional Sports: How the Major Leagues Respond to Market Conditions.* Westport, CT: Quorum, 1999.

Keat, Paul G., and Philip K.Y. Young. *Managerial Economics: Economic Tools for Today's Decision Makers.* Fifth Edition. Upper Saddle River, NJ: Pearson Prentice Hall, 2006.

Keri, Jonah, and James Click. *Baseball Between the Numbers.* New York: Basic Books, 2006.

Kun, Michael, and Howard Bloom. *The Baseball Uncyclopedia: A Highly Opinionated, Myth-Busting Guide to the Great American Game.* Cincinnati, OH: Emmis Books, 2006.

Lenehan, P. *Anabolic Steroids and Other Performance-Enhancing Drugs.* London: Taylor & Francis, 2003.

Lewis, Michael. *Moneyball: The Art of Winning an Unfair Game.* New York: Random House, 2003.

Marburger, Daniel R., ed. *Stee-Rike Four! What's Wrong with the Business of Baseball?* Westport, CT: Praeger, 1997.

McCarver, Tim, and Danny Peary. *Tim McCarver's Baseball for Brain Surgeons and Other Fans: Understanding and Interpreting the Game So You Can Watch It Like a Pro.* New York: Villard, 1999.

Miller, Marvin. *A Whole Different Ballgame: The Sport and Business of Baseball.* New York: Birch Lane, 1991.

Noll, Roger G., ed. *Government and the Sports Business: Studies in the Regulation of Economic Activity.* Washington, D.C.: The Brookings Institution, 1974.

Noll, Roger G., and Andrew Zimbalist, eds. *Sports, Jobs and Taxes: The Economic Impact of Sports Teams and Stadiums.* Washington, D.C.: The Brookings Institution, 1997.

Perrin, D. *American Fan.* New York: Avon, 2000.

Powers, Albert Theodore. *The Business of Baseball.* Jefferson, NC: McFarland, 2003.

Putnam, D. *Controversies in the Sports World.* Westport, CT: Greenwood, 1999.

Quirk, James, and Rodney D. Fort. *Pay Dirt: The Business of Professional Team Sports.* Princeton, NJ: Princeton University Press, 1992.

Reston, James. *Collision at Home Plate: The Lives of Pete Rose and Bart Giamatti.* Lincoln, NE: Bison Books, 1997.

Rose, Pete, and Rick Hill. *My Prison Without Bars.* New York: Rodale Books, 2004.

Rosentraub, Mark S. *Major League Losers: The Real Costs of Sports and Who's Paying for It.* New York: Basic Books, 1997.

Sands, Jack, and Peter Gammons. *Coming Apart at the Seams: How Baseball Owners, Players, and Television Executives Have Led Our National Pastime to the Brink of Disaster.* New York: Macmillan Publishing Company, 1993.

Schaaf, Phil. *Sports, Inc.: 100 Years of Sports Business.* Amherst, NY: Prometheus, 2004.

Schwarz, Alan, and Peter Gammons. *The Numbers Game: Baseball's Lifelong Fascination with Statistics.* New York: St. Martin's Griffin, 2004.

Scully, Gerald W. *The Business of Major League Baseball.* Chicago: University of Chicago Press, 1989.

Shropshire, Kenneth L. *The Sports Franchise Game: Cities in Pursuit of Sports Franchises, Events, Stadiums, and Arenas.* Philadelphia: University of Pennsylvania Press, 1995.

Simon, R. *Fair Play: The Ethics of Sport.* Boulder, CO: Westview, 2004.

Sokolove, Michael. *Hustle: The Myth, Life, and Lies of Pete Rose.* New York: Simon and Schuster, 2005.

Sommers, Paul M., ed. *Diamonds Are Forever: The Business of Baseball.* Washington, D.C.: The Brookings Institution, 1992.

Staudohar, Paul D., and James A. Mangan, eds. *The Business of Professional Sports.* Champaign: University of Illinois Press, 1991.

Szymanski, Stefan, and Andrew Zimbalist. *National Pastime.* Washington, D.C.: The Brookings Institution, 2005.

Voight, David Q. *American Baseball: From Gentlemen's Sport to the Commissioner System.* Norman: University of Oklahoma Press, 1966.

Weiner, J. *Stadium Games.* Minneapolis: University of Minnesota Press, 2000.

Weiss, Ann E. *Money Games: The Business of Sports.* Boston: Houghton Mifflin, 1993.

Will, George F. *Bunts: Curt Flood, Camden Yards, Pete Rose and Other Reflections on Baseball.* New York: Scribner, 1999.

Winfield, Dave. *Dropping the Ball: Baseball's Troubles and How We Can and Must Solve Them.* New York: Basic Books, 2007.

The World Almanac and Book of Facts. New York: World Almanac Books, 1950–2005.

Zimbalist, Andrew. *Baseball and Billions: A Probing Look Inside the Big Business of Our National Pastime.* New York: Basic Books, 1992.

_____. *In the Best Interests of Baseball? The Revolutionary Reign of Bud Selig.* Hoboken, NJ: Wiley, 2006.

_____. *May the Best Team Win: Baseball Economics and Public Policy.* Washington, D.C.: The Brookings Institution, 2003.

Dissertations

Corzine, Nathan M. "American Game, American Mirror: Baseball, Beer, the Media and American Culture, 1933–1945." M.A. diss., University of Missouri-Columbia, 2004.

Jozsa, Frank P., Jr. "An Economic Analysis of Franchise Relocation and League Expansion in Professional Team Sports, 1950–1975." Ph.D. diss., Georgia State University, 1977.

Snyder, Todd Keith. "The Unaccountability of Organized Baseball: A Sport Turned Business." B.A. diss., Tulane University, 1980.

Government Publications

"Statistics Canada, Canada's National Statistics Agency." http://www.statcan.ca cited 23 January 2007.

Internet Sources

"AP: Players Could Scrap New Drug Policy." http://www.mlb.com, cited 9 May 2006.

"Attendance." http://www.baseball-statistics.com, cited 18 September 2006.

"Average Salary Climbs 9 Percent to Nearly $2.7 Million." http://www.si.com, cited 21 December 2006.

"Ballparks." http://www.ballparks.com, cited 15 December 2006.

Barzilai, Peter, and John Follaco. "What's the Problem with Baseball?" http://www.usatoday.com, cited 15 September 2006.

"The Baseball Archive." http://www.baseball1.com, cited 30 December 2004.

"Baseball Payrolls List by Team." http://sportsillustrated.netscape.cnn.com, cited 6 April 2006.

"The Battle of the Sexes — Fifty Million Women Avidly Follow Professional Sports." http://www.arbitron.com, cited 24 September 2006.

Bauman, Mike. "A Great Year for the Grand Old Game." http://www.mlb.com, cited 27 December 2005.

_____. "Baseball Labor Peace in Our Time, Great for the Game." http://www.sportsbusiness news.com, cited 27 December 2006.

"Behavior Modification.Glavine: Amphetamine Testing Changing Culture." http://www.si. com, cited 29 September 2006.

"Biggest Cheaters in Baseball." http://www.espn.com, cited 6 November 2006.

Bloom, Barry M. "Diversity in Baseball Remains Priority." http://www.mlb.com, cited 2 February 2007.

_____. "Mitchell Asks Owners For Cooperation." http://www.sportsbusinessnews.com, cited 19 January 2007.

_____. "MLB Owners Approve Latest National TV Agreements." http://www.sportsbusi nessnews.com, cited 17 November 2006.

_____. "MLB Owners Unanimously Approve Labor Deal." http://www.sportsbusiness news.com, cited 4 November 2006.

_____. "MLB Selects D.C. for Expos." http://www.mlb.com, cited 30 September 2004.

_____. "MLB, Union Announce New Labor Deal." http://www.mlb.com, cited 25 October 2006.

_____. "No Penalty Changes to CBA Expected." http://www.mlb.com, cited 18 January 2007.

_____. "Selig Shares Thoughts on Bonds." http://www.sportsbusinessnews.com, cited 9 February 2007.

Bloom, Howard. "Baltimore Orioles Fans — When Not Enough Is Too Much." http://www. sportsbusinessnews.com, cited 26 September 2006.

_____. "Bud Selig, Good or Bad for Major League Baseball?" http://www.sportsbusiness news.com, cited 9 April 2007.

_____. "From the Top to the Bottom: The MLB Outhouse Franchises." http://www.sports businessnews.com, cited 25 April 2007.

_____. "Glory Days — the Yankees Are Losing Bucks." http://www.sportsbusinessnews.com, cited 24 August 2006.

_____. "The Good News a New MLB Labor Accord." http://www.sportsbusinessnews.com, cited 24 October 2006.

_____. "In 2006 — What a Year for MLB and Bud Selig." http://www.sportsbusinessnews. com, cited 28 December 2006.

_____. "Inside the Latest MLB CBA." http://www.sportsbusinessnews.com, cited 27 October 2006.

_____. "Jeffrey Loria — the Major League Baseball Franchise Killer!!" http://www.sportsbusi nessnews.com, cited 15 August 2006.

_____. "Major League Baseball — 2006 Attendance Trends." http://www.sportsbusinessnews. com, cited 2 October 2006.

_____. "Major League Baseball 2007 — the Haves vs. the Have Nots." http://www.sportsbusi nessnews.com, cited 14 December 2006.

_____. "Miami Ballpark Deal Progressing." http://www.mlb.com, cited 7 January 2007.

_____. "The New York Yankees — as Evil an Empire as Ever." http://www.sportsbusiness news.com, cited 30 September 2006.

_____. "Senator Mitchell — There Is No Gas in His Engine I." http://www.sportsbusiness. news.com, cited 4 December 2006.

_____. "Senator Mitchell — There Is No Gas in His Engine II." http://www.sportsbusiness news.com, cited 5 December 2006.

_____. "Time to Have Barry Bonds Back (Again)." http://www.sportsbusinessnews.com, cited 19 January 2007.

_____. "The Yankees Lose and So Do Their Fans." http://www.sportsbusinessnews.com, cited 6 October 2006.

Bodley, Hal. "Baseball Facing Big-League Debt." http://www.usatoday.com, cited 24 March 2005.

_____. "Baseball Officials Announce Tougher Steroids Policy." http://www.usatoday.com cited 27 October 2006.

Bowman, Mark. "Liberty Media Buys the Braves." http://www.sportsbusinessnews.com, cited 13 February 2007.

"The Boys of Summer." http://www.forbes.com, cited 9 November 2004.

"The Brand Keys Sports Loyalty Index." http://www.brandkeys.com, cited 18 September 2006.

"Brandweek Customer Loyalty Awards Powered by Brand Keys." http://www.brandkeys.com, cited 16 January 2007.

Chass, Murray. "Baseball in D.C., They Have a Name But No Money." http://www.sports businessnews.com, cited 30 November 2004.

"Cisco and Athletics Announce Cisco Field." http://www.sportsbusinessnews.com, cited 15 November 2006.

"City and Area Population." http://www.world-gazetteer.com, cited 17 October 2006.

"Club Co-Owner Expands Search for New Stadium Site." http://www.si.com, cited 16 January 2007.

"Computer-Imaging Firm Says '98 Balls Were Juiced." http://www.si.com, cited 4 January 2007.

"Court: Feds Entitled to Testing Data." http://www.mlb.com, cited 28 December 2006.

Crasnick, Jerry. "Is MLB Held to a Higher Standard?" http://www.sportsbusinessnews.com, cited 7 August 2006.

_____. "It Really Does 'Suck' to Be a Baltimore Orioles Fan These Days." http://www.sports businessnews.com, cited 21 September 2006.

"Crowd Pleaser: MLB Sets Attendance Record." http://www.si.com, cited 1 October 2006.

Dahlberg, Tim. "Column: Fan Loyalty Stretches Only So Far." http://www.netscape.com, cited 19 April 2006.

Davidoff, Ken. "BALCO — Sheffield Tells SI He Took Steroids." http://www.sportsbusiness news.com, cited 8 October 2004.

"Decline Is First Since 1965." http://www.sports.espn.go.com, cited 5 January 2005.

"Dodgers Opening All-Your-Can-Eat Right Field Pavilion." http://www.si.com, cited 12 January 2007.

Donovan, John. "Globalization of the Grand Old Game Hits All-Time High." http://www.cnnsi.com, cited 17 July 2003.

_____. "MLB Considers Making Coors Field Cooler Mandatory." http://www.cnnsi.com, cited 15 February 2007.

_____. Negotiate This: Baseball Has Lots of Problems That Need Fixing, Too." http://www.cnnsi.com, cited 27 October 2006.

Doyle, Paul, and Matt Egan. "In Hartford, a Look at the Challenges Youth Baseball Is Facing." http://www.sportsbusinessnews.com, cited 17 September 2006.

_____. "The Diamond Doesn't Cut It for African American Kids Anymore." http://www.sportsbusinessnews.com, cited 17 September 2006.

"Economic Block: Baseball Panel Urges Increase in Revenue Sharing." http://www.cnnsi.com, cited 1 December 2002.

"Fading Images: Bonds, Giambi, Sosa Tumble in Marketability Survey." http://www.cnnsi.com, cited 5 April 2005.

Falkoff, Robert. "Baseball Witnessing Field Leveling." http://www.mlb.com, cited 30 January 2006.

"Fans Conflicted About Bonds." http://www.usatoday.com, cited 14 March 2006.

"Feds Close to Getting Proof of Steroid Use in Baseball." http://www.si.com, cited 30 December 2006.

"Fitch Upgrades $1.3B Major League Baseball Trust Securitization to 'A' from 'A-.'" http://www.sportsbusinessnews.com, cited 13 December 2006.

"Forbes Financial 2004 Valuation For MLB Franchise." http://www.sportsbusinessnews.com, cited 5 October 2004.

Fordin, Spencer. "Orioles Fans Have Had Enough." http://www.sportsbusinessnews.com, cited 22 September 2006.

Forrester, Paul. "Fan Value Index 2006: Readers Rate Which Parks Offer Best Value, Experience." http://www.si.com, cited 23 September 2006.

Frisro, Joe. "Marlins Inspired by FanFest Turnout." http://www.sportsbusinessnews.com, cited 12 February 2007.

_____. "Marlins Meet with Las Vegas Mayor." http://www.mlb.com, cited 10 December 2004.

"Game 5 Finishes 12th in TV Ratings." http://www.cnnsi.com, cited 2 November 2006.

"Game of Shadows." http://en.wikipedia.org, cited 27 October 2006.

Gillette, Gary. "MLB Not as Popular as It Once Was." http://www.sportsbusinessnews.com, cited 6 August 2006.

Golen, Jimmy. "Goodman Tries to Lure Baseball to Vegas." http://channels.netscape.com, cited 15 December 2004.

"A Great Year For the Grand Old Game." http://www.mlb.com, cited 27 December 2005.

Harrow, Rick. "Biz of Baseball Pretty Good Right Now." http://www.sportsbusinessnews.com, cited 18 October 2005.

_____. "Overall Good Times for the Biz of Baseball at the LCS." http://www.sportsbusinessnews.com, cited 15 October 2006.

"Hearing on First Drugs Grievance Begins." http://sportsillustrated.netscape.cnn.com, cited 18 June 2005.

Heller, Dick. "The Birth of the American League Led to Modern Baseball." http://www.sportsbusinessnews.com, cited 24 November 2006.

Heyman, Jon. "Selig Finally Appreciated for His Work as Commissioner." http://www.si.com, cited 6 January 2007.

Hoch, Bryan. "Yanks Partner with Chinese Baseball." http://www.mlb.com, cited 30 January 2007.

Howard, Johnette. "Well Worth Nothing — Small Market MLB Owners Are Angry." http://sportsbusinessnews.com, cited 4 February 2005.

"Is the 2006 World Series All About Parity?" http://www.sportsbusinessnews.com, cited 24 October 2006.

Isidore, Chris. "Baseball Ticket Prices: Supply, Not Millionaires." http://cnnmoney.com, cited 15 April 2006.

_____. "In Search of an Athlete to Market." http://www.sportsbusinessnews.com, cited 12 July 2005.

"Juicy Controversy." http://www.si.com, cited 26 December 2005.

"Lapchick Study — Racial and Gender Report for Major League Baseball." http://www.sportsbusinessnews.com, cited 21 April 2006.

Lemke, Tim. "Major League Baseball Enjoys Winning Season." http://www.sportsbusinessnews.com, cited 24 July 2006.

"List of Major League Baseball Figures That Have Been Banned for Life." http://www.answers.com, cited 30 October 2006.

"List of Major League Baseball Players Suspended for Performance-Enhancing Drugs." http://en.wikipedia.org, cited 27 October 2006.

Lopresti, Mike. "Has MLB Recovered from Its 1994 Strike?" http://www.sportsbusinessnews.com, cited 5 October 2004.

"Major League Baseball." http://www.teammarketing.com cited 10 September 2006.
_____. http://www.mlb.com, cited 9 October 2006.
"Major League Baseball Properties Selects Scarborough Sports Marketing for Consumer and Fan Research Services." http://www.arbitron.com, cited 24 September 2006.
"Major League Baseball Scandals." http://en.wikipedia.org, cited 30 October 2006.
"Major League Baseball's Record Attendance Reaches Nearly 75 Million." http://www.sportsbusinessnews.com, cited 4 October 2005.
"Major League Soccer." http://www.mls.com, cited 9 October 2006.
Marlin, Brooks. "Major League Baseball's 'Permanently Ineligible' List (Thing)." http://everything2.com, cited 30 October 2006.
McCauley, Janie. "Bonds Finally Signs Contract with Giants." http://www.usatoday.com, cited 15 February 2007.
"Metropolitan Areas." http://www.census.gov, cited 9 October 2006.
"Miscommunication? Language Problems Complicate Drug Policy for Latins." http://www.cnnsi.com, cited 11 May 2005.
"Mitchell Says Probe Has Been Delayed by Lack of Power." http://www.si.com, cited 2 December 2006.
"MLB and Steroids — This Could Get Very Interesting." http://www.sportsbusinessnews.com, cited 28 December 2006.
"MLB Attendance Report." http://www.sports.espn.go.com, cited 3 October 2006.
"MLB Attendance Report: 2004." http://sports.espn.go.com, cited 19 September 2006.
"MLB Attendance Report: 2005." http://sports.espn.go.com, cited 19 September 2006.
"MLB Attendance Report: 2006." http://sports.espn.go.com, cited 3 October 2006.
"MLB Cash Flows." http://www.baseballguru.com, cited 9 November 2004.
"MLB, MLBPA Reach Five-Year Labor Accord." http://www.sportsbusinessnews.com, cited 25 October 2006.
"MLB Owners Unanimously Approve Labor Deal." http://www.sportsbusinessnews.com, cited 4 November 2006.
"MLB Steroids Rules Trip Up Latin Americans." http://www.cnnsi.netscape.com, cited 6 May 2005.
"MLB Teams: 2005 Valuations." http://www.forbes.com, cited 12 September 2006.
"MLB Ticket Prices Going Up for 2006." http://www.sportsbusinessnews.com, cited 4 April 2006.
"MLB Wants China to Host Games." http://www.cnnsi.com, cited 2 November 2006.
Morgan, Jon. "Baseball in D.C., Camden Yards May Cost More." http://www.sportsbusinessnews.com, cited 29 September 2004.
"National Basketball Association." http://www.teammarketing.com, cited 10 September 2006.
_____. http://www.nba.com, cited 9 October 2006.
"National Football League." http://www.teammarketing.com, cited 10 September 2006.
_____. http://www.nfl.com, cited 9 October 2006.
"National Hockey League." http://www.teammarketing.com, cited 10 September 2006.
_____. http://www.nhl.com, cited 9 October 2006.
"National Survey Ranks Baseball Fans." http://forums.nyyfans.com, cited 24 September 2006.
"The 1980s." http://www.cbaforfans.com, cited 30 October 2006
"The 1990s." http://www.cbaforfans.com, cited 30 October 2006.
"1998 Team Payrolls." http://www.usatoday.com, cited 19 May 1999.
O'Connell, Jack. "Selig Receives Business Honor." http://www.mlb.com, cited 22 December 2006.
O'Connor, Ian. "Baseball Fuels Disparity." http://www.usatoday.com, cited 5 January 2005.
"An Open Letter to Baseball Fans from Commissioner Allan H. (Bud) Selig." http://www.mlb.com, cited 19 September 2006.

"Owners Approve New TV Contracts." http://www.si.com, cited 17 November 2006.

"Owners Content with Amphetamines Penalties." http://www.si.com, cited 18 January 2007.

"Paper Defends Right to Confidentiality." http://www.si.com, cited 4 December 2006.

Pappas, Doug. "Summary of the [2002] Collective Bargaining Agreement-Analysis." http://www.businessofbaseball.com, cited 5 January 2005.

Passan, Jeff. "Playing Connect the Dollars." http://www.sportsbusinessnews.com, cited 21 December 2006.

"Payroll Comparison." http://si.printthis.clickability.com, cited 2 January 2005.

"Payrolls for Every MLB Team." http://www.augustasports.com, cited 6 September 2001.

"Peaceful Coexistence: Players, Owners Reach Tentative Five-Year Labor Deal." http://www.si.com, cited 24 October 2006.

"Personal Income and Per Capita Personal Income by Metropolitan Area, 2003–2005." http://www.bea.gov, cited 9 October 2006.

"Players, Owners Settle Collusion Claim." http://www.si.com, cited 7 November 2006.

"Poll: MLB Too Soft on Steroids." http://www.si.com, cited 25 April 2006.

Porretto, John. "Baseball Commissioner Sees More Parity." http://www.cnnsi.netscape.com, cited 12 April 2005.

"The Principal Agglomerations of the World." http://www.citypopulation.de, cited 17 October 2006.

"Professional Football Continues to Be the Nation's Favorite Sport." http://www.sportsbusinessnews.com, cited 1 January 2006.

"Professional Football Leads Baseball by 2-to-1 as Nation's Favorite Sport." http://www.sportsbusinessnews.com, cited 15 October 2004.

"Proof That Baseball Fans Could Care Less if the Players Are Juiced." http://www.sportsbusinessnews.com, cited 20 October 2006.

"Readers: Dirtiest Pro Players." http://www.espn.com, cited 10 November 2006.

"Readers: Most Disruptive Players." http://www.espn.com, cited 10 November 2006.

"The Readers' List: Least Likable Ballplayers." http://www.espn.com, cited 10 November 2006.

"Report: Bonds Failed Amphetamine Test." http://www.mlb.com, cited 12 January 2007.

"Report: Giambi Used Steroids." http://www.mlb.com cited 7 December 2004.

"Revenue Sharing (by the Numbers)." http://www.sportsbusinessnews.com, cited 5 October 2004.

"Revenue-Sharing System Bothers Bosox Owner." http://www.netscape.sports.com, cited 16 February 2006.

Rosenthal, Ken. "Baseball's Problems Can Be Solved — Baseball/Insider." http://www.sportingnews.com, cited 15 September 2006.

_____. "Can Money Really Buy Happiness in Baseball?" http://www.sportsbusinessnews.com, cited 15 October 2004.

Rovell, Darren. "Baseball Needs to Wake Up to HGH." http://www.sportsbusinessnews.com, cited 8 June 2006.

Rutter, Joe. "Wow, the Pirates Sure Are Making a Lot of Money." http://www.sportsbusinessnews.com, cited 19 June 2006.

Seepersaud, Steve. "Cheapest Owners in Sports." http://www.askmen.com, cited 3 March 2006.

"Selig: No Changes to the Record Book." http://www.si.com, cited 14 March 2005.

"Selig Plans to Retire When Contract Ends in 2009." http://www.si.com, cited 1 December 2006.

Shea, John, Henry Schulman, and Susan Slusser. "Integrity for Baseball in Question." http://www.sportsbusinessnews.com, cited 19 October 2004.

"Sign of the Times: World Series TV Ratings Plunge Again to Record Low." http://www.si.com, cited 30 October 2006.

"Sports Loyalty Index." http://www.brandkeys.com, cited 17 September 2006.

"Sports Loyalty Systems (SLS) Launches an Interesting Sports Branding Program." http://www.sportsbusinessnews.com, cited 29 July 2005.

Stark, Jason. "MLBPA, Sen. Mitchell at Odds Over Former Player Interviews." http://www.sportsbusinessnews.com, cited 6 June 2006.

"Steroids in Baseball." http://www.answers.com, cited 30 October 2006.

Street, Jim. "Salary Arbitration Still Performs Key Role." http://www.sportsbusinessnews.com, cited 17 January 2007.

"Table Containing History of CPI-U U.S." at http://www.bls.gov, cited 11 September 2006.

"Teams." http://www.mlb.com, cited 27 September 2006.

"Teams History." http://www.mlb.com, cited 17 January 2007.

"Three Clubs Set Example with Private Ballpark Funding." http://www.si.com, cited 15 November 2006.

"Toronto's Economic Profile." http://www.toronto.ca, cited 23 January 2007.

"Tuning Out: Fans to Pay Price for Declining Postseason Ratings," at http://www.si.com, cited 24 October 2006.

"29.2 Percent of Major League Baseball Players Born Outside the United States." http://www.mlb.com, cited 12 April 2005.

"2001 Team-by-Team Revenues and Expenses Forecast." http://www.usatoday.com, cited 24 January 2007.

"2005 Baseball Final Payrolls, List." http://sportsillustrated.netscape.cnn.com, cited 7 January 2006.

"2006 Salaries." http://www.sportsline.com, cited 23 January 2007.

"2006–2007 Local Television Households: Local Market Universe Estimates." http://www.nielsenmedia.com, cited 9 October 2006.

"Union Moves to Overturn Steroid Ruling." http://www.mlb.com, cited 13 February 2007.

Verducci, Tom. "Blackout: The African-American Baseball Player Is Vanishing. Does He Have a Future?" http://www.cnnsi.com, cited 17 July 2003.

Voorhis, Scott Van. "Are the Red Sox Paying the Tigers to Win — the Cost of Revenue Sharing." http://www.sportsbusinessnews.com, cited 17 August 2006.

Waldman, Ed. "Baseball in D.C., Mr. Angelos Goes to Visit Mr. Selig." http://www.sportsbusinessnews.com, cited 8 October 2004.

Walker, Ben. "Poll: Half of Fans Rooting Against Bonds." http://www.capecodonline.com, cited 21 October 2006.

Walker, Don. "Wanted: Younger Fans." http://www.jsonline.com, cited 25 September 2006.

Walker, Don, and Drew Olson. "Roids in MLB — Bud 'Shout–Out' to MLBPA." http://www.sportsbusinessnews.com, cited 9 December 2004.

Weisman, Jon. "Tuning Out: Fans to Pay Price for Declining Postseason Ratings." http://www.si.com cited, 24 October 2006.

Wentworth, Bridget. "$7,500 for Five Minutes with Barry Bonds — Think They Cared About Roids." http://www.sportsbusinessnews.com, cited 13 December 2004.

"What Else Is On? Series Ratings Low for Opener, Rebound for Game 2." http://www.si.com, cited 24 October 2006.

"What Was the GDP Then?" http://www.en.net, cited 11 September 2006.

"Who Wants to Be a Millionaire?" http://www.cnnsi.com, cited 5 April 2001.

"Yankees Ask to Play First Major League Baseball Game in China." http://www.sportsbusinessnews.com, cited 15 February 2007.

"Yankees Luxury Tax — Their Bill Comes Due." http://www.sportsbusinessnews.com, cited 23 December 2006.

"Year in Review." http://www.baseball-almanac.com, cited 25 January 2007.

Media Guides

Official Major League Baseball Fact Book 2004 Edition. St. Louis, MO: The Sporting News, 2004.
Official Major League Baseball Fact Book 2005 Edition. St. Louis, MO: The Sporting News, 2005.
Washington, Kelli D., and Richard K. Miller. *The 2004 Entertainment, Media & Advertising Market Research Handbook.* Sixth Edition. Norcross, GA: Richard K. Miller & Associates, Inc., 2004.

Reports

Anderson, Stuart, and L. Brian Andrew. *Coming to America: Immigrants, Baseball and the Contributions of Foreign-Born Players to America's Pastime.* Arlington, VA: National Foundation For American Policy, October 2006.
Shapiro, Sebastian. *The Most Valuable Brands in Sports: The 2002 Report.* New York: FutureBrand, 2002.

INDEX